Women EMERGING ...
A Decade of Irish Feminist Scholarship

Alan Hayes, Rebecca Pelan
EDITORS

National University of Ireland, Galway
Ollscoil na hÉireann, Gaillimh
women's studies
Centre
Ionad Leann na mBan

Chapters © Individual contributors, 2005
Collection © Women's Studies Centre, 2005

The moral rights of the authors and editors have been asserted

First published in September 2005 by

Women's Studies Centre
10 Upper Newcastle Road
NUI, Galway

ISBN 0–9549924–0–7, *paperback*

The views expressed in this book are not necessarily those of the editors or the publisher.

We are grateful to all authors and copyright holders for their permission to reprint material in this anthology. We will endeavour to address any omissions or correct any mistakes in future editions.

Cover image 'In Nature Looking at Three Birds', by Pauline Bewick, courtesy of the artist
Printed by: Cahill Printers, Dublin

Contents

Acknowledgements	12
Introduction *Rebecca Pelan*	13
A Personal History *Alan Hayes*	15
Mother of Eros *Eva Bourke*	19
The K.K.K. of Kastle Park *Rita Ann Higgins*	22
The Pit *Hannagh McGinley*	24

Equality, Rights, Society

Oral History *Catríona Crowe*	27
Women in Ancient Europe *John Waddell*	28
Athenian Women *Brian Arkins*	32
Roman Women *Brian Arkins*	34
Roman Imperial Women *Constantina Katsari*	36
Medieval Irishwomen *Aoife de Paor*	39

The Drennan-McTier Letters *Maria Luddy*	41
Lola Montez: A Multiography *Grainne Blair*	44
Inghinidhe na hÉireann *Alan Hayes*	47
Suffrage in Galway *Mary Clancy*	50
The Ulster Women's Unionist Council *Diane Urquhart*	52
Mary Strangman (1872–1943) *Irene Finn*	55
Rural Economy and Female Emigration *Peter Moser*	58
Women Teachers in Clare, 1922–1958 *Mary Kierse*	60
Equality in Local Development *Anne Byrne*	63
Women and Trade Unions *Nuala Keher*	64
Equality and Women Academics *Celia Davies*	66
Mismeasured and Misunderstood? *Eileen Kane*	69
Migrant Women in Ireland *Marian Tannam*	71
Black Irish Women *Philomena Mullen*	73

After the Burial 76
Moya Cannon

"With One Continuous Breath" 77
Anne Kennedy

Fáilte Ui Dhonnchú 78
Louis de Paor

From the Creative to the Critical

Women and Embroidery 81
Jo. George

Lady Morgan 83
Riana O'Dwyer

Käthe Kollwitz 86
Eoin Bourke

Camille Claudel 89
Angela Ryan

Una Troy and Siobán Piercy 91
Wanda Balzano

Marina Carr's Plays 94
Catherine Kelly

Sylvia Plath 96
Bernadette Fallon

Female Musical Creativity 98
Nóirín Ní Riain

Women Composers 101
Jane O'Leary

Women and Dance 103
Berni Divilly

Art and 'Women's Work' 105
Catherine Marshall

Interview with Alice Maher 106
Sheila Dickinson

A Conversation with Carmel Benson 110
Luz Mar González Arias

Alternative Representations create Alternative Possibilities 113
Helen O'Donoghue and Catherine Marshall

Latin American Women Writers 117
Catherine M. Boyle

Marguerite Yourcenar 118
Francesca Counihan

Algerian Women Writers 121
Christine O'Dowd-Smyth

Gayl Jones' *Corregidora* 124
Ana Paula Leal Nabais Nunes

Italian Feminist Filmmakers 126
Áine O'Healy

The *Femme Fatale* on Film 131
Christiane Schonfeld

Creativity Workshop 133
Chris Head

After Twenty Years 136
Mary Dempsey

Refugees 137
Jessie Lendennie

Women Watching the Door 138
Joan McBreen

From the Personal to the Political

'Experience' in Recent Feminist Thought 141
Liz Stanley

Citzenship 144
Sylvia Walby

National Specificities in European Feminisms 146
Karen Offen

Feminist Research Methodologies 150
Ronit Lentin

Single Women in Ireland 153
Anne Byrne

A Journey Into the Women's Prison 156
Christina Quinlan

Entering the Field Day 158
Siobhán Kilfeather

Women and Volunteering 161
Freda Donoghue

An Interview with Phoebe Jones, Global Women's Strike 165
Maggie Ronayne

Feminist Moral Psychology 169
Stephen Mannix

Feminist Identities in the Irish Context 172
Jane Tynan

Aunt Katy 173
Mary Mangan

Mama 175
Sharon Murphy

Dauernarkose 176
Mary O'Donoghue

From the Local to the International

Rural Women in Ireland   179
Mary Owens

Rural Women in Ireland   181
Anne Byrne

Oral Research in Ballyconneelly   182
Terri Conroy

Poetry, Presidents and the Centre   185
Victor Luftig

Women and Employment   188
Mary Quinn

North American Indigenous Women   189
Mary C. Pruitt

East German Women   191
Rosaleen O'Neill

Global Exploitation   194
Rose Tuelo Brock

Nicaraguan Women's Movement   196
Lorna Shaughnessy

Beijing 1995   199
Nóirín Clancy

Residents at the Chateau Lavigny   203
Kerry Hardie

from Borderline Crosstalk   205
Ailbhe Smyth

Health and The Body

From "Guest Introduction" Cecily Kelleher	209
Blasket Island Traditions Pádraig Ó Héalaí	210
Women Health Workers Anne MacFarlane	215
Social Care Workers Margaret Hodgins and Cecily Kelleher	217
Staff in Domestic Violence Shelters Catriona Brennan	220
Women's Attitudes to Health Jane Sixsmith, Ethna Shryane, Emer McCarthy	222
Body Image Helen Mortimer	224
Osteoporosis Mike Power	227
HRT Cecily Kelleher	230
Able-Bodied Women Esther-Mary D'Arcy	232
Women and HIV Sheila Street	234
Female Genital Mutilation Lorna Shaughnessy	237
Women and Health in Nicaragua Margaret Brehony	240

Bridget Lyons-Thornton 242
Timothy Collins

Lady Dudley Nurses in the West of Ireland 245

from Visa to Rejoin the Human Race 249
Mary Dempsey

Irish Women's Movements

Feminist Activism in Northern Ireland 253
Myrtle Hill

Women's Equality in West Belfast 255
Eilish Rooney

Obstacles to Peace in Ireland 258
Caitríona Ruane

The Cork Lesbian Community, 1975-2000 260
Orla Egan

Rural Women's Lives 263
Mary Owens and Anne Byrne

Networks of Women's Groups and the Women's Movement 265
Eilís Ward and Orla O'Donovan

Lesbian and Gay Visions of Ireland 269
Maria Gibbons

Women and Disability 270
Ann O'Kelly

Domestic Violence in Galway 273
Claire McDonagh

Women Engineers 276
Catherine Cronin

Travelling Women   278
Mary O'Malley-Madec

Irish Journal of Feminist Studies   280
Liz Stanley

Women Publishing Feminism   281
Alan Hayes

The Maighdean Mhara   284
Mary O'Malley

Notes on Contributors   285

The Women's Studies Review 1992–2004   307

Acknowledgements

For excellent administrative support we thank former Women's Studies Centre staff Caitriona Keane and Sinead Coyne. Many thanks to Vivienne Batt and Ann Lyons for their support in a wide number of ways throughout this project.

The cover image is from a previously unseen watercolour by Pauline Bewick and we thank her for permission to use the image.

To all the authors who responded so promptly and so encouragingly to our requests.

All the previous editors of *UCG Women's Studies Centre Review* and the *Women's Studies Review*, and for all those who kept the publishing vision of the WSC alive.

Introduction

In 2003, as a result of significant changes within the Women's Studies Centre (WSC) at NUI, Galway, it was decided that a new feminist journal, to be called *Irish Feminist Review*, would be launched in 2005, as a replacement for the existing *Women's Studies Review*. Whilst it is the case that the new is, in so many ways, always a continuation of the old, it was generally felt that the time had come to begin a new era in feminist publishing in Ireland. Some very fine Irish feminist journals existed over the years, and yet none but the *Women's Studies Review* survived. And so it seemed an appropriate time to take a fresh look at an old face. At the same time, there was a very strong sense that the work that existed in the *Women's Studies Review* should be marked or acknowledged in some way. The result is *Women Emerging*, a celebration of nine volumes of feminist research in Ireland, published in the *Women's Studies Review* between 1992 and 2004. It is hoped that the selection will serve not only as a tribute to work done in the past, but as a useful reference for future research.

In their Introduction to Volume 1 of the *Women's Studies Review* in 1992, editors Anne Byrne, Jane Conroy and Sean Ryder pointed out that, "the Women's Movement, feminism and Women's Studies are often misunderstood and held in suspicion by many people" (vii). I'd love to be able to say how quaint that sounds today, but, sadly, the truth is that, some thirteen years later, we're in much the same state now as we were then. The Women's Movement has given way to a broad-based feminism that reveals, every day, just how far removed we are now from any sense of collective consciousness; feminism has, in the most positive way, given way to feminisms and yet has, in the process, forfeited any possibility of forming a united front from which to fight the many and varied, yet integrally connected feminist issues, including the regular attacks from openly hostile and conservative forces within our society; and Women's Studies remains perched precariously between its radical potential and its realistic limitations – an evolving discipline that is, like other disciplines, at the mercy of economic rationalist policies, within and without the University system, as well as ignorance, apathy and self-interest. And, yet, feminism and valuable feminist research continues to be produced.

As a conduit for both a feminist world-view and its accompanying research output, the *Women's Studies Review* also prevailed. From humble beginnings as a collection of papers, published in 1992, and based on the seminar series organised by the Women's Studies Centre in University College, Galway (now NUI, Galway) between 1988 and 1992, the *Review* has had an illustrious career. Volumes 1 to 4 were published under the journal's original title, *U.C.G. Women's Studies Centre Review*. From Volume 5, the title became *Women's Studies Review*, and the journal moved to produce a number of specialist volumes on topics such as 'Women and Health' (Vol. 5), 'Oral History and Biography' (Vol. 7), 'Women and the Creative Arts' (Vol. 8), and 'Women's Activism & Voluntary Activity' (Vol. 9). Throughout, it retained a commitment to the dissemination of feminist research, so evident in the early writings of those involved in the first seminar series. The excerpts contained in *Women Emerging* provide just a sample of the breadth and depth of Irish feminist research over the recent period. It is, I think you'll agree, a fine body of work which is deserving of further attention.

Dr Rebecca Pelan

August 2005

The *Women's Studies Review*
A Personal History

Coming to UCG in 1989 as a first arts student, I immediately joined the newly founded Women's Studies Centre. The WSC had no location, only pittance funding and no staff, yet it was energetic, politically open and eager to engage in feminist activities. The Seminar Series was one of the main activities of the centre in those early days, and its aim was to bring feminist knowledge and discussion to as wide an audience as possible.

Terrifyingly I was asked to give a public lecture in the seminar series, and afterwards invited to contribute to the planned publication which was germinating in the minds of a subcommittee. The next summer, sitting on a beach on the Isle of Wight, each evening I hand wrote that little article on Maud Gonne and sent it to Sean Ryder, the editor I was working with, who must have typed it up. Less than 2 years later, on 8 May 1992, Jane Conroy handed me the first copy of the new journal straight out of the box and just delivered from the printers to her office. I can still remember the excitement of that moment, the joy of seeing my first article in print, as we both admired the high production standards and quality of Volume One.

Over the next decade we published 9 volumes of the *Women's Studies Review*, the final report of the Rural Women's Research Project and an Equality conference proceedings. Our *Review* alone has sold over 3000 copies and has journeyed around the world. We have published local, national and international authors, women and men, leading scholars and students, professors and poets, articles we agreed with, some we didn't. There were many teams of editors, some volumes were published fast, others took longer.

We had some hairy moments, some occasions of great laughter and a few proud successes. One volume made it onto page one of the *Irish Times* and was picked up by the London and American media. Many volumes got great reviews for both content and presentation. Our distribution was never as bad as we thought it was – we managed to circulate the work far and wide, and even bring in some decent amounts in sales! After a few years the university management began to better support the research and publishing work of the WSC. We gained some 'status' and recognition in the academy – some of us cared about that. Some of us were interested in high academic research, others were interested in changing the world through political activism. Yet I believe that working on the *Review* helped all of us to develop our feminist agendas in our own many diverse ways.

There was a lot of work. All voluntary work. It resulted in what has now become a major archive of feminist research and dialogue which will always be a credit to the work of the Women's Studies Centre in Galway University and will remain a great resource for the feminist community in Ireland and abroad.

Alan Hayes

Equality Activist, NUI, Galway

August 2005

Women Emerging …

Eva Bourke

Mother of Eros

She's lost among the trivia collected,
bills, headaches, heartaches, disconnected
phone calls, postcards from forgotten places,
hopeless letters full of cautious phrases
like 'nice to see you sometime' and 'when
you pass through here, do call again',
but can't think for the life of her which 'here',
the writer's signatures become a blur;
she treads so lightly, watching cracks with care,
keeps to a thin line, counts each greying hair,

she pins a smile on for each face she meets,
she talks about the cold, she feels it so, she greets
endearments in a language long deferred
with every kind of frosty effort, in a word
she's lost all nerve and thinks that all despise
her, gauche and unwanted, with her tired vice
of putting on a false front that belies
the *cri de coeur,* the tears, the drugs, the booze.
It's omissions and cold routine that kill
the frozen months of Januaries, Februaries till

a March that thaws and flowers seems just a blunder
of seasons bent on getting on with it. But under
the iced-up weeks, notes of dismissal, dates
not kept and messages not replied to stir
the plosive sounds of pulp and peach and pear,
for laid out in silkpaper-cushioned crates,
net-covered like old gentlewomen's faces,
rest these univalves, ripe ovaries in their juices.
And like a somnambulist that's being led
I want to take her down the length of Henry Street

into the tranquil darkness of a shed
that's lined with shelves of every type of fruit

where this comfortable woman moves, with apple head,
ample arms, in striped, open-necked shirt.
This is a neighbourhood garden of paradise
not just some vegetable shop, she presides
over an unseasonal summer of tastes. She'll call
us past bags of onions, spuds and swedes,
the earth-bound caretakers of our needs
into her inner sanctum where with all

the sly bravura, the relish of the gourmande
she picks from varied piles luxuriant
outlandish things, hands us, maybe a mango,
to taste its blushing flesh with total sang-froid
and then demands to know how we'd describe
the jungle tangs beneath its smooth cool endocarp.
For years we've been at naming games together,
test uglies, lychees, kumquats, puckered leather
bags of granadills for the lip-closing labials,
they yield a serpent's sting of graded vowels,

from jujube, pampelmousse, to pippin, passion fruit,
the hushed-up sibilants, the glottal stops
of pleasure, honey dew melons flattened at the tops
like planets, plums and cherries full of sweet blood,
tangerine, pineapple, pawpaw, papay,
we say it over and again like a lullaby,
and harshness softens and the ice gives way,
as morning peels the rind of night from day,
as tongues that tell sweetness from bitterness
repeating palatals of yes and yes and yes

and the aspirates of an entire phonetic
of heaven and heart and him and her, the erotic
richness we find on pulling back the skin
on the secret luscious flesh within,
hidden like feelings, segments, pips and drupes,
the pod-bags, scent-bags, clustered seeds, the globes,
and like a sudden miracle, the neat
geometry of the Chinese lantern fruit
sheltering inside its hexagonal tapered sphere
the acid burning flame of Demeter.

And last but not least she unearths from her trove
pomegranates, the archetypal fruit of love,
whose scarlet seeds are tightly parcel-packed
in vellum-wrap and spill out as from the cracked
shell of the broken world-egg once did spill
out all creation, earth and sea and sky,
the shell to which the goddess hoists her sail
to skim an ocean of milk. Moon-mother stand by
her, Danae, all-giver open your jar
of grains and fruit, Mother of Eros – help her.

Rita Ann Higgins

The K.K.K. of Kastle Park

from Volume 6, pp. 100-101

At a K.K.K. meeting
in Kastle Park
you could
walk into a dark garden
void of roses
or an after-Easter lily
but reeking with thorns,

briars too
that smoked
and choked
with shouts of
'Get them out,
we don't want them,
they're dirty,
cut off their water.'

These briars
have big brothers
and heavy-bellied husbands
(who are really thistles)

who know only
about foam-backed carpet
and curtains
that go up and down
with a string.

These prickly thistles
have roots
in other parts of town,
where they never saw
foam-backed carpet
or curtains
that went up and down
with a string

Now these deep roots
spoke often
at peak thistle times
about the lessers
who are dirty
on the outside,

of them they warned,
'My prickly sons,
you are better
than this sort,

so if they cross
your path
step on them
Nip them in the bud,
know you are superior.'

And the thorny briars
who smoked and choked
had cacti problems
with their male thistles
and with money
and with awkward-shaped light
bills.

Sometimes these thistles
chased other briars;
some played cards
with the briar money
others played the horses
the evil ones drank jungle juice

All the time
the anger
of the frustrated briars

and thistles
was building up
under the stairs
in the houses
with the foam-backed carpets
and the curtains
that went up and down
with a string.

And the
heavy-bellied husbands
of the thorny briars,

sent out
in the dead of night
their children,
to inform
all the other
briars and thistles
about the Midnight Court at
Kastle Park,

where they would
nip in the bud,
the lesser
their fathers spoke about
at peak thistle times.

And all
the under-stair anger
burst forth
and was spread evenly
over the streets
and over the caravans,

and a chalice full
seeped into
a hive-shaped chapel.

After that
all the thistles and briars
went home
and danced
on their foam-backed carpet,

and pulled the string
and the curtains
came down and down
(but no one took any notice).

And they all
slept soundly
knowing they did a good job,
nipping the lessers
in the bud.

Hannagh McGinley

The Pit

from Volume 6, p. 95

Give me back those stolen years,
wipe away these growing fears.
I have risen from the pit
but keep falling back in
Am I just so weak
I can't reach the top?
Is sadness caving me in?
I feel the boulder bruise my head
The sides are coming too close
Suffocating, but I'm trying to breathe
I'm down here, please somebody hear
Just give me a hand, I'm too tired to climb

The pit bottom is catching up.

Equality, Rights, Society

Catríona Crowe

Oral History

from 'Guest Introduction', *Volume 7*, pp. xi–xiv

My paternal grandmother lived her life on the banks of the river Shannon in county Clare, on the farm she married into in her thirties. She had 10 children, of whom 8 survived to adulthood (she lost her only daughter to diphtheria at the age of two). Her life was dominated by hard work, in the home, rearing children, and doing farm work. I spent most of my childhood holidays on the farm, and like every other child in such circumstances, was allotted certain tasks in the household economy. My favourite was bringing tea and bread and jam to the men saving the hay in the fields. Food has never tasted so good as at the foot of a newly constructed hay stack.

I remember sitting with my grandmother as a young girl, when she was in her seventies, listening to her accounts of her wedding day, an event to which she often returned as her short-term memory began to fail. I have a photographic image in my head of her appearance on the day, down to the pearl buttons on her blouse, and the half-veil on her hat. I can see her vividly, even though there were no photographs taken at the time. But I do not have her voice telling the story, and this is a cause of great regret to me. Not just the sound of her voice, but her idiomatic phraseology, her accent and the aspects of her life she chose to talk about, are things I miss now more than I ever thought I would. [....]

It is vital that the voices of Irish women from the last century, one of dizzying change, be captured and preserved in a systematic and accessible way. [....] The documentary record is immeasurably enhanced by personal testimony.

The variety of subjects and individuals covered in these pieces serves to underline how much still remains to be done in the area of oral history collection, preservation and dissemination. In 100 years time, the voices of women living today will seem very distant, but at least there is a chance that they will be heard, if the necessary resources are provided to preserve them. When we hear the voices of Maud Gonne, Kathleen Clarke, Cathleen Delaney or Frankie Byrne now, they have a value above the information they convey. They bring with them an intangible aura of the time in which they spoke, as well as the unique stamp of the individual's mode of expression.

John Waddell

WOMEN IN ANCIENT EUROPE

Abstract: The historical evidence for the subordination of women in ancient Europe is manifest. The prehistoric evidence is more difficult to interpret but, while some women achieved high status, patriarchal domination may have been the norm since the beginnings of agriculture some over 6000 years ago. While pre-agricultural, hunting and foraging societies were, in all probability, egalitarian, evidence for a matriarchal era at any time is lacking.

from 'Women in Ancient Europe', *Volume 1*, pp 29-37

The large number of books and articles now being published about the role of women in every aspect of society testifies in quite a dramatic way how the fossilized conceptual edifice of a patriarchal ideology is being slowly chipped away. This ideology is so ancient and so pervasive that many men and women fail to recognize it or to appreciate the distorted perceptions it has engendered. The weird misogyny of the Christian Fathers and some of their successors is an obvious instance and when Paul declared that woman should not teach nor use authority over man he was probably echoing a belief spawned millennia before. [....] Their general subordination may have had a long pre-history and those instances, in different cultures and a different times, when individual women acquired great wealth and status and even exercised direct authority over men, should not obscure the wider picture. This wider picture is a patriarchal one which, in Europe at least, may be over 6000 years old. [....]

In early Ireland the power of women was much restricted and, according to Fergus Kelly in *A Guide to Early Irish Law*, 'exaggerated claims have sometimes been made about the degree of power and freedom [they] enjoyed'. [....]The notion of the *imbecillitas* of women is a cliché repeated over and over again in the religious and juridical literature of the Middle Ages. [....]

What the situation was in late prehistoric Ireland is unclear. Some believe that the relative prominence of women in early legend and pseudo-history indicates that they had a considerably greater degree of social and political prominence than in later times. There may be some truth in this but the exhaltation of women in ritual or myth may not be the most reliable reflection of their status in real life. Thus the exploits of the legendary Queen Maeve in the *Táin Bó Cuailnge* do not necessarily mean that warrior queens were a feature of Irish Iron Age society. The original Maeve was a goddess and it is a moot point whether the events of the *Táin* should be seen as the accumulated literary trappings of a fictive female deity or as the accretion of mythical motifs around an historical figure. However, there is evidence elsewhere in Celtic society for powerful female leaders. Early British history provides two famous examples:Cartimandua, Queen of the tribes of the Brigantes in northern England [and] Boudicca, Queen of the Iceni in East Anglia. [....]

That some women achieved high status is also seen in the archaeological evidence. [....] The most famous of the Continental burials is undoubtedly that at Vix, near Chatillon-sur-Seine, where, about 500 BC, a forty year old woman was buried with a ceremonial four-wheeled wagon, rich personal ornaments and imported Mediterranean pottery and bronze vessels. A great Greek *krater* or wine container with a capacity of over 1000 litres was an exceptional and splendid funerary offering. The great majority of rich graves are those of males, however, and the occurrence of some rich female burials, interesting and significant as they may be, does little to alter the impression of a male dominated society.

The same seems to be true of the preceding later Bronze Age where male weaponry sometimes in graves, often in hoards, is a fairly prominent and consistent feature of the archaeological record. Female personal ornaments do occur in both hoards and graves in various parts of Europe but, except for Scandinavia, relatively few studies have attempted to analyse what the material might reveal about the respective roles and status of men and women. This sort of study is fraught with difficulty but now at least questions about gender are being posed which were unthought of a decade or two ago. [....] Margaret Ehrenberg, in her book *Women in Prehistory,* discusses the numerous interpretative difficulties presented here and concludes that even if women of higher status had a better deal in this society, it is impossible to argue that they actually held power. Indeed various writers have suggested that there could be an inverse relationship in cultures of this sort where women may be celebrated in art and ritual but nonetheless controlled as reproducers with limited status. [....]

Neolithic Europe offers evidence of a very different sort. Now there is relatively abundant settlement evidence and from south-eastern Europe in particular a fascinating series of small human figurines. These figurines, from the Balkans and from Greece, seem to echo fashions in Asia Minor (Anatolia) and the eastern Mediterranean. [....]

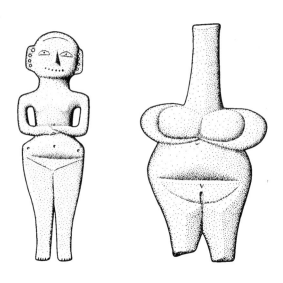

Female figurines (left) from Blagoevo, Bulgaria, and (right)
Cernavoda, Roumania (after Georgiev and Berciu).

The majority are stylised (Fig. 1) with buttocks emphasised and over many years they have generated a large body of literature preoccupied with Mother Goddesses or Fertility Goddesses and related beings. [....] However, the general significance of these various female figures is debated. A magico-religious explanation, even a fertility significance, does seem reasonable in many instances but most scholars seem sceptical of any suggestion of a widespread European 'Mother Goddess' cult. Detailed regional studies, as in Neolithic Crete, imply the possibility of a range of functions. Figurines thrown away on settlements may have been 'teaching aids' to depict characters in myths or to illustrate appropriate behaviour in certain realms of society. The predominance of female figurines might reflect the prevalence of women's ceremonies or initiation rites such as explaining pregnancy to girls at puberty. Some figurines may just have been dolls, others — particularly those buried in graves — may have had some commemorative significance. Others still may have been used in sympathetic magic ceremonies, to help cause a pregnancy, for instance. A Fertility Goddess cult is by no means the only possibility. Nonetheless this relative wealth of female iconography does raise the question of the role women played in these Neolithic societies and has also led to claims, particularly in the last century, that at this early date theirs was a crucial role in ritual and political activity and that the structure of society may have been matrilineal or even matriarchal.

Most people would hesitate to accept this claim and indeed there may again be an inverse relationship as far as women's status is concerned. Since the cultures in question are all well-established agricultural societies a patriarchal structure is more likely. [....]

In fact in modern agricultural communities a remarkably consistent pattern emerges: in societies where plough agriculture is practised and animals kept on a significant scale most of the agricultural work is done by men, with women playing no direct part. In horticultural societies (i.e. simple technology with shifting agriculture — no plough or traction or irrigation and using hoes or digging sticks) women are usually almost wholly responsible for production. This is a continuation of their role in hunting and foraging societies, for in virtually all such societies of relatively recent times women are responsible for plant food gathering. Men hunt and women gather. Usually a high proportion of plant food supplements a smaller proportion of meat and it has been estimated that two-thirds of foraging societies depend on gathered food for 60-70% of their diet. Because they have such a significant economic input the standing of women in modern foraging societies is correspondingly greater with equality of status between men and women.

Various writers have suggested that this may have been the case in the hunting and food gathering societies of pre-farming Europe before 4000 BC and that the advent of sedentary patterns of settlement and an economy based on cereal cultivation and animal husbandry saw a major shift in the role of women (Fig. 2). [....]

A rock-carved scene of a ploughman followed by a woman with a child on her back (?) from the Val Camonica region of northern Italy (after Anati).

Factors such as land, property and inheritance will all assume an obvious importance in a settled agricultural community and, if gradually appropriated by male interests, will have equally obvious consequences for the other sex. Equally important may be a greater emphasis on child bearing. [....] In agricultural societies [....] more and more children are desirable both as eventual and important additions to the labour force and as a means through marriage of forging and extending kinship links (and thus perhaps acquiring other land rights or other economic or social benefits). Here, paradoxically, in what archaeologists for years have described as the Neolithic Revolution may lie both the basis of civilization and the basis of the subordination of women. In the pre-farming foraging societies, of the Mesolithic and Palaeolithic, where a measure of equality of status is assumed, there is no hint of the pre-agricultural matriarchal society postulated by writers such as Friedrich Engels. Indeed the limited evidence from burials seems to suggest a degree of gender differentiation, but this could conceivably be an echo of those different subsistence roles of men and women, roles perhaps as old as hunting and foraging humanity. One of the values of archaeology is the long perspective it offers and if, as is now assumed, the Neolithic period saw the development of significant inequalities between the sexes, then [....] 6000 out of 500,000 years can perhaps be seen as a relatively short-term aberration in the human story of Europe.

Brian Arkins

ATHENIAN WOMEN

Abstract: This paper explores how aristocratic women were excluded from all political, military, and legal power, and were defined by the social significance of their bodies, that is by their capacity to give birth to boys who would become adult male citizens.

from 'The Reign of the Phallus: Women in Fifth Century Athens', *Volume 3*, pp. 63-68

Athenian society epitomises what Eva Keuls terms "the reign of the phallus".[1] By that is not meant primarily that it was a society that specially privileged the phallus, the male sexual organ – though that is certainly true – but that it was a society that accorded men, as opposed to women, extraordinary power. If it is true that in any society the position of women cannot be assessed without examining the position of men, it is *a fortiori* true of Athens, a city ruled by men for men. Athenian men, not having read Lacan, knew full well that they possessed the phallus: they had absolute power, of which sexual power formed a part.

The literal importance of the phallus can be seen in the casual display of male genitals: men exercised nude, could be nude at other times, gloried in their naked masculinity. In front of both public buildings and private houses, statues of the god Hermes boasted an erect phallus (contrast the covered genitals of the goddess Athena, born, in male fantasy, out of her father's head). Vase paintings constantly depict the phallus, in both erect and non-erect states, as an object of desire. The pillar, that staple of Greek architecture, has obvious phallic associations.

But the reign of the phallus was at its most effective in the organisation of Athenian society. To begin with, Athens was ruled by adult male citizens and no woman was allowed to play any role in politics, the army, the navy, or the law courts; women were also excluded from the Olympic and other Games, from agriculture and from trade. Respectable women were also banned from that important social occasion, the symposium, where men gathered to talk, drink, and have sex with prostitutes. In other words, the *public world* of the *polis,* the city state, was completely out of bounds for all women (except prostitutes at the symposium).

The domain of aristocratic Athenian women was, therefore, the *private world* of the *oikos,* the house, to which they were almost literally confined. This fact shows how democracy at Athens was a system of gender as well as of politics; women were defined by the social significance of their bodies, i.e. by their capacity to bear male children, who would ensure continuity of the system; remained at home to look after these boys; and were not let out, in case they might meet men and bring the legitimacy of the children into question (a form of Mediterranean social control). All of this is made clear by the statement made to the groom at the engagement ceremony by the bride's father: 'I give you this woman for the ploughing of legitimate children'.

Women, therefore, spent their lives *in inner space,* cooking food, supervising slaves, spinning clothes (considered an archetypal female activity). This very restricted life style was exacerbated by the fact that women were not properly educated; most may have been literate, but they did not enjoy the sort of literary and musical education men had; as Shelley said, this led women to acquire "the habits and qualities of slaves".[2] A further disadvantage women endured was that they had to be legally subject to some guardian *(kurios),* a man who was father, husband, brother. And women were often deprived of their names, named in relation to some man; indeed there is no Greek for Athenian woman.[3]

Even in the restricted private lives they led, Athenian women fared very badly. They entered an arranged marriage at a very young age – about 14 – to a much older man – about 30 – and this increased the risk of death in child-birth, which, in the ancient world, was already high. There was, therefore, no question of romantic love between a woman and a man or of regard for the woman's sexual pleasure: marriage existed to procreate males. Indeed, men and women lived in separate parts of the house, had meals apart, slept apart, only getting together briefly for sexual intercourse (for this it appears women did not undress fully). [....]

Notes
1   Eva Keuls 1993. *The Reign of the Phallus: Sexual Politics in Ancient Greece*, Berkeley: University of California Press. See also Roger Just. 1991. *Women in Athenian Law and Life*, London.
2   Quoted by Nathaniel Brown 1979. *Sexuality and Feminism in Shelley*, Cambridge, MA: Harvard University Press, p. 11.
3   Nicole Loraux 1993. *The Children of Athena: Athenian Ideas about Citizenship and the Division Between the Sexes*, Princeton, pp. 111–143, esp. pp. 116–117.

Brian Arkins

ROMAN WOMEN

Abstract: This paper outlines a variety of ways in which women in Rome, from the first century B.C. on, enjoyed a very considerable degree of freedom. Roman women were educated, sometimes to the same level as men, and were free to mingle with men on a variety of social occasions, including the symposium. Roman women could divorce men easily, and could inherit property. It is in this kind of social context that romantic love between women and men came into existence, and is chronicled by male poets such as Catullus, and female love poets such as Sulpicia. Women also played an important *indirect* role in politics through the manipulation of men. [....]

from 'Women in Rome', *Volume* 6, pp. 115-121

Virtually the only role played by women in fifth-century Athens was to produce legitimate children.[1] But in Rome from the first century B.C. onwards, aristocratic women enjoyed a very considerable degree of freedom, perhaps more than any other group of European women until the nineteenth century. These women were educated; they were free to attend social gatherings with men; they could inherit and own property; and they could easily divorce their husbands. For women lower down the social scale, life was much harder, as the matter of housework attests: aristocratic women ran the house, with others doing the work; poor women had to do this work themselves.[2]

Even for aristocratic women in Rome, there were difficulties. Average life expectancy was about 27 (death coming from disease, poor nutrition, and childbirth). For centuries, women did not have a proper name of their own, but were given the feminine form of their father's family (*gens*) name: Julius Caesar's daughter was called *Julia*; in the first century A.D., women acquired a second name, as in *Julia Drusilla*. Women were largely excluded from politics, the army, the navy, and the law-courts, areas felt to belong to men. While Athenian women were not educated like men (and may even have been illiterate), aristocratic Roman women were often educated to the same level as men. Girls could attend an elementary school, and then receive further education at home from private tutors. This meant, to a large extent, the study of Greek and Latin literature, a field the Sempronia attacked by Sallust is well versed in.[3] So the women loved by male love poets such as Catullus and Propertius had to be *doctae*, 'learned', 'educated'.

The history of advances for women in the nineteenth century shows that education is a necessary (though not a sufficient) condition for women to achieve equality with men. The fact that Roman women were educated enabled them to meet men on equal terms, especially in social situations. Such women could not be confined to the private life of the house (*domus*), but moved out into the public world of the city (*urbs*) where men operated.

Central to the social emancipation of Roman women was their attendance at dinner-parties/symposia and at the games. Whereas the Greek symposium (like that described in Plato's dialogue *Symposium*) was confined to men, in Rome, the symposium was open to women also. The mixing of the sexes in this relaxed social setting will have ensured that men took women seriously, and will have created the conditions in which romantic love between women and men could develop.[4]

Major advances were achieved for Roman women in the areas of sexual relationships, marriage and divorce, and of property rights. In Rome in the first century B.C., a huge shift takes place in the relationship between women and men: because women were educated and socially free, romantic love between men and women became a recognised mode of being.

It is true that in the first century B.C. in Rome, aristocratic marriages were still arranged – the man being about 25, the girl as young as 12 – but this form of arranged marriage, which was often used to cement political alliances between families, began to come under intense pressure. Divorce became more and more common, and when people remarried (as they often did), they then got married to someone they *wanted* to marry. We know, for example, that about 40% of the consuls (chief magistrates) between 80 and 50 B.C. remarried. [....]

The women of the Roman aristocracy were precluded from taking an active part in politics, but often played an important role through the indirect mechanism of influencing men. One important group of women was the Vestal Virgins, whose task was to watch the fire on the State hearth *(vesta)* in the Temple of Vesta in Rome. When Julius Caesar was proscribed by the dictator Sulla for refusing to divorce his wife Cornelia (the daughter of Sulla's enemy, Cinna), the Vestal Virgins ensured that he was forgiven. When the radical politician Clodius profaned the all-women Bona Dea festival by attending dressed as a woman, the Vestal Virgins ruled that this was an evil act *(nefas)*, and Clodius was brought to trial (he was acquitted). [....]

Notes
1   Brian Arkins 1995. *UCG Women's Studies Centre Review,*3 pp.63–68.
2   John P.V.D. Balsdon 1962. *Roman Women,* London: Bodley Head; S.B. Pomeroy 1994. *Goddesses, Whores, Wives and Slaves,* London, Pimlico; Mary R. Leftovitz and Maureen B. Fant, (eds) 1982. *Women's Life in Greece and Rome,* London, Duckworth.
3   Sallust, *Catiline,* p.25
4   For romantic love in antiquity see Niall Rudd 1981. *Ramus* 10 pp. 140–158.

Roman Imperial Women

Constantina Katsari

Review essay: Charles Brian Rose, *Dynastic Commemoration and Imperial Portraits in the Julio-Claudian Period,* Cambridge UP 1997; Elizabeth Bartman, *Portraits of Livia: Imaging the Imperial Woman in Augustan Rome,* Cambridge UP, 1998; Susan E. Wood, *Imperial Women: A Study in Public Images, 40 B.C.–A.D. 68,* Brill, 1999.

from a review article, *Volume 8*, pp. 1-12

[....] Currently, researchers deem it necessary to 'contextualise' the material culture. As a consequence, they examine catalogues of artifacts and study their typology and style in relation to the ideological, military and economic background of the society in which they were produced.[1] This methodological approach facilitates the exploration of private and public aspects of people's lives and enhances the study of the role of women as an integral element of historical evolution. The most important study that analyses in detail the function of Roman art and contextualises it as a means of visual communication, is the book by P. Zanker, *The Power of Images in the Age of Augustus*, published in 1990.[2] The author successfully explains the way public monuments projected the image of the emperor and the honours that had been bestowed on him. The creators of the emperor's image used a popular 'visual language' or 'visual imagery' that characterised means as different as buildings, statues, poems, religious rituals, clothing, state ceremony, the emperor's conduct and various forms of social intercourse. This 'visual imagery' reflected aspects of society and revealed values of individuals, which are often not depicted in literary sources. [....] The trend established by Zanker has inspired a series of studies on Roman art history, among which are the three books under review. Although art, especially in the Julio-Claudian period, has been studied thoroughly in the past years[3], there is always room for different perspectives in the study of old problems. [...]

Charles Brian Rose's *Dynastic Commemoration and Imperial Portraiture in the Julio-Claudian Period* examines dynastic images on public monuments from circa 31 B.C. to 68 A.D. in Rome and the provinces. The examination of literature sources, inscriptions and coins is essential for the study of public representation of the Imperial Family. One of the main aims of the book is to distinguish between private initiatives and imperial propaganda in regard to the dynastic ideology in both eastern and western provinces; therefore, the author deems it essential to analyse the factors that controlled the production of dynastic statuary groups. It has been suggested that the form of the statues was defined by the donor's perception of the emperor's attitude towards his family. Because of the changing relationships within the Julio-Claudian family, though, these perceptions altered from time to time. Adoptions, remarriages, divorces and the *damnatio memoriae* became increasingly important factors in the composition of new schemes or in the repetition of older ones [....]

Still, if Roman women were not supposed to play an important role in the political life of the Principate, how can we explain their numerous and prominent representations in public spaces? Elizabeth Bartman's

Portraits of Livia may have clues in regard to the answer to this question. Even the structure of Bartman's book suggests that Livia, the most powerful Roman woman in her own time, existed only in relation to other men [....] It is important to remember that Livia was above ordinary Roman women, since she eventually became a *diva*. Women in antiquity, even before the Augustan period, held certain religious freedoms in the public sphere. These freedoms, though, were accentuated when Augustus became *primus inter pares* and his wife became the first woman among equals. Elizabeth Bartman dedicates a relatively small part of her book to the interpretation of Livia's new religious role. [....]

The importance of the religious role played by imperial women is an important theme in the book by Susan E. Wood, *Imperial Women : A Study in Public Images, 40 B.C-A.D. 68*. [....] In her book … she emphasises the dificult task of identifying the statues and portraits of Roman women, and she does not ignore the political, ideological or religious aspects of their public images. Her views of the politcal significance of imperial women roughly coincide with the views of previous researchers, even though she delves deeper into the study of the participation of these women in religious rituals. [....]

In conclusion, the three studies under review indicate that the public images of women in ancient Rome served well the political and ideological purposes of the State/emperor. Both Hellenistic and Roman Republican traditions were significant in the process of formation of a new imperial ideology that facilitated the perpetuation of the Julio-Claudian dynasty. The women of the *Domus Augusta* played an exceptionally important role in enduring the stability of the State and the continuation of the dynasty. On one hand, their images in the public sphere advertised this exceptional role; on the other hand, these same images became archetypes for all women in the Roman empire. The deification of imperial women was the highest point of their political career, even though their divine status only served the purpose of helping the emperors who wished to justify their hereditary claim to the throne. The comparative analysis of the three studies under review shows that they are essential for the reconstruction of the ideological, political and social history of women during the Julio-Claudian period. Using the above studies as a source of inspiration, modern researchers should also examine the public images of women who lived during the second and third centuries A.D. The study of third century imperial women in particular will prove extremely interesting, since dominant female characters, such as Julia Domna, Julia Mammaea and others, played a key role in the Roman empire at a time in which it was incessantly threatened by military disorder and political instability.

Notes

1   A. Wallace-Hadrill, 'The social structure of the Roman house', *Proceedings of the British School at Rome,* 56, 1988, pp. 43-97; E. Gasda, *Roman Art in the Private Sphere*, Ann Arbor, Michigan University Press, 1991.
2   P. Zanker, *The Power of Images in the Age of Augustus*, transl. by Alan Shapiro, Ann Arbor, University of Michigan Press, 1990.
3   N. Kampen, Image and Status: Roman Working Women in Ostia, Berlin, Mann, 1981; K. Fittschen, P. Zanker, Katalog der römischen Porträts in den Capitolinischen Museen und der anderen kommunalen Sammlungen der Stadt Rom. 3. Kaiserinnen und Prinzessinnenbildnisse, Frauenporträts, Mainz am Rhein, Verlag Philipp von Zabern, 1983; N. Kokkinos, Antonia Augusta: Portrait of a Great Roman Lady, London, Routledge, 1992; R. Winkes, Livia, Octavia, Julia, Louvain, Art and Archaeology Publications, 1995.

Aoife de Paor

MEDIEVAL IRISHWOMEN

Abstract: This paper argues that the status of woman in medieval Ireland was essentially that of subordinate. Though a woman might have, in rare cases, inherited property, and though she might possess her own money, she was generally debarred from tangible power. The patriarchal mode operated so much more visibly in medieval Ireland than today and yet paradoxically, was probably unseen by those who laboured under it.

from 'The Status of Women in Medieval Ireland', *Volume* 3, 69-79

The Anglo-Norman invasion of Ireland in 1169 and the colonisation that followed, resulted in two diverse 'nations' co-existing in this country.[1] The Anglo-Norman settler society lived under the English Common Law and the Gaelic Irish operated under traditional Irish or Brehon law, and even while each society was inevitably, or, more accurately perhaps, eventually influenced by the practices and customs prevailing in the other, there were many and glaring differences between them. [....]

Brehon law was the native, traditional and Gaelic law and under it a woman held a position of perpetual dependence. After a woman married, and she must marry if she was to have any security, she did not pass completely under the guardianship of her husband, but some portion of responsibility for her actions still rested with her family. If she committed a crime her guardians were held responsible; protection perhaps, but a protection certainly bordering on tyranny.[2] It was a law implying a person with no mind, no self-control and no sense of responsibility, restraint or reason. It reduces the status of woman to that of child, a status arguably imbued with less dignity than a child's. She lived in a state of tutelage under father, brother, husband or son from the cradle to the grave, in effect portions of her being handed out amongst the males surrounding her. [....]

An Irish woman under Irish law could not usually own land and she did not have the right to pass it on to her children, but she could hold a life interest in some of her own family's or her husband's estate. She could possess moveable goods and when she married she did not surrender this property completely into her husband's hands. If divorce occurred, as was permissible under Irish secular law, she was normally entitled to receive her marriage portion back again. Under English common law, a woman's property passed wholly into the hands of her husband when she married, and he became her sole guardian.[3] [....]

Under common law, when there were no surviving sons, a daughter could inherit her father's estate, although in late thirteenth-century Ireland, with an eye to defence, a number of Anglo-Irish families devised ways of preventing daughters inheriting.[4] Obviously a daughter's place was not as 'King of the Castle'. Under Irish law a male heir would be chosen from amongst the wider kinship network.

Under common law, only legitimate children, born after marriage, could be their father's heir, and a man could not marry again while his first wife was living. Under Irish law legitimacy was of no concern as long as the child was recognised by the father.[5] According to Archbishop Lanfranc of Canterbury, the traditional Irish law of marriage and divorce was nothing more than 'a law of fornication',[6] with divorce and remarriage allowed at will, and the tenuousness of Irish marriages in the period makes it hard to argue against him. Reading Katherine Simms' article you are left with the overwhelming impression that men married in a flurry of lust and passion, and when that petered out, as it mostly did, wives were cast aside easily to make way for newer models. [....]

Notes
1   Art Cosgrave, 1995, "Marriage in Modern Ireland", in Art Cosgrave (ed.) *Marriage in Ireland*, Dublin, College Press, p. 25.

2   Katharine Simms, 1975, "The legal position of Irishwomen in the later Middle Ages", *The Irish Jurist*, New Series, vol 10, p. 110.
3   *Ibid*, pp. 104-105.
4   Donncha O Corrain, 1978, "Women in Early Irish Society", in Margaret MacCurtain and Donncha O Corrain (eds) *Women in Irish Society: The Historical Dimension*, Arlen House, Dublin.
5   Simms, *op cit*, p. 15.
6   Cosgrave, *op cit*, p. 28.

Maria Luddy

THE DRENNAN-MCTIER LETTERS

from 'The Women's History Project', *Volume* 7, pp. 67-80

[Another publication undertaken by the Women's History project was the editing and annotating of] the correspondence of William Drennan and his sister, Martha McTier between 1776 and 1819.[1] The original letters are held in the Public Record Office of Northern Ireland. There are just over 1,400 letters, mainly between Martha McTier and her brother William. Drennan is renowned as a political activist and writer, his sister is less well known. Through these letters William and Martha provide us with direct accounts of their life experiences, their domestic, social and political preoccupations. The letters are a vital source for the politics of the period. But they can also be used to deepen our understanding of life for the middle classes at this time. Through them we can explore the world of domesticity, investigate the intimacy of marriage and personal relationships, observe the impact and importance of reading on a woman's life, and witness the development of political views. We can investigate attitudes to servants, to health, to the profession of medicine. We can assess contemporary views on childbirth and children. Martha's and William's letters were a forum for the exchange of political ideas, family news, gossip, advice, information and feelings. I wish to focus on two aspects of life evidenced in the letters to give a flavour of the range of information that they contain.

Marriage was a significant feature of life and a subject that caused concern, gossip, and much interest. Needless to say for women and men love, companionship or attraction were not always the motivations for marriage. Throughout the correspondence marriages of all types are referred to. Writing to William in December 1777, Martha told of a recent marriage in Belfast which:

> caused much surprise and diversion—a young lady who has lived all her life in Belfast and of one of the best families in it, but without fortune, to an old brute of the same place, rich you may believe and above eighty, a town house, country house and carriage, and a number of angry disappointed relations.[2]

The best kind of wife to have, as evidenced in the correspondence, was a 'sensible' one. This implied a wife who would be 'prudent' in her expenses, and who would support the endeavours of her husband, and care for him and their children.[3] There were men and women who fought, who were violent to each other, vindictive in life and even in death. Daniel Marsden, for instance, died "immensely rich", but, according to Martha, had:

> fixed a blot on his wife, not undeservedly, by leaving her not a penny beyond her settlement of a hundred a year and £2000 a piece to each of her daughters …[4]

There was also the case of a Mrs Atkinson who had run away to marry a doctor but was "taken mad" on her wedding night.[5] There were affairs, divorce and even murder. Martha was to write to William informing him that an acquaintance had murdered his wife, for which she observed "there is never any punishment in Belfast".[6] There was also of course a deal of fortune hunting and money often made up for what appeared to be physical or even intellectual deficiencies. Lennox Biggar's wife was considered by Martha a "fright, ugly and vulgar", and older than her husband. However she believed that "money perhaps makes up for this".[7] That some sympathy was given to a hard-done-by wife is evident from another case observed by Martha, though she retains her sympathy for perhaps more deserving causes. Martha's caustic wit is evident in her portrayal of Mrs Hyde who has been widowed:

> Mrs Hyde also adopts the same form since her return (not home), for in such a country she will only stay to dispose of her house in town and Cabin Hill, weep in the meeting house, and be affected at the *first* meeting of each acquaintance who knew she was married to a disgusting tyrant, that to the very last acted as such and left her as little as he could, though certainly in the character of a wife she was for above thirty years *perfection*. By her father and sister chiefly she has £800 a year, and freedom from a brute, so that I think at a *convenient time, her spirits will recover*.[8]

Bad marriages were as common an occurrence as good marriages. Financial considerations were a major priority for many individuals who sought to marry, particularly women, who required some form of financial security. It was money that decided independence, and independent choice, it did not guarantee happiness.

Another aspect of the correspondence that is significant in the area of women's history is the insight it provides into the intellectual and political ideas current at the time. One of the more extensive commentaries within the letters refers to the work of Jean Jacques Rousseau, William Godwin and Mary Wollstonecraft. Martha, like a number of Irish women of the period, was familiar with the work of Mary Wollstonecraft. Wollstonecraft was the author of two famous works by the early 1790s. Her *Vindication of the Rights of Man*, published in 1790 in response to Burke's reflections on the French Revolution is less well known than her *Vindication of the Rights of Woman*, published in 1792. The latter work calls for the rights of women. It seems likely that Martha read both works. Martha encouraged William to read Wollstonecraft. On 5 January 1793 she asked:

> Have you read Mrs Wollstonecraft? I suppose not, or surely you would have mentioned her to me—you ought, even as a politician, and *she* too conspires to make an important change. I wish they would order her book to be burned.

Martha realised that to order a book burned would immediately increase its sales. A review of *The Vindication of the Rights of Woman* appeared in the *Northern Star* on 22 December 1792 and it was noted as a work that:

> ... abounds with ingenious observations ... it affords a variety of judicious instruction for the early management of the female mind, and frequently, and pertinently, corrects the assumptions of the *tyrant man*.

While the 1790s were a time when the rights of Irish men were constantly being urged there was little concern with the rights of women. The correspondence is an invaluable source for the history of the period and this short account does not do justice to its richness. [....]

Notes
1 Jean Agnew (ed.). 1998, 1999. *The Drennan-McTier Letters, 1776–1819*, 3 volumes, Irish Manuscripts Commission/Women's History Project.
2 Letter 18, 8 Dec.1777. Martha McTier [Belfast] to William Drennan [Edinburgh].
3 Martha wrote to William about "our stubborn friend Bruce [who] is a hen-pecked ninny and called so to his face by an ignorant unfeeling shrew of a wife who is hurting

him in his Academy and the opinion of the world, poor fellow". Letter 334, ND 1792. Martha McTier [Belfast] to William Drennan [Dublin].

4 Letter 435, Mon. 29 Apr.1793. Martha McTier [Dublin] to Sam McTier [Belfast].

5 Letter, 145, Thurs.1785. William Drennan [Newry postmark] to Martha McTier [Donegall Street, Belfast].

6 Letter 52, Mon. franked by John Blackwood. Martha McTier [Belfast] to William Drennan [Mr Maxwell's, Newry].

7 Letter 543, 4 Oct. postmark, 1794. Martha McTier [Belfast, postmark] to William Drennan [11 Dame Street, Dublin].

8 Letter 892, 29 July 1799[?] Martha McTier [Belfast] to William Drennan [33 Marlborough Street, Dublin].

Gráinne Blair

LOLA MONTEZ: A MULTIOGRAPHY

Abstract: This article looks not only at the life and times of Lola Montez, but at various different ways of looking at the biography of such a colourful and elusive figure. It is suggested that the term multiography makes more sense than biography in the case of somebody like Lola, whose life is subject to a variety of interpretations. It is only through multiography that the complexity of Lola Montez as a woman of her time, can be understood.

from 'Looking for Lola: I, Lola Montez and Others – A Multiography', *Volume* 7, pp. 123-142

In truth one might ... take all the remarkable women in history and legend and stir them all up in an effort to find the receipt of that popular mystery Lola Montez.[1]

She is known as Lola Montez or Marie Dolores Eliza Rosanna Gilbert, Mrs James, Mrs Head, Mrs Hull, Baroness of Rosenthall and Countess of Landsfield, (c. 1818/20–1861). She has been the subject of numerous biographies, novels, newspaper articles, court cases, ballets and movies. She has had sonatas and polkas written for her and named for her. Irish, dancer, notorious, infamous, magnificent, divine, eccentric, divorcee, lecturer, actress, diplomat, international spy, horsewoman, horse whipper of humans, liberal reformer, adventuress, choreographer, smoker, bigamist, charitable, revolutionary, linguist, penitent, gold miner, angelic, counsellor, intrepid traveller, animal lover, loyal friend, lover of Franz Lizst, friend of George Sand – all of these and more descriptions were applied to this woman called Lola. Was she extraordinary or was she an 'ordinary woman' whose deeds and actions made her a good copy for the cultural constraints of the times in which she lived? Montez is important as a subject for multiography on two levels: her achievements and the way in which she has been demonised.

[LOLA MONTEZ.]

This paper is based on research in progress, and is exploring ways of (re) writing, (re) reading, (re) seeing, (re) looking at the 'story' of a woman, sometimes called Lola Montez. Upon Notification of her death in New York in January 1861 *The Irish American Weekly* dismissed her by writing that: "Her life was neither creditable to her native land nor useful to society, so we choose not to inquire further into it".[2]

Such sentiments, applied to many women, have ensured that they were excluded from the record, and negated in life. Isolation of such women both in historical and cultural terms, effectively created a false record, disconnecting and obscuring the reality. It is well documented that biographies involve turning the iconoclastic spotlight onto the persona, with a white heat that often ignores the shadows or grey lines between the subject and their social and cultural gendered constructions of time, place and other people. Multiography means replacing the spotlight with a peripheral two-way lens, examining the context and recognising the importance of all these elements to the subject. It is putting gender first and listening in this case to the woman's life, and distilling them to obtain the essence of the real self. The ways in which scholars have incorporated their lives into their research, have transformed feminist scholarship itself. Historians currently engaged in writing women back onto book shelves and into reading lists, utilise these skills in plumbing the depths of personal narratives to understand the construction of power and gendered identities. Heilbrun wrote that:

> There are four ways to write a woman's life: the woman herself may tell it, in what she chooses to call an autobiography: she may tell it in what she chooses to call fiction: a biographer, woman or man, may write the woman's life in what is called a biography; or the woman her own life in advance of living it, inconsciously, and without recognising or naming the process.[3]

Multiography is simply the word I use to convey my ideas about contextualising the ways in which we historiographise the people who contributed to events in the canons of history that we remember. For myself as a feminist historian, the importance of the (non)/ relationships of people add to the wealth of why and how an event came into being. Mutliography comes closer to presenting a holographic character than previously available. Multiography does not reconstruct or create a character with hindsight. It does, however, use our modern knowledge of the time and the place to construct the most likely scenario, similar to reconstructing character profiles using gender as the analytical tool.

I was nine when I first came across Lola in a book. I do not remember the title but that was before I understood the value of fleeting sentences or scouring footnotes for mentions of 'throw away women'. The dilemma facing me as an Irish historian in writing the life of a 'notable woman', is defining the research premise. Am I any better or worse than those who have written her life before me? Why has she generated so much copy? She is universally admired, reviled, ignored and unknown. If I were to ask a group what they know of her, some would know a little, others may say they have never heard of her. However, no one seems to know the multiplicity that was Lola Montez. What some may know is the more infamous parts of her life, her connections and interactions with others. What I propose is to tell Lola's complete story, in my voice, her voice and others – with the full understanding that we are all socially constructed by the patriarchy which has not only limited my life, limited Lola's life but limited the way in which she wrote about her self, how others wrote about her and how I will write about all of us. But knowing this limitation is the value, the limitation of Lola's life as defined by the strictures of nineteenth century society, the revolutionary times in which she lived, and the continents, states, nations, and realms in which she moved. The paradox is that if Montez really defined social ideas, why did she attract such huge audiences, both female and male? As Ward says, "Our task is to write a very different script".[4]

The numerous biographies and dramatic presentations of Montez's life have chosen to portray what they consider extraordinary in her life. Writing women back into history has shown that Montez is the norm, not the abnormal. Traditional male history opposed this – a view which Montez recognised, as she wrote in her autobiography in 1858:

> Such is the social and moral fabric of the world, that woman must be content with an exceedingly narrow sphere of action, or she must take the worst consequences of daring to be an innovator and a heretic. She must be either the servant or the spoiled plaything of man; or she must take the responsibility of making herself a target to be shot at.[5] [....]

Notes
1 *New York Herald Tribune Books*, Sunday 4 Oct. 1936, p. 8.
2 *The Irish American Weekly*, New York, 26 Jan. 1861.
3 Carolyn G Heilbrun. *Writing a Woman's Life*, London: The Women's Press, p. 11.
4 Margaret Ward 1994. 'Writing Biography: No Script to Follow', *Irish Association for Research in Women's History Bulletin*.
5 Lola Montez 1858, *Lectures of Lola Montez (Countess of Landsfeld) including her Autobiography*, New York, Rudd and Carleton.

Alan Hayes

Inghinidhe na hÉireann

Abstract: Many people are familiar with the name Maud Gonne. We almost certainly recognise her as the person about whom William Butler Yeats wrote many passionate and bitter poems. She may also be remembered as the wife of the executed patriot John MacBride, and as the mother of the famous Seán MacBride. Finally she is renowned for being a great beauty. These aspects may be true, but they are also very minor. Maud Gonne was a significant person in her own right, who played an important role in the Irish and European political arenas. The truth about her is difficult to come by, but I think it is worth knowing. I hope to show what I believe to be the *real* Maud Gonne.

from 'The *Real* Maud Gonne', *Volume 1*, pp. 55–68

Maud Gonne in Paris c. 1890s

[....] Maud Gonne could never forget that she was working alone, without the backing of any organisation behind her. She had been refused membership of all nationalist groups on the grounds of her sex, and so she decided it was time to set up her own group. She believed that it would be a group that could make use of the vast armies of women who were never allowed to offer their talents for the nationalist cause, and whose talents were needed if there was to be any hope of independence. On Easter Sunday 1900 she founded *Inghinidhe na hÉireann* (Daughters of Eireann), a nationalist group made up of a committee of women, many of whom were to become famous in Irish political affairs afterwards. They had an ambitious list of aims:

– The re-establishment of the complete independence of Ireland;

– To encourage the study of Gaelic, of Irish literature, History, Music and Art, especially among the young, by organising the teaching of classes for the above subjects;

– To support and popularise Irish manufacture;

– To discourage the reading and circulation of low English literature, the singing of English songs, the attending of vulgar English entertainments which is doing so much injury to the artistic taste and refinement of the Irish people.[1]

Even in its first phase of formation, *Inghinidhe na hÉireann* proved to be a major success. During Queen Victoria's visit to Ireland there had been a free treat given to 5,000 children in the Phoenix Park. The Committee realised that they would make a major contribution if they organised a similar treat for those children who had shown their allegiance to Ireland by not "being bribed into parading before the Queen of England."[2] The so called 'Irish Patriotic Children's Treat' took place in the summer of 1900 for 30,000 boys and girls. It was an outstanding success, being at that time the largest ever nationalist demonstration in Dublin. It is significant that even though it was women who organised the event and made all the food, during the Treat, Maud Gonne was the only woman who spoke on stage. Perhaps at that time very few women had the self-confidence to address such a crowd – even though it was composed totally of children. *Inghinidhe* was responsible for developing the qualities of confidence, courage and determination for many members, including Helena Moloney and Constance Markievicz.

Inghinidhe na hÉireann launched weekly classes teaching illiterate boys and girls about the culture of their land and the part they would play in a free Ireland. They received from most of the children an enthusiastic promise never to join or mix with members of the British Army. They conducted an intense campaign against enlistment in the Army, concentrating on direct action rather than public meetings. On O'Connell Street in Dublin, the women handed out leaflets warning Irish girls "against consorting with enemies of their country", and which graphically described the dangers of venereal disease, unwanted pregnancies and illegitimate babies to those girls who were seen associating with soldiers. The *Inghinidhe* even followed recruiting sergeants into pubs where they then distributed leaflets stating the Catholic Church's doctrine on unjust wars. The result of this campaigning was that almost every night there were fights in O'Connell Street when irate soldiers tried to attack the women and were stopped by passers-by sympathetic to the nationalist cause.[3] [....]

Notes
1 Margaret Ward 1990, *Maud Gonne: Ireland's Joan of Arc*, London: Pandora, p 48.
2 *United Irishman*, Apr. 1900.
3 Margaret Ward 1983. *Unmanageable Revolutionaries: Women and Irish Nationalism*, Dingle: Brandon, p. 52.

Mary Clancy

Suffrage in Galway

Abstract: This paper will attempt to evaluate the story of the women's suffrage debate as expressed in County Galway. Specifically, it will assess the configuration of the Connaught Women's Franchise League (1913) and consider the range of its appeal, strategies, and influence. The paper will examine earlier attempts to address the suffrage question and will attempt to situate the Galway campaign in the context of the national suffrage debate. [....]

> from '"... it was our joy to keep the flag flying": A Study of the Women's Suffrage Campaign in County Galway', *Volume 3*, pp. 91-104

[....] The launch of the Galway society took place at a public meeting, held in January 1913, in Galway Town Hall, and addressed by Helen Chenevix and Miss Moser. The meeting was told that the Federation was non-militant, and, as with so many organisations in these years, 'non-political and non-sectarian'. Among the topics covered by the guest speaker, Cork Poor Law Guardian, Susan Day, there was reference to the origins of trade unions, the Franchise Reform bill, those regions where women were enfranchised (US, New Zealand and China) and the benefits of a woman's perspective in areas of legislation, including the education of children. Day was to compare the situation of disenfranchised women with that of a previously disenfranchised Catholic male population regretting, as a Protestant, the abuses of her class.

from *Galway Express*, 18 January 1913

Susan Day and her colleagues of the Irishwomen's Suffrage Federation may not have had the same dramatic appeal as a personality like Christabel Pankhurst but they too would attract a large crowd. As reported in the *Galway Express,* the meeting was "packed", with "some hundreds" having "to go away disappointed owing to the great congestion". Even allowing for some exaggeration, it would seem that the meeting did attract significant local interest, but there the similarity with the IWFL/Pankhurst meeting ends. For if the latter was a model of efficiency, then the ISF meeting was its opposite. All accounts describe the interruptions which befell the meeting; even the *Galway Observer,* which rarely covered suffrage events, devoted half of its paragraph to the ructions. As described by a *Galway Express* columnist, there was "whistling, singing, and cat calls", causing continuous interruption which Miss Day could not manage to stop.[1] The culprits, male undergraduates at play, were attracted possibly, among other things, by the absence of an entrance fee and the notion that suffragists were easy and ready targets on their soapboxes and platforms.

The Galway branch would become known as the Connaught Women's Franchise League (non-militant) and the picture that emerges suggests that there was little deviation from the original objectives described in May 1913, i.e. the holding of monthly meetings "to discuss how they might educate and help those who have not yet formed any decided opinion on the subject".[2] The main approach, therefore, was educative, with the suffragists discussing the question during members' meetings and communicating information to the Press.

The size of the group is more difficult to estimate; descriptions like 'many Galway women' are vague although the figure of thirty members may be estimated from one report in 1914. If this is accurate, then it would suggest that there was something of a healthy interest in the question. Further, the Connaught Women's Franchise League appeared to be able, when required, to attract a significant local audience. There is no evidence to suggest that the League extended into the countryside but there is occasional newspaper reference to suffrage events. Gretta Cousins, for instance, mentions Clifden in a report of November 1911.[3] A number of women in Clifden were involved in local government, the Women's National Health Association and the United Irishwomen, so it is possible that there was an interest in women's suffrage too. Also, Gretta Cousins, along with her husband James, spent some months near Clifden in the summer of 1910 and, although not mentioned in their recollections, there may have been some contacts made locally.[4] There is an account of a "vigorous minded" suffragist who tried to organise the women of Annaghdown, a nurse who spoke of women's slavery and

'Votes for women for the Irish Parliament' – but the columnist is so taken by the concept that the piece is smothered in the florid imagery that a title such as 'Captious Corkers' might suggest and its accuracy is uncertain.[5] Suffrage leaflets and pamphlets were distributed in Tuam in May 1913 by Helen Chenevix, Irishwomen's Suffrage Federation and Miss Helen Fraser, a visiting suffragist. The open-air meeting appeared to be good-humoured with suffragists countering the heckling by successfully pinning posters claiming 'Votes for Women' on the backs of some listeners, including the police. The Tuam report would suggest that there were a number of women involved in organising the meeting, but again, information about Tuam and Ballinasloe (where another branch was reportedly established) is lacking.[6] Given that a link may be discerned between suffrage and moral and social reform, again, it is possible that there was some interest in Ballinasloe, which had its share of reform activists. [....]

Notes
1   *Galway Express*, 25 Jan. 1913.
2   *Galway Express*, May 1913.
3   *Freeman's Journal*, 6 Nov. 1911.
4   James Cousins and Margaret E. Cousins 1950, *We Two Together*, Madras, pp 141-144.
5   *Connaught Tribune*, 15 Mar. 1913.
6   *Connaught Tribune*, 3 May 1913.

Diane Urquhart

THE ULSTER WOMEN'S UNIONIST COUNCIL

Abstract This paper aims to analyse the way in which members of the Ulster Women's Unionist Council both defined and defended their citizenship through the third home rule crisis, the First World War and the establishment of a separate Northern Irish state.

from 'In Defence of Ulster and the Empire:
The Ulster Women's Unionist Council, 1911–1940', *Volume 4*, pp. 31–40

[....] The establishment of the Ulster Women's Unionist Council (UWUC) in January 1911 formalised and augmented the efforts which had been made from the late nineteenth century to enlist women's support in the anti-home rule campaign. In Ulster, the earliest permanent organisation of unionist women was prompted by the first home rule crisis of 1886, when a branch of the London-based Women's Liberal Unionist Association was instituted in Belfast.[1] Despite the establishment of this association, the efforts of female unionists during the first and second home rule crisis remained both sporadic and largely dependent upon individual initiative.[2] In 1907 the first indigenous Ulster women's unionist association was established in North Tyrone. This organisation mirrored the later activities of the Ulster Women's Unionist Council by electioneering both in its own locality and in English constituencies, updating electoral registers, distributing unionist propaganda and fund-raising.[3]

The formation of the UWUC was one consequence of the increased sense of crisis which followed the removal of the House of Lord's power of veto by the Parliament Act of 1911.[4] The political significance of this legislation lay in the fact that it erased the last constitutional bulwark against home rule. In practical terms this meant that any future bill, unlike its predecessors of 1886 and 1893, could only be delayed by the lords and not defeated outright. The women's council became the first mass-based, female political organisation in Ulster. During the first month of the council's existence over 4,000 women joined its West Belfast branch. By March 1911, women's unionist associations affiliated to the council were active throughout Antrim, Armagh, Belfast, Londonderry, Monaghan and Tyrone.[5] The UWUC had become not only an important component within unionism, but the largest politically active female force in Ireland. To place the UWUC's membership in its contemporary context – the women's nationalist association, *Cumann na mBan*, had an estimated membership of 4,425, whilst there were approximately 3,500 Irish suffragists.[6]

The explanation for the UWUC's success, in numerical terms, lies in unionism becoming truly popular for the first time in its history during the third, and most severe, home rule crisis of 1912–14. The protestant clergy, the family unit and women all became politicised.[7] Like the establishment of the UWUC, this can be explained by the heightened sense of political crisis in the aftermath of the removal of the House of Lord's power of veto, coupled with the popular appeal of unionists' anti-home rule arguments. By publicising a multi-faceted entreaty which underlined the constitutional, economic and imperial consequences of imposing home rule, unionists succeeded in maximising support amongst all classes and both sexes of protestant Ulster. Unionists' definition of citizenship, which focused on Ulster and the empire, therefore formed an important part of the popularisation process.

Unionist women adopted the general arguments which were forwarded by their male colleagues, by emphasising that home rule would curtail the freedom of religious practice and ruin Ulster's economic prosperity. Unionist arguments were not, however, based wholly on self-interest. Indeed, unionists attempted to cultivate sympathy in Britain, where they were only too aware that the ultimate decision to implement home rule would be taken by highlighting the imperial implications of home rule. The rhetoric which focused on their rights as citizens of the British empire formed an important constituent of their popular appeal, persuading many that they were not only defending the province of Ulster, but were helping to preserve the British empire. [....]

To conclude, defending their rights as loyal citizens of Ulster and the empire was partially responsible for enabling the UWUC, within a year of its establishment, to develop into a truly popular organisation. The women's organisation certainly became the largest, and, arguably, one of the most important associations of its type in early twentieth-century Ireland. Lady Cecil Craig, the president of the women's council from 1923–42, outlined that the organisation initially experienced "great difficulties ... prejudices were very strong against women taking any part in politics".[8] The resistance towards women's participation in politics gradually declined as a result of the increasingly visible public role which women took in society and the legislative advances which facilitated this departure. However, another significant component in this process was the impact of organisations, like the UWUC, who provided a positive and influential example of how women could effectively exercise their powers of citizenship. Therefore, the significance of the council lay not only in popularising the unionist cause, but also in spreading the unionist message throughout and beyond Britain and inculcating a sense of political responsibility and community amongst unionist women. Indeed, the long term effect of women publicly defending and exercising their rights as citizens of the imperial province of Ulster was considerable. The change which occurred in public opinion was recognised by one contemporary observer, who claimed, with some justification, that women had been taken "away from ... home duties by ... [the unionist] crusade far more than the ... granting ... of the Parliamentary Franchise".[9]

Notes

1   The first home rule bill was introduced by W. E. Gladstone in April 1886. This proposed the establishment of an Irish legislature with restricted functions. The bill was defeated in the Commons in June 1886.

2 The second home rule bill was introduced by Gladstone in January 1893. It was defeated in the Lords in September 1893.
3 Minute book of North Tyrone Women's Unionist Association 1907, (Public Record Office of Northern Ireland, D. 1908/2/1/1). In 1909, another women's unionist association was established in Londonderry. In 1911 both of these associations became affiliated with the UWUC.
4 For an analysis of the UWUC's activities see D. Urquhart 1991. 'The Ulster Women's Unionist Council, 1911–1940', MA, QUB, and 1994. "The Female of the Species is More Deadlier Than the Male?' The Ulster Women's Unionist Council, 1911–1940' in Janice Holmes and Diane Urquhart (eds), *Coming into the Light: The Work, Politics and Religion of Women in Ulster, 1840–1940*, Belfast: Institute of Irish Studies, pp. 93–123.
5 *Belfast News-Letter*, 22 Sept. 1913 and *Darlington and Stockton Times*, 22 Nov. 1913.
6 Figure for *Cumann na mBan* from David Fitzpatrick 1987. 'The Geography of Irish Nationalism, 1910–1921' in C. H. E. Philpin (ed.), *Nationalism and Popular Protest in Ireland*, Cambridge, Cambridge UP, pp 421–2. Figures for suffragists from *Irish Citizen*, 30 May 1914. Appropximately 1000 women in Ulster were members of suffrage societies.
7 T. A. Jackson 1992. 'Unionist Myths, 1912–1985', *Past and Present*, 136, pp 164–185.
8 *Northern Whig*, 9 May 1930.
9 *Irish Citizen*, 9 May 1914.

Irene Finn

Mary Strangman (1872–1943)

Abstract: This paper outlines some of the problems and possibilities encountered in writing a biography of Mary Strangman. She was one of Ireland's first woman doctors, a prominent figure in the suffrage movement, and an energetic campaigner in the cause of public health, first in the Women's National Health Association, and later as Waterford's first woman councillor. Because she was a woman in a man's world, there is enough relevant information on record to reconstruct the more public aspects of her life. The scarcity of information about her private life makes it difficult to move beyond a purely factual account to the heart of the subject. As a method, the biographical approach proved to be indirectly useful as a means of opening up new areas of research in women's history, and identifying the connections between them. The main objective, a biography which adequately portrays Mary Strangman in a local setting, within the broader context of early twentieth century Ireland, is proving to be more elusive.

from 'From 'Case Study' to 'Life': Mary Strangman (1872-1943) Doctor, Suffragist, Public Health Activist, Town Councillor', *Volume 7*, pp. 81-98

I first heard of Mary Strangman in connection with the women's suffrage movement. Curious to know what impression she had made in Waterford, her native city, I made enquiries, only to discover that this aspect of local history was uncharted territory. Mary Strangman, it seemed, had been forgotten. I was intrigued when further investigation revealed that on 15 January 1912, Mary Strangman became Waterford's first woman councillor. The election of a suffragist in the stronghold of John Redmond, MP for Waterford, leader of the Irish Parliamentary Party and certainly not a supporter of women's rights, seemed to offer the basis for an interesting case study. [....]

Speaking at a suffrage meeting in Waterford in April 1911, Mary Strangman acknowledged that most Waterford people saw the suffrage campaign as "a very far off thing ... an English movement". She insisted however, that the franchise could make a difference in Waterford too: women were 'sweated' in Waterford, as they were in London and Manchester. She knew of:

> Numerous instances of girls and women employed at a skilled work which it took years to learn, not earning a wage on which they could be independent of their people ... girls working fourteen hours for the miserable sum of 2s 6d a week.[1]

As I read her speech in its entirety, almost a century later, the immediacy of her words seemed to open a local window on the history of feminism in early 20th century Ireland – a topic which is still generally considered somewhat 'far off' and irrelevant. Before long, however, it became obvious that Mary Strangman's thoughts and actions, far from being simply the provincial echoes of a larger movement, were her own. My eagerness to create a local point of entry to women's history gave way to misgivings about exploiting Mary Strangman for this purpose. Frances Power Cobbe's warning about the 'absurdity of supposing ... that we can talk about "Woman" ... with a capital W'[2] came to mind. While it is clear that Mary Strangman saw gender as a defining feature of existence, this was only one aspect of her identity within the local community. Rather than attempting to place her within an existing body of knowledge, it seemed that the only valid approach was to focus on Mary Strangman as an individual and, in so far as possible, to retrieve and record her story. [....]

Contemporary publications reveal some of the background to Mary Strangman's public life. As a medium of information, propaganda and debate, as well as an administrative tool for record-keeping and reporting, the printed word was an integral part of Mary Strangman's environment. The 'male' domains of medicine and local government were documented in many official and professional publications. Women's organisations, too, used the printed word to further their cause. Specific reference to Mary Strangman herself can be found in the annual reports of the various organisations to which she belonged, and in the newspapers of the day. As a useful documentary source, the local newspapers surpassed all expectations. In contrast with the official Waterford Corporation council minutes, for example, press reports give vivid, verbatim accounts of council proceedings as they would have been heard by those present in public gallery. Mary Strangman's contributions to these debates, like her occasional letters to the editor and her addresses to public meetings, were always direct and incisive in tone. She appealed to reason rather than emotion. The content was concrete and practical, laced with facts and figures. Although only a few thousand of her words are on record, her voice is quite distinctive. In the absence of personal papers which might give some insight into the private, reflective side of her life, these few thousand words, representing the active, public woman, are as close as we can come to the real Mary Strangman. [....]

Unexpectedly, the only manuscript source that has come to light, the census form which she completed in April 1911, brought her to life. This official document gives a glimpse of Mary Strangman in action, engaging with the events of the moment. In England, plans for a highly organised 'census strike', with slogans such as 'NO VOTE NO CENSUS', had brought the suffrage cause into the headlines. The response in Ireland was more muted. Acting apparently on her own initiative, Mary Strangman decided that census night was an opportunity to take a stand against 'government without consent'. Having supplied full details of her servant, Julia Gibbons, she neatly added the word 'unenfranchised' in the 'infirmities' column of the census form – a particularly apt touch on the part of a Fellow of the Royal College of Surgeons. Concerning herself, she simply declared that she was 'absent in protest against unenfranchisement'. The enumerator, Constable Maurice Kelliher, noted in red ink: 'Head of Family is a Suffragette and states that she did not sleep in the house on 2 April but in Enumerator's opinion she did and probably was not enumerated elsewhere that night'. He completed the form correctly, apart from underestimating her age by four years.[3]

Mary Strangman's act of 'passive power' marked the beginning of open suffrage activity in Waterford. Her decision to run the risk of a £5 penalty, and compromise her position as a pillar of respectable Protestant middle-class society, gave a local dimension to the suffrage question. A public meeting on 20 April attracted a large crowd. In a speech punctuated by laughter and applause, she ably defended not only her own act of civil disobedience, but the entire movement, describing English Suffragettes, jailed for "the breaking of a few windows", as "no more militant than the Salvation Army". She drew attention to the facts: they had never "done damage to a single person in life or limb … a few pounds would cover the whole damage they had done".[4]

Notes
1 *Waterford Standard*, 22 April 1911
2 Frances Power Cobbe, 'The final cause of woman', in Josephine Butler (ed.), 1869, *Woman's Work and Woman's Culture*, London, Macmillan, pp 5-6.
3 Census of Ireland, 1911, 80/53
4 *Waterford Standard*, 22 April 1911

Peter Moser

Rural Economy and Female Emigration

Abstract: The substantial production alterations within the agricultural sector in the West of Ireland in the 1930/1940s affected men and women differently and provoked a gender-specific behaviour pattern. While men tried to save their socio-economic interests through the formation of their own political pressure groups, women acted more individually and more often emigrated. This emigration pattern was also influenced through the gender-oriented (emigration) policy of Church and State.

from 'Rural Economy and Female Emigration in the West of Ireland 1936-1956', *Volume 2*, pp. 41-51

We are all perturbed to discover that rural girls today are not inclined to settle on the land. The whole future of this country is at stake.[1]

While comprehensive research on emigration from rural Ireland in the post-war period has been done,[2] the causes for the significant differences between male and female emigration patterns in the 1940s have received little attention so far.

There were 19,000 female relatives working on the farms in Connacht in 1936. Fifteen years later, in 1951, the figure was less than 9,000. While the number of women relatives declined by more than half, only about a quarter of the male relatives left in the same period.[3]

In this article I will discuss the question why proportionally so many more women than men left the farms in Connacht in that period. In the first section I will argue that a large part of these women's economic basis eroded due to substantial changes in the production structure. The women who left Connacht and mainly, though not exclusively, went to Great Britain are the topic of the second part, where I look at the reasons they put forward for their decision to emigrate. In the third part the influence which this female exodus had on those (males) who were left behind is examined. And, finally, the gender aspect of the policy on emigration of both the State and the Catholic church is examined very briefly.

1. Women in the Rural Economy

On Saturday, 12 September 1942, the following incident happened in Belmullet, Co. Mayo:

> A farmer's son from Emlybeg, in the Mullet, was approached by a Ballina fowl dealer who requested him to convey with his horse cart a few boxes from Mr. O'Reilly's yard in Chapel St. to Mr. Hurst's premises in Main St. for conveyance to Ballina. The young farmer was courteous enough to oblige, but when he went to load the boxes he discovered they were two crates of old hens. Errismen as a rule do not engage in the fowl traffic, leaving this as a legacy to the opposite sex, and much as he disliked his engagement he drove off as fast as he could to get rid of his burden, and to escape the observation of many farmers' daughters who were on shopping errands in the town. Rounding the post office corner, and turning into Main St., the captives began to scream violently. The shame-stricken farmer's son drove faster and faster, but the uproar still grew, and excitement followed when the old 'cluckers' broke through the bars, some flying on to the horse's back, infuriating the animal, and others flying to the roof-tops of the nearest houses. The round-up went on for several hours before order was restored.[4]

The incident may have been unusual – and therefore got the necessary attention to be reported in the local paper. But it contains a precise description of the division of labour between men and women on one side and the strong social hierarchy within this rural society on the other. While we were told that certain aspects of the rural economy were strictly left by men 'to the opposite sex', we also get the message that the farmer's son was concerned about the impact this episode had on the group of 'farmers' daughters', not on women generally. Both aspects, the division of labour and the social hierarchy, are crucial for the understanding of rural society and the emigration pattern in Connacht in the 1940/50s. [....]

Notes
1. A member of Mayo Vocational Education Committee commenting on the fact that in 1957 only 4 girls applied for 6 scholarships for a month's course in poultry keeping, butter-making and domestic science at St. Vincent's School of Domestic Science. *Mayo News*, 18 May 1957.
2. *Cf*, for example, Damian Hannan. 1970, *Rural Exodus*. London.
3. In 1936 there were 18,973 female and 61,577 male relatives assisting on the farms in Connacht [....] If the figures are broken down according to the size of the farm it becomes clear that the smaller the farm, the more likely the women were to leave.
4. *Western People*, 19 Sept. 1942.

Mary Kierse

WOMEN TEACHERS IN CLARE, 1922–1958[1]

Abstract: I was interested to find out about Clare women teachers, and to explore the impact of the marriage bar. By doing so I uncovered information that suggested that Clare's female teachers 1922-1958 made an active choice to determine their future. They did this by choosing to work as teachers and spurn marriage (as combining both marriage and career in this period was made more difficult) or by ensuring that their daughters especially would not have such a stark choice. There were, of course, some who sought to combine marriage and family with teaching, something that was only feasible for females who were already teaching before the marriage bar.

from "'We Taught and Went Home': Women Teachers in Clare, 1922-1958', *Volume* 7, pp. 41-52

The testimonies that are recounted here are personal stories: individual women talking about their lives, how they saw themselves, what they remember, and what significance they give to personal and political events. [....]

From the very beginning of their careers, some lengthy, some cut short, the women told of how they were subjected to low pay, public vigilance, and frequent isolation in draughty classrooms. As in the home, a female teacher's work in the classroom was never done. Their duties frequently went beyond preparing lessons and marking work, often involving washing floors, emptying bins and grates, lighting fires and cleaning classrooms. This sort of domestic work did not cause problems for the women I interviewed, it was never a topic that they highlighted as unfair, rather they accepted this work as part of the school day.

Being a teacher, especially a female teacher entailed many responsibilities not only towards the school and the children but also to the church and the community. This was especially true of national teachers. The personal conduct of teachers was closely monitored, and not only during school time. Indeed, they were advised to avoid all public gatherings, including fairs and political meetings—the key events in social life.

Mrs Liddy and Miss Keane had varied opinions on how they were regarded in the community. Mrs Liddy found it hard to be herself as she felt that most of the time she was viewed as 'the teacher', and not just 'Susan':

> It was hard to be at ease, I was always conscious of position ... there was a strict mode of conduct. I think it meant that other people felt they had to be on their best behaviour ... it wasn't easy to keep a bit of dignity or distance or whatever ... we had great fun but still you knew people were looking on.

She did, however, find that when she got married, things eased a little:

> There was a small bit of release ... as a farmer's wife; I could talk about things more easily. As a married woman, I still had to be a respectable person.

Miss Keane, who enjoyed a quiet life and took great comfort in her religion, did not agree that teachers were subject to great scrutiny while Mrs Liddy felt that there were enough restrictions on teachers without further confining the limited opportunities for a happy social life. These restrictions continued in the classroom with a rigid and unimaginative curriculum. Mrs Liddy remembers the teaching of Irish:

> There was a set way of teaching Irish and you dare not deviate from that, I had to stick pictures of the word on the board and say the word, then more pictures would be introduced and stuck on ... of course you rarely got halfway through the lesson and the pictures would fall off and you would spend a good ten minutes sticking them up again. [....]

Mrs Monahan was the most forthright with regard to the perceived position of the teacher, especially the male teacher:

> In our community the teacher held a position of prestige, not due entirely to his personality, character or attributes, but because of the noble vocation he represented. He was treated with respect by young and old. His presence was requested at all social events. His advice was sought and his influence great. I considered it to be a privilege to become a teacher. I also considered the mundane factor of security. I was becoming a member of a very influential, powerful Teachers' Organisation.

However, she noted that in teacher training she was forever reminded that she should be a model of good behaviour, every word, thought and action should conform to a high standard; she believed that the profession restricted women teachers significantly:

> A vigilant community and eager pupils forever reminded us that we were teachers and so we stood lonely and apart. [....]

Eleanor Daly, who was married, warned of the necessity of carefully assessing any prospective partners, as some unscrupulous men would see an earning woman teacher as an asset to their lifestyle if not a meal ticket. It would seem that in Clare prudence held sway and many women decided on a life alone:

> I was as happy on my own to tell you the truth. I could come and go on as I pleased. Of course, sometimes the neighbours or someone would say, well, you'd get people wanting to make a match for you. My father always said, God bless him, there's two of you here and none for sale. [....]

The women that I interviewed were keen to point out that the discrimination that they suffered at school was simply accepted as their lot, even though the rest of society was not *overtly* prejudiced. Similarly, many of the women referred to the marriage bar as the 'marriage ban' or simply the 'ban' and marked periods in their lives as 'pre-ban' and 'post-ban'. The term is loaded with significance. Did they insist on calling the marriage bar a ban because of its absolute restrictions and prohibitions that it placed upon women? Was the ban a more accurate term for the veto that was imposed on married women teachers? [....]

Note

1 All quotations are from interviews with various women teachers. See Mary Kierse, 'Women and National Teaching in Clare, 1922–1958: A Marriage of Convenience?', MA Thesis, NUI, Galway.

Anne Byrne

Equality in Local Development

Abstract: This paper raises questions about the commitment to equality issues in local development programmes. Previous local development programmes are critiqued for their lack of attention to gender. The commitment to gender equality in the 1994-1999 local development programme presents a challenge to partnerships and to community groups. It is argued that proactive strategies are required in order to feminise the development process and one example of a targeting strategy used in a rural development programme is outlined.

from 'Making Development Work for Women', *Volume 3*, pp. 201-213

Introduction

There is no doubt that many women have always been and continue to be involved in community and voluntary activity. This is evident, for example, in their participation in school boards and parent-teacher organisations, sport and leisure clubs, branches of political parties, charitable institutions, in adult education organisations and in the recent growth of extensive women's networks throughout the country. But rarely are women involved at formal decision making levels or rarely do they occupy leadership roles in community and voluntary organisations that are committed to a developmental or entrepreneurial brief. Women are also acutely under-represented at key decision making levels in many organisations which claim to represent their interests – for example, in farming organisations, trade unions, community councils, local authorities, health boards and educational bodies. In addition, many local development schemes do not actively include women, seek their direct participation or promote women's interests. Explanations pertaining to organisational/administrative factors and family/societal factors abound for the segregated participation of women in development, ranging from women's lack of interest in leadership, the demands of family and others on already 'busy' women, the exclusionary procedures of organisations themselves, women's lack of financial independence, relative immobility and lack of access to transport, particularly in rural areas.

There are at least four issues which need to be addressed in order to 'feminise' development. Strategies are required to facilitate the promotion of women on boards of management; to encourage the advancement of women in leadership roles at local, regional and national level; to assist the participation of women in local development schemes; and to encourage the involvement of women who are not currently active in development schemes, but who do wish to become involved. This article examines one strategy which targeted rural women in a development programme within a partnership context and evaluates the outcome in terms of an equal opportunities framework. [....]

Nuala Keher

WOMEN AND TRADE UNIONS

Abstract: This essay examines women's participation within the Irish trade union movement. It attempts to place a study carried out in 1987 in the context of recent trade union restructuring which was in part a response to 'new' forms of work emerging in the 1990s. It argues that the trade union movement to date has failed to adequately address the barriers to women's participation in the movement and concludes that unless this failure is addressed, the degree of relevance which the trade union movement holds must inevitably decline.

from 'Women and Trade Union Restructuring: Women Must Wait?', *Volume 2*, pp. 15–31

Introduction

> Women must ... be integrated at every level of trade union structure, including the social and economic policy-making level, and they must be integrated on an equal footing, not merely for 'women's questions' or 'family questions', even if that means modifying structures, rules or the traditional means of access to these levels.[1]

These words, written twenty-five years ago, reflect the aspirations of a trade union movement which had as a priority the elimination of inequality within its own structures. However, despite the positive action programmes adopted by ICTU, women continue to play a subordinate role within the movement, particularly at executive decision making level. There are seventy-three ICTU affiliated unions with over 250,000 (37%) women members, yet women constitute only 24% of themembership of the executives. This number is much lower in the larger more influential unions (see ICTU *Programme for Progress* 1992).

ICTU has made a number of recommendations to its affiliated organisations in an attempt to respond to the low level of women's participation. These include a proposal that the number of women on decision making bodies be increased, either through the creation of additional seats for women or through co-option. It has recommended also the setting up of special structures such as women's committees. There have been some limited successes. Of the seventy-three unions in ICTU, twenty have national women's committees and ten organise women's conferences. The vast majority of unions have, however, resisted the option of power sharing at executive level. Only four (5%) unions have reserved seats for women.

There are mixed views as to whether the creation of women's committees is the most appropriate method of redressing the gender imbalance. Some writers believe that these committees can be organised in a democratic way which may be more appropriate to women's participation than the traditional hierarchical organisation of the male dominated movement (see Beattie 1986). Likewise, it is argued that women's committees are an important medium for monitoring the progress of women within society and within the movement. They can also be seen as a valuable educational forum for women who wish to progress within the traditional union structures.

Conversely, women's committees could prove to be divisive as it can be argued that workers should unite in common cause for better conditions for all workers. By putting their energies into special structures, women activists, it has been said, can easily become marginalised from the central activity of unions or alternatively can be co-opted by the union hierarchy. [....]

In order to provide an effective response it is, perhaps, first of all necessary to explore some of the reasons for women's low level of union participation. It has been suggested that women are less inclined than men to join trade unions and when they become members they are less active and have different priorities (Siltanen and Stanworth 1984). Clancy and McKeogh (1987) discount this view. They connect the low level of participation with the position of women in the labour force which, they argue, is in turn largely determined by the position of women within the family. This essay attempts to develop this theme and makes connections between the hierarchal structure of the movement and the low level of participation by women. A study carried out in Galway in 1987 (Keher 1987) and presented in Part 1 looks at the 'divide' between the union leadership and the membership, which it is said adversely affects women's participation. Part 2 raises issues in relation to the debate on the restructuring of work in the 1990s and asks if the trade union movement's response to such restructuring has in any way bridged the gap between the unions and their female membership. [....]

In conclusion, I am suggesting that a gap continues to exist between the vision of equality espoused by the male-dominated movement and the reality facing women members, despite the restructuring process that has taken place within the movement. This gap can only be bridged if the organisation is prepared firstly to accept that barriers to women's participation exist and secondly, to work energetically towards breaking them down. The experience and contribution of women workers is fundamental therefore to the success of the movement. The participation of women at all levels can only benefit and strengthen a trade union movement which not only has to respond to management initiatives must also shape future developments in the workplace.

Celia Davies

EQUALITY AND WOMEN ACADEMICS

Abstract: This paper argues that a more critical perspective is needed in considering the integration of women academics into the university and the degree of power and privilege they enjoy. Based on in-depth interviews with five women academics in the North of Ireland, it suggests that an 'equality mystique' prevents us from a confident articulation of the problems we face and blinds us to the depth of the threat that women can present to the unwritten rules in the university.

from 'The Equality Mystique, The Difference Dilemma and the Case of Women Academics', *Volume 2*, pp. 53-72

[....] This paper will argue that an equality mystique, in the shape of a celebration of sameness and an adherence, as far as possible, to a principle of equal treatment for the two sexes, has replaced the feminine mystique of the 1950s and 1960s, and this equality mystique has now been in the ascendant for some considerable while. Just as Betty Friedan argued that the feminine mystique reified and rigidified a concept of the feminine, giving an apparently attractive but ultimately narrow prescription of what it was to be a woman in the postwar era, cutting women off from areas of experience that would add to their sense of esteem and selfworth – so I shall argue a parallel case for the equality mystique. Like the feminine mystique it is a 'problem with no name', and like the feminine mystique it confuses and frustrates. [....]

The data for this paper are drawn from a study [....] the core of which involves lengthy and in-depth interviews with five women who hold academic posts in my own university in Northern Ireland. [....] The project owes its being to the unprecedented step that the University took in 1987 in appointing me as Professor of Women's Opportunities, with an academic brief to develop teaching and research, and a more managerial, roving brief to comment on the university's policies as they affected its female employees. [....]

My colleagues, or perhaps more strictly, given the research design, my co-researchers, vary in ages from early 30s to mid-50s. They were all born on the island of Ireland, two in the South and three in the North. Four of the five are Catholic, one a (Southern) Protestant. They all work broadly in the fields of social sciences. They are all people who showed an interest in the University's Women's Opportunities initiative, but they are not all working in Women's Studies, nor are they all necessarily especially familiar with the debates raised in this paper. They are known, but not necessarily well known, to each other. Three of the University's four campuses are represented. [....]

All five women emphasised that to be accepted and heard in the academic setting it can be necessary to deflect men's attempts to impose their own stereotyped views of women's contribution. [....] The dilemmas of being seen as less serious, and of being discounted in various ways, can mean getting the lower status work or getting responsibility on a temporary basis. Housework imagery recurred. [....] Differential expectations of women academics can arise when behaviour is, on the face of it, the same. [....] These interviewees report much pressure to behave like men. Anything else is felt to count against you, even though very little is actually being said. If women are going to put so much effort into the quest not just to get in, but to fit in, should we not also pay more attention to what it is that we are fitting into, and the nature and form of resistance we face? [....] Women, in the university world at least, seem to make their male colleagues uneasy. [....] Elsewhere, the interviews show women as being mystified and disillusioned as to how the system functions at all – especially in relation to committees. [....]

The women I have spoken to feel highly committed to the enterprise that is higher education and feel that its rewards, both personal and financial, are so great that they are privileged to be able to take part in it. They have made strenuous efforts to fit in and to contribute, and this can mean juggling responsibilities at home and work, feeling guilt in ways that are not the same for men. Despite the positive side of university work, however, [....] there is a sense among them – among us – of not really understanding the system, of not belonging, and, in the particular instance where a woman is placed in a man's shoes, of amazement about the 'easy' fashion in which the work is actually done. Such a picture seems a long way from actionable discrimination and a long way too from any simple account under the heading of sexist behaviour on the part of a male minority.

The puzzlement present here should, I would contend, be seen in terms of the power of the equality mystique. It seems self-evident that the doors to advancement are no longer closed to women; it seems incontrovertible that the accepted injunction is that women and men should be treated in exactly the same way, and hence that opportunity is there for women to demonstrate their merit and to gain suitable recognition and reward. If women are unhappy – as clearly on many counts they are – if they are not rising to senior positions – as is again demonstrably true – there is little in the current language of equality that can address this. Few would want to undo legislative moves towards formal equality, but formal equality, I maintain, does much to obscure the real conditions which women face. And indeed for these women, far from such equality enhancing their self-esteem and respect, the effect can be the reverse. If women's inclusion is so partial, their integration so imperfect, what are the rules that we break?

I find glimpses of an answer in several of the events and incidents reported here: in the distaste over displays of emotion, for example, in the negative messages around women's pregnancy and around the presence of children, in the managed and formal agenda of committees, and also in the story of the protected space of the head of department. All relate to the separation of the public and the private spheres and the creation of a link in the public sphere with a particular style, a particular behaviour which is culturally linked with the male. [....] Women's presence in the University is more than a challenge to exclusion from a sphere populated by the other sex, it is a challenge to men's way-of-being in that sphere, and to the rules that constitute that way-of-being. If we challenge that, we challenge something very fundamental.

Three components of this challenge can now be highlighted. First, women break the rules because we *pollute public space*. [....] Second, women *demonstrate that transgressing or perhaps permeating the boundary between the public and private spheres is possible*. [....] Third, some women's presence in the public space denotes the *danger of defection of other women from the private space*. [....]

Eileen Kane

MISMEASURED AND MISUNDERSTOOD?

Abstract: This essay offers an analysis and critique of theories of biological determinism as a way of explaining gender differentiation. It demonstrates that there is no easy way of objectively measuring biological and psychological differences, and that such measurements do not in any case provide conclusive evidence for an exclusively 'biological' basis for women and men's behaviour.

from 'Women: Mismeasured and Misunderstood?'
Volume 2, pp. 1–13

That women are 'defective', biologically and intellectually inferior to men, rather than merely different in some respects, is an idea which enjoys a long tradition in western philosophy. Historically, the words of Aristotle, 'The female is a female by virtue of a certain lack of qualities; we should regard the female as afflicted with a certain natural defectiveness,' are reflected repeatedly in the words of theologians, politicians and social commentators. [....]

Women, it is said, are less 'intelligent' than men; more subjective, passive, sociable, compliant, obedient, dependent and better at jobs requiring attention to sequence and detail; leadership, while it can be acquired, does not come easily to the average woman; girls who dream erotically have a male brain pattern; that perhaps women are paid less money because money interests them less; and that, even given equal opportunities, women are less likely to excel. [....] On the other hand, men are more intelligent than women; they have 'the simple stuff of genius' (could this be testosterone?); they are more analytical, better at theorising and are more natural leaders; more objective, independent, achievement oriented, dominant and single-minded. It is not simply that men have more of these characteristics; these are male characteristics. Women who possess them must also possess suspiciously high levels of male hormones, or be genetically misprogrammed.

Underlying all these ideas, historical, scientific and popular, are two assumptions: that behavioural differences between men and women are the inescapable result of biology, and that the differences reflect some lack or defect in women. [....]

The fact that societies must socialise for these characteristics indicates that they are not innate, but rather based on activities which, in technologically-simpler societies, each of the sexes is likely to perform. Just as superior strength and fecundity are not particularly adaptive characteristics in modern societies, nor are these special activity-related characteristics, when applied exclusively to one sex or the other. [....]

Many of the sex-related customs which we in the western world assume are universal or near-universal are not: the majority of world cultures do not express a preference for male children, for example. Male witches are more common or more powerful in the majority of societies. Women spend either the same amount of time and effort, or more, on the subsistence activities of society, in a majority of cultures (while at the same time doing all or most of the domestic work in all cultures). At marriage, when goods or money change hands, the more frequent direction of the exchange is from groom's family to bride's, not the other way round, as we who are familiar with the dowry might expect. In nearly half of all cultures, both sexes initiate pre-marital sex equally, or females do. Finally, divorce is equally possible for both males and females in three quarters of world cultures, as is re-marriage (Whyte 1980).

The popular model of physical difference as the basis for psychological and cognitive differences, which in turn are the basis for culturally assigned differences, appears not to be the best explanation for sex roles and activities. While not ruling out the possibility that cross-cultural research may yet lead to the delineation of some universal sex-linked psychological attributes, the evidence at the moment points to a simpler explanation; that in the brief span of our evolutionary history, physical attributes related to childbearing and childcare dictated the range of economic activities most compatible with that activity; and most of these are assigned to women, cross-culturally. Work requiring superior physical strength and immediate energy fell to men.

Marian Tannam

Migrant Women in Ireland

Abstract: The main focus of this paper is to examine the 'everyday lived experiences' of some migrant women in Ireland with reference to the wider frameworks of migrancy and racism. This will be done through using the accounts of personal interviews with migrant women, examination of some of the literature, private and public discourse and media representations. Migrant women can be both 'invisible' and 'visible'. Even though from very diverse backgrounds and cultures, they are often perceived and their identities defined as similar by the 'host' society. They are often regarded as 'other'. Ireland's role as 'Mother Ireland' to her adopted daughters will be examined and how elites such as the media contribute to racist ideology which results in inappropriate policy and practice.

from 'At Home from Abroad: The Experiences of Some Migrant Women in Ireland', *Volume* 6, pp. 19-32

Introduction

[....] For many migrant women, their identities are constructed and defined by the 'host' society. Through the analysis of the research data the extent to which this happens in Irish society will be examined with reference to the larger frameworks of migrancy and racism. [....] The migrant is often forced to examine the 'host' society's definition of their identity and consequently is made aware of and accountable for their identity in a way that they were not in their country of origin. Gone are the familiar landmarks and cultural markers which once mapped their identity. The past is an integral part of exploring 'Who am I?' [....] Being somewhere else often means one's identity becoming a focus, which must be explained to others and to oneself. [....]

Ireland has a long history of emigration rather than immigration, a country whose children have travelled to many corners of the world in search of work, adventure or a better way of life. In the past thirty years there has been a visible increase of people residing in Ireland of African, Asian, Middle and East European origin. Ireland as a 'host country' is a relatively new phenomenon. The term 'host country' usually denotes a country in which migrants reside. Often used in relation to 'guest workers', the term is by nature a signifier of a temporary event (guests usually leave after a given period). Uninvited guests, those who do not behave (i.e. do not keep the host's rules) and those who overstay, risk being unwelcome. [....]

Focus on Media

Watson and Hill quote Alvarado et al. as identifying four main areas of media representation of Black people: the exotic, e.g. tribal dancing and rituals to welcome visiting dignitaries or royals; the dangerous, e.g. immigrants and refugees presenting a threat; the humorous, e.g. humorous stereotypes in television shows at the expense of Black people; the pitied, e.g. media coverage of famines.[1] We can see that the exotic and dangerous representations are a direct result of early Eurocentric attitudes. Tales of 'paradise' and 'the uncivilised' formed the binary opposites often presented by travellers. The other two areas of representation are newer developments in media reporting but are equally based on the Eurocentric/ethnocentric concepts that are part of racism. Recent media reporting in Ireland has focused on immigrants and refugees as a threat and constantly links immigrants and refugees with racism and social problems. This linking and juxtaposing of foreigners/problems and more recently refugees/racism is misguided as it wrongly identifies foreigners and refugees as the cause of problems and racism, and gives Ireland an excuse for not addressing its racism in the wider and historical contexts. A fifth category, that of sexual representations, could be added. Marshall says that "Portraying Black women as sexually denigrated has been central to the ideological justification for systems of racism, sexism, heterosexism and class oppression".[2] [....]

Sister Ireland

Living in a patriarchal society it might be expected that migrant woman would engage in mutual support with Irish woman. The 1993 Commission on the Status of Woman (2nd Report) gives the impression that "women who experience exclusion are working together to gain equal rights with other women and towards equal rights with men",[3] however there is no specific mention of migrant women in the whole report. Nor to my knowledge have migrant women featured in any published comprehensive texts on women in Ireland. It is hard to give or receive support when you are 'invisible'. [....] The intersection of sexism and racism can be explored and challenged, and women supported through activities of women's groups, and other broader support groups can help challenge stereotypes.

Conclusion

Looking at discourses of migrancy, racism and difference and relating them to an Irish context through the eyes of migrant women in Ireland

and available literature, we can see that despite the constant denial at all levels of society, racism is central to the lives of migrants in Ireland.

This denial is indicative of xenophobia and a wish to keep our country homogeneous instead of facing the fact that Ireland cannot exist in isolation from the rest of the world. Before we can go beyond racism we must stop denying its existence. Only then can we start to change the structures in our society that reproduce racism, only then can we enter into meaningful dialogue. [....] [Since the original article was written the National Women's Council of Ireland have worked in partnership with their members, including minority ethnic women's groups such as AkiDwA and the Louth African Women's Support Group on challenging racism in Irish society. They were one of forty-four NGOs who signed up to the NGO Alliance Shadow Report to the UN Committee on the Elimination of All Forms of Racial Discrimination. However access to funding for minority ethnic groups continues to limit their activities and keep the power within the minority ethnic group].[4]

Notes

The author wishes to thank the women who were interviewed for this article for sharing their experiences.

1. James Watson and Anne Hill 1993. *A Dictionary of Communication and Media Studies*, London: Edward Arnold, pp. 120, 154.
2. Annecka Marshall 1996. 'From Sexual Denigration to Self-respect: Resisting Images of Black Female Sexuality,' in Delia Jarrett-Macauley (ed), *Reconstructing Womanhood, Reconstructing Feminism*. London: Routledge, p.5.
3. Second Commission on the Status of Women: Report of the Government. 1993. Dublin: G.P.S.O., p. 163.
4 NGO Alliance (Nov. 2004). Shadow Report.

Philomena Mullen

BLACK IRISH WOMAN

from 'On being Black, Irish and a Woman', *Volume* 6, pp. 45–50

Within the ongoing debate on immigration into Ireland, a once homogeneous island that tended to export people rather than import them, I wish to give a brief but personal appraisal of some of the factors that go into the make-up of a Black Irish woman. A minority group (to say the least) in Ireland, which has felt at times as a minority of one. One can argue that there is nothing particularly significant about being a Black woman, but the relevance of my identity to this discussion is the Irish part of the Black equation and how, with no pun intended, this places me outside the Pale of most current feminist dialogues within this, my own country.

My mother and I are very similar in character and in many ways her values are still my values. Her personality is carved deep inside me. I now recognise, as I grow older, that I am very much her daughter. The one thing, however, that intractably separates us, informing our very different views of the world, is our colour. My mother is a stereotype of Irish beauty. Red hair, fine aquiline features and grey-blue eyes. Her skin is so white I am sure that it reflects the sun. I am, in contrast, a deep coffee colour, with typical Black features: flat nose, big lips, kinky Afro hair and dark brown eyes. [….]

I was raised as a typical Irish girl, with very conservative traditional values. I was good at Irish dancing (pre-Riverdance, of course) and competed in Slógadh and the Feis. I grew up with the concerns of the 'Kennedys of Castleross' on the radio every day at lunchtime and the outrages 'perpetrated' by the 'Late Late Show' on the people of Ireland, with its constant discussion of sex. My education was a good convent schooling in the history and geography of Ireland. I studied Vinegar Hill and the 'terrible beauty' of 1916; I knew my *Buntús*, the height of Carrantouhill and the length of the Shannon by heart. I can still recite my Yeats and Pearse, Clarke and Kavanagh. To my mind I was exceptionally unremarkable, being just as Irish as everyone else.

When I was a child watching *Sesame Street* on the little b&w in the corner, they used to play a song called 'one of these kids is not like the other'. My anthem. From the vantage point of the passage of more than 30 years, one thing that seems remarkable to me about the verbal abuse I elicited by my presence, was its wide variety. In the Ireland of the 1960s, which had no multiracial society, there was no paucity of racial slurs when it came to name-calling. It ran the entire gamut from coon to nigger to wog, and this was without the benefit of the inspiration that vast hordes of 'scrounging immigrants' would have afforded the Irish inventive genius. I often reflect that, given our natural ability for word-smithing, now that Ireland teeters on the brink of becoming multicultural, we may well enlarge the vocabulary of abuse. [….]

In secondary school my mother attended a parent-teacher meeting and was asked by one of my teachers where my 'real' mother was. She stated that she was my real mother, but the teacher persisted and rephrased the question, asking where my 'natural' mother was. Often I was questioned about whether I was adopted, not just by classmates but by their parents and my teachers. Incidents such as these have cut across my relationship with my mother, making me feel that some terrible fraud had been perpetrated and that I was 'unnaturally' hers. I began to wonder myself if I was adopted and if I wasn't then, perhaps, I ought to have been. These occasions stick out in my mind, as they served to make me feel uncomfortable in settings which included my mother. I could not look out and see myself reflected back in anyone's eyes and most especially not in my mother's. I began at this time a process of rejection and started to look outside for an identity, a place where I might fit in and not be my mother's 'little darkie'.

As a teenager I searched for and discovered Black heroes and heroines with whom I believed I could identify. By definition I had to search in the annals of other countries though I did read of the visit of the leader and ex-slave Frederick Douglass to Ireland during the last century, and of how he came away "deeply affected".[1] [....] Sojourner Truth, Ida B. Wells, James Baldwin, Harriet Tubman, and Maya Angelou. They became as real to me as my own native Yeats or Pearse. I searched for the experiences of Black women around the world and through them I thought I would discover my 'natural' mother and myself. [....] I lived daily the lines of Chandra Mohanty, believing that beyond sisterhood there was still racism.[2] Black liberation became my focus, I saturated myself in every aspect of it. Slavery, Apartheid, lynching, the independence days of various African countries. [....] My sense of reality has always been informed by my outstanding racial characteristic – my Blackness. It has led me to be treated differently. [....]

Ireland is on the brink of experiencing multiracialism first hand for the first time. Race and class, race and gender are issues that will have to be addressed within the Irish context. Women as the main transmitters of culture will be playing leading roles in the dissemination of the racial ideology that takes hold in this country. Here, the role of the women's movement must be to promote constructive debate on the issues by adding race to their agenda, and so protecting all Irish women, regardless of class, race or any other sociological or political stratification. The only certain means of accomplishing this is by first recognising the problem and then by discussing it. [....]

Notes
1   Robert L. Factor, *The Black Response to America: men, ideals and organisation from Frederick Douglass to the NAACP*, London, Addison-Wesley, 1970, p. 80
2   Chandra Mohanty, 'Under Western Eyes', in Mohanty, Russo and Torres (eds), *Third World Women and the Politics of Feminism*, Bloomington, Indiana UP, 1991, p 53

Moya Cannon

After the Burial

from Volume 2, p. 76

They straightened the blankets,
piled her clothes onto the bed,
soaked them with petrol,
then emptied the gallon can
over the video and tape recorder,
stepped outside their trailer,
lit it, watched until only the burnt chassis was left,
gathered themselves
and pulled out of Galway.

Camped for a week in Shepherd's Bush,
then behind a glass building in Brixton,
he went into drunken mourning for his dead wife,
while their children hung around the vans,
or foraged in the long North London streets
among other children, some of whom also perhaps understood,
that beyond respectability's pale,
where reason and civility show their second face,
it's hard to lay ghosts.

Anne Kennedy

'With One Continuous Breath'

from Volume 2, p. 80

I have stepped out
onto that same patch of grass
a thousand times,
it is my Heraclitean stream.
You, jingling your car keys
me, wearing the low-cut lilac dress,
eager for the Italian meal,
unsure, always unsure.
Only your hieratic gestures
tipping the head waiter
calling him by name
assure me you too are uncertain.

Up on the hill our house
dissolving in a sea of lights,
under chaparral, granite decomposing
our oranges slightly sour
more lemons than we could ever use
the jacaranda
life in such profusion.

Again and again I step
out of the car your father gave us
too posh
too grand for newly marrieds.
The grass springs sere under my lilac sandals,
petal sleeves, beehive, eyes absurdly kohled.
With one continuous breath
I absorb the pungent night air
never dreaming
that from all our years together
this moment only will sting.

Louis de Paor

Fáilte Uí Dhonnchú

from Volume 6, p. 90

Ar shráideanna naofa
chathair na dtreabh
mar a bhfuair Cromail,
de réir an tseanchais,
lóistín dá chapall
i sanctóir eaglaise,
tá boladh spíosraí san aer
a chuirfeadh faobhar
ar ghoile Céile Dé.

Tá port feadóige ag séideadh
as bolg an tseanbhaile,
anáil na staire isteach
tré fhallaí fuara
dheisceart Chonamara.

I lár an aonaigh
lena súile bó tá bean
ón Rúmáin ina suí le geata
meánaoiseach an tséipéil,
cárta mór faoina muineál
mar a bheadh peaca marfach
á admháil aici i láthair na bhfíréan.

– Ladies and gentlemen ...
adeir an pheannaireacht chaol,
is ní scoithfi níos tapúla í
dá nochtfadh sí cíoch
nó géag theasctha.

– Ladies and gentlemen ... please.

Tá an cupa polystyrene os a cornhair
ag cur thaI maoille dea-rnhéin
an Aire Dlí agus Cirt (sic),
a goile ag ceolle hocras.

From the Creative to the Critical

Jo. George

WOMEN AND EMBROIDERY

Abstract: This article aims to show how needlework, as well as evoking a medieval ideal, played a crucial part in the definition of Victorian femininity. Two 'approaches' to embroidery are presented – that of Jane Morris and her daughter May.

from 'The Women's Art:
May and Jane Morris and their Embroidery',
Volume 1, pp. 99-106

[....] For many in the nineteenth century, embroidery was indissolubly linked to an idealised view of the past. [....]

The Victorians' view enshrined a nostalgia for a mythical era of pre-capitalist production. Embroidery's evocation of medieval practice made it attractive to William Morris and the other members of the Arts and Crafts Movement. The Holy Grail series of tapestries, executed by Morris and company between 1890 and 1895, reflects an idealisation of the Middle Ages. The seven tapestries of this series contain the all-important themes of love, war, death, and 'the spiritual life'. But their chief significance lies in their demonstration of the skills of individual workmen. In an interview for *Studio* in 1894, Morris said that in the Grail tapestries:

> a considerable latitude in the choice and arrangement of tints in shading etc. was allowed to the executants themselves, who were in fact by nature and training, artists, not mere animated machines.[1]

Janey, Morris' wife, shared her husband's enthusiasm for needlework and, later, their daughter May became an accomplished needlewoman in her own right. In fact, of the many women who worked embroidery for the Arts and Crafts revival – Evelyn De Morgan, Marianne Stokes, Elizabeth Siddal and Georgina Burne-Jones, to name but a few – May and Janey were perhaps the most distinguished. May was also exceptionally open when it came to discussing the place that needlework held in her life. For these reasons I have chosen here to look at the responses of these two women to embroidery.

There exists a painting of May Morris done in the 1920s which shows her at her house in Hammersmith Terrace in the Tapestry Room. Solitary, seated in a flowery boudoir in front of a tapestry, May reminds one here of the 'silent embroiderer' of the Victorian period. Very much her father's daughter, May was a staunch individualist, principal figure in the Arts and Crafts Movement, and prominent member of the Hammersmith Socialist Society. Under these circumstances, May hardly strikes one as a woman who would wish to be portrayed in such a passive pose.Like Christina Rosseti, May Morris could easily have felt herself running the risk of compromising, indeed even sacrificing, her womanhood to an involvement in an area that was looked upon by the majority of society as being exclusively masculine. For the former this area was poetry, for the latter, politics and the visual arts. Thus, the painting, on one level, can be seen as a subtle vindication of the subject's femininity, even if this was only realised in the unconscious of May herself. [....]

Curiously, upon Morris' death, [his wife] Janey's health, and interest, seem to have revived. This indicates perhaps that whilst her husband lived she allowed him to be the vital, creative member of their union. In the years following Morris' death Janey began to exhibit her needlework and subsequently gained much acclaim for it. Her obituary in *The Times* described Janey as 'an exquisite embroideress' and then went on to praise a piece of needlework shown in Ghent in 1913, which had been worked on by Janey, as:

> remarkable for its poetic feeling and breadth of handling ... her eye for colour and design was by nature, or became by training, almost as unerring as that of Morris himself.[2]

Perhaps May did not get all her ideas for *Decorative Needlework* from her father alone.

From what we have seen, Janey's attitude towards her needlework was, at best, ambivalent. One reason for this may be that, on the symbolic level, it represented something that she never quite managed to come to terms with: the fact that she came from a social station inferior to that of her husband. Bloomfield alludes to this and mentions that as the daughter of a man who hired out horses, Janey could not have been oblivious to the differences between her social class and the one which she was marrying into. 'That he [Morris] was a gentleman and well off' Bloomfield writes, "were considerations that weighed heavily with her".[3] Forever aware of her 'inferior' station, Janey may have adopted the characteristics and accomplishments of the ideal middle-class lady in an attempt to gain the approval of Morris and the more elitist of his circle of friends. Knowledge of embroidery would, of course, have been one such accomplishment.[4]

Notes

1 Interview with William Morris in *Studio*, July 1894.
2 *The Times*, Wed. 28 Jan. 1914.
3 Paul Bloomfield 1932. *William Morris*, London: Arthur Baker, p. 86
4 It is worth mentioning how often embroidered articles were used to gain male approval. One immediately thinks of all those domestic articles–bedroom slippers with fox heads embroidered on the toe, cushion covers etc.–worked by women in attempts to show 'their men' that they were the object of love and admiration.

Riana O'Dwyer

LADY MORGAN

Abstract: Lady Morgan's interest in feminist protest has usually been overlooked when considering her writings. This paper will examine the contribution she made to the literature of feminism in her text *Woman and Her Master: A History of the Female Sex From the Earliest Period*, 1840. While Lady Morgan wrote from an essentially conservative social position, she was outraged by two areas of inequality, namely women's education and women's position under the law, and she undertook this 'herstory' in order to highlight the injustices which had been and were still tolerated in these areas. She was by temperament a novelist, however, and her tendency to convert historical figures into romantic heroines will also be considered, using as examples the narratives of Agrippina and Zenobia.

from 'Woman and her Master:
Lady Morgan and Feminism',
Volume 3, pp. 117–127

Dale Spender, in her book *Mothers of the Novel* (1986), makes the following summary of the reputation of Lady Morgan:

> Despite her many novels and works of non-fiction, despite the huge (if harassing) exposure her work received in the *Quarterly Review*, the furore that her fictions on Ireland fermented, her well-publicised controversies with prominent figures, despite her feminist protest in the two-volume *Woman and her Master* (1840), and the fact that her writings were placed on the Index of forbidden books, Lady Morgan has no place in the political, literary, religious – or feminist – history of her time.[1]

Recent work by Tom Dunne and Joep Leerssen, among others, has begun to recuperate Lady Morgan in the political and literary spheres. This paper will attempt to do the same for Lady Morgan the feminist. [....]

Throughout her career Lady Morgan had used the novel to comment on Irish affairs, and had had some influence through *The Wild Irish Girl* (1806), *O'Donnel, A National Tale* (1814), *Florence MacCarthy: An Irish Tale* (1818), and *The O'Briens and the O'Flahertys: A National Tale* (1827). It was therefore a logical step to use her pen to advance the cause of women, when Catholic Emancipation had been achieved for Ireland and the Morgans had taken up residence in London. The publication by Lady Morgan, already in her sixties, of *Woman and her Master: A History of the Female Sex From the Earliest Period,*[2] represented a deliberate attempt on her part to get involved in the feminist debate. Two guiding themes run through the text: the disabilities which women have suffered under the law throughout history, and their lack of educational opportunities. [....]

We can regard Lady Morgan's text as an early attempt at 'herstory'. Subtitled *A History of the Female Sex from the Earliest Period,* it was dedicated to revealing women's secret and difficult agency through all the centuries of legal and intellectual oppression. For Lady Morgan, product of the Englightenment, admirer of the French Revolution, advocate of political and social reform, there was a direct connection between the exposure of an injustice, and the initiation of steps to remedy it. She therefore emphasised the:

> large and formidable sum of suffering ... in the bosom of the most civilised communities, untouched by science, unmitigated by laws. Some great impediments to the working of the social machinery ... require to be eliminated, before the interests of humanity can be based upon a system, consonant with nature, and conducive to general happiness. (I, 7–8)

The greatest impediment to human progress, as Lady Morgan saw it, was the unequal status of woman:

> Has one half of the human species been left... where the first [i.e. earliest] rude arrangements of a barbarous society and its barbarous laws had placed it? ... Has Woman been forgotten? ... And is man still 'the master', and does he, by a misdirected self-love, still perpetuate her ignorance and her dependance? [Has he] brightened instead of breaking the chain of his slave? (I, 10)

To this question Lady Morgan's implicit answer was yes, and her text would therefore be dedicated to illustrating the consequent injustices of the status quo, especially in the areas of legal status and of education. She asserted that both sexes are "moved by common desires, and subjected to common necessities. Their rights in all these respects are therefore equal; their claims to protection before the law, for property and person, equal; their claims to a full development of their intelligence, by education, equal" (I, 325).

To prove her case Lady Morgan wrote a narrative of woman's past, based on widely available sources such as the Bible, classical texts in translation (including translations into French which she read fluently) and Gibbon's *Decline and Fall of the Roman Empire*. She searched these texts for accounts of woman's actions, which then became the central events of her *History of the Female Sex From the Earliest Period*. Her sources provided her with material for two volumes, and she meant to bring the history up to the present in two more, but in the *Advertisement* she refers to eyesight problems and she never did complete the task – she was already in her sixties when she began it. Her methodology involved a retelling of familiar material, but with an emphasis on the agency of women rather than that of men. She wrote it, firstly for the benefit of those who had not had a satisfactory education, that is women themselves, and secondly for the benefit of those who may not have noticed the contribution of women in the past, that is the 'masters' themselves, men. [....]

There are limitations to Lady Morgan's feminism, especially related to her acceptance of class as a factor in what women might achieve, and her acceptance of respectability, in its narrowest sense, as a desirable social value. Nevertheless, in the context of her time, and of her own failing health and advancing years, *Woman and her Master* was a significant undertaking, and within its limits, an effective one. I think it is time we recognised that Ireland, as early as 1840, had contributed a spokesperson to the movement which Lady Morgan would have called Female Emancipation.

Notes

1   Dale Spender 1986. 'Lady Morgan and Political Fiction', *Mothers of the Novel: 100 Good Women Novelists Fefore Jane Austen*, Pandora, pp. 301–303.
2   Lady Morgan 1840. *Woman and her Master: A History of the Female Sex From the Earliest Period*, 2 vols., Colburn. Page references are given in the text.

Eoin Bourke

Käthe Kollwitz

Abstract: The socialist Käthe Kollwitz spent much of her artistic career depicting women. In her relatively carefree youth she frequently presented them as revolutionary in spirit and deed, but later on, as a result of close and continuous contact with the proletariat of the North Berlin district of Prenzlauer Berg and in the context of the brutally suppressed Spartacist revolution of 1919, she began to portray women as victims of social and political forces, feeling increasingly obliged to gear her artistic talents to the publicising of the plight of the working classes. After the senseless death of her younger son Peter in the very first stages of the First World War, she turned more and more to the theme of victims of war at home, i.e. the grieving mothers, widows and children. Her poster art became a prominent feature of Berlin street life.

from 'From a Proletarian Aesthetic to Social Agitation. Käthe Kollwitz's Portrayal of Women as Revolutionaries, Victims and Protectors in her Art and Poster Work', *Volume 9*, pp. 117-134

One could sum up Käthe Kollwitz's entire artistic production as being essentially representational rather than abstract, realist rather than expressionist, graphic and sculptural rather than painted, narrative rather than symbolic, more urban than rural, always depicting humans rather than landscapes or still life, peasants and proletarians rather than members of the middle or upper classes, and portraying women and children more frequently than men. This characterises her art from the very beginning when she was studying in 1888/89 at the Ladies' Academy of the Munich Female Artists' Association. Women were not yet admitted to the Royal Academy of Fine Arts in Munich (and hardly anywhere else), being referred to contemptuously by the male art establishment as 'Malweiber' ('painting hussies').

Kollwitz scored a first success with an illustration in pencil and charcoal of the scene from Part 6, Chapter 3 of Émile Zola's novel *Germinal,* set in the coal-mining district of the Borinage. The scene takes place in Madame Rasseneur's bar, where Étienne and Chaval fight it out for the favour of Catherine:

> She stood with her back against the wall, silent and so paralysed with anguish that she no longer trembled, but simply stared with her great eyes at these two men who were going to kill each other for her sake.[1]

Kollwitz went on to do a series of etchings on this theme, based on sketches she had made in her native Königsberg (Kaliningrad) in a sailors' pub called 'Das Schiffchen' (The Little Boat) which she visited with the consent of the owner only in the mornings, as she would have been in 'mortal danger' there in the evenings, when "a furious din was to be heard inside and knife fights were everyday occurrences".[2] At this early stage of her work she interpreted this preoccupation with the labouring classes in terms of aesthetics, writing later in a memoir of 1941:

> The actual motivation for my choosing from then on to depict almost solely the life of workers was because the motifs that I selected from that sphere simply and unconditionally provided me with what I felt to be beautiful. What was beautiful for me were the Königsberg carriers, the Polish Jimkies on their barges, the grandiose momentum of the common people. Members of the middle classes never had any appeal for me. The life of the bourgeoisie always struck me as being stuffy. The proletariat, on the other hand, had panache.[3]

This preoccupation was soon to propel her into the midst of a controversy on the function of art. In 1893 she experienced the premiere of Gerhart Hauptmann's naturalist drama *The Weavers* at the *Freie Bühne* on the topic of a spontaneous riot of weavers in the Silesian villages of Peterswaldau and Langenbielau in June 1844 that was savagely crushed by Prussian troops. She immediately dropped the theme of *Germinal* and began work on her now famous cycle *A Weavers' Revolt,* consisting of three lithographs and three etchings. Kollwitz depicts the womenfolk here not only as passive sufferers, but as active rebels. In Print No. 4, *The March of the Weavers,* the foreground is taken up by a woman carrying – instead of a pickaxe or hatchet over her shoulder like the men – a sleeping child on her back, denoting her double role as insurgent and carer (fig. 2).

The March of the Weavers

In Print No. 5, *Attack*, women, again in the foreground, are loosening cobbles to supply the men with missiles, while one of the women is prevented from doing so by literally 'having her hands full' with a child on each arm. The Belgian sculptor Constantin Meunier exclaimed that he had never seen the likes of such a work of art done by a woman's hand[4] [....] Kaiser Eilheim II reacted to the Berlin Salon's plan to award Kollwitz a gold medal for her work with the misogynist remark "I beg you, gentlemen, a medal for a woman? That would be going much too far! That would amount to a belittling of every distinguished decoration. Orders and medals of honour belong on the breasts of outstanding *men*!"[5] [....] The Court must have been further appalled by Kollwitz's next success, an etching of the Carmagnole, the dance of the French Revolution [....]

Notes
1   Émile Zola 1954. *Germinal*, transl. Leonard Tancock, London: Penguin, p. 385.
2   Käthe Kollwitz 1999. *Die Tagebücher 1908–1943*, ed. Jutta Bohnke-Kollwitz, Berlin: Siedler, p. 740. (This and all further translations by Eoin Bourke.)
3   *Ibid.*, p. 741.
4   Cit. Catherine Kramer 1981. *Käthe Kollwitz – mit Selbstzeugnissen und Bilddokumenten*, Reinbek b. Hamburg: Rowohlt, p. 37.
5   *Cit*, Jurgen Schutte & Peter Sprengel (eds), 1987. *Die Berliner Moderne 1885–1914*, Reclam, pp. 572–573.

Angela Ryan

Camille Claudel

Abstract: Full recognition of the artistic achievement of Camille Claudel, one of the greatest sculptors of the late nineteenth/early twentieth century, has been somewhat overshadowed by the tragic aspects of her biography. Her sculpture L'Age mûr, in particular, has been reduced to a representation of her desertion by her teacher Rodin. Over-attention to the biographical, in interpreting the art, has paradoxically been accompanied by a relative lack of emphasis on the significance of the historical under-mentoring of female creative artists. This paper attempts a semiotic reading of L'Age mûr 'in its own right' and, at the same time, a re-evaluation of the role of mentor in the reception of the female artist.

from 'Camille Claudel: The Artist as Heroinic Rhetorician' *Volume* 8, pp. 13-28

Camille Claudel's group sculpture L'Age mûr is usually given a biographical interpretation. [....] While this is a possible reading, critical trends since the late twentieth century open possibilities of interpreting works of art without necessarily referring to the artist's life. The group's plasticity and configuration might give rise to a multiplicity of discrete and linked possible interpretations: not only in terms of different generational groups, but also as different symbolic beings, the left-hand figure being represented on a different level to the others, semiotically bisexualised, and symbolically mythologised by the wing-like drapery. No statement of Claudel's, nothing in the work's title gives credence to the reductive autobiographical reading (whose only source is her brother, the poet Paul Claudel).

The very prevalence of the biographical interpretation of the love triangle is a sign of Claudel's artistic merit being greater than her reputation. Sixty-seven years after her death her artistic reputation is still in the popular mind inextricable from her unhappy love relationship with her teacher (Rodin) and its destructive effect upon her life. The museum in which the greater part of her work is exhibited does not bear her name. [....] Yet Claudel's contribution to Rodin's work should be acknowledged as part of her own. Parallel readings of their works on comparable themes are useful in order to gain a better understanding of each artist, and also contribute to the study of the evolution of the imaginaire and its reception. Claudel's reputation has been rising for some time and is not merely a function of Rodin's. [....]

L'Age mûr no 2, Camille Claudel 1889, bronze 120.8 x 181.2 x 70cm. Photo Benôit Schaeffer

That women's artistic talent and genius is represented by fewer examples is a fact of reception, of the making of reputations and of curation. The idea that they are inferior is no longer accepted. That they are equal to men as a fact of reality cannot be disproved by a quantitative difference of number of works or market price. There are many examples, from Anne Bradstreet or Margaret Cavendish to Virginia Woolf, of the specific obstacles to female artistic success. These include the glass ceiling, the difficulty of being accepted by one's peers, the incomprehension and jealousy of those who seek to defend an establishment heretofore without female rivals, and even the reappropriation of their work.

Camille Claudel's story is that of a woman of genius who has not had the reputation she deserved, who suffered from mentoring which, in today's terms, would be considered abusive, from the abuse of masculine power in the family and from the period's abusive treatment of psychiatric cases. If the third and fourth of these abuses do not persist today, for women artists or anyone else—one cannot say as much for the second—then the solution to the first is in the hands of this generation. Claudel's misfortunes ought not be better known than her work. Claudel's sculptures may be seen in the musée Rodin in Paris and in the National Museum of Women in the Arts in Washington D.C., as well as in a number of museums in France and in private collections.

Wanda Balzano

Una Troy and Siobán Piercy

From "The Veiled Subject: Figuring the Feminine Through
Una Troy's/Elizabeth Connor's 'The Apple'
and Siobán Piercy's screenprints"
Volume 8, pp. 71-86

[....] Una Troy's 'The Apple',[1] written in 1942 under the pseudonym of Elizabeth Connor, provides a useful literary paradigm to explore the notion of the feminine in Irish terms. 'The Apple' places its protagonist in the rich and illustrious tradition of the 'thieves of fire'. [....] It is the story of a forty-nine-year-old nun who surrenders to her hidden desire, and sins by entering the forbidden territory of her original family home, thus falling into freedom. Mother Mary Aloysius – who is described at the beginning of the story in her disarming simplicity as one who "was not afraid of being happy" because "she was used to it"(p.35) – is one of the four nuns chosen by the Reverend Mother to go with her to the Order's new house at Youghal, County Cork. Seeing that the doctor has prescribed a change for the Reverend Mother, the Bishop – having already altered the strict rule that forbade any member of the order to set foot outside the Convent grounds – urges her to go to the new house of the Order at Youghal. Notwithstanding Reverend Mother's initial reluctance, which must be noted as a sign of resistance to the higher power by an (in)subordinate female member of the Church, they all set off, as Obedience to the higher religious authorities, in this case the Bishop, was one of the Vows. [....]

While metaphorically retracing the Biblical myth from *Genesis* (especially the story of Eve) to *Revelation*, this piece of short fiction literally represents the status of confinement and femininity in Ireland, that is (if we regard sin as a creative act, an act of transgression that escapes the transcendental or patriarchal Law and embraces instead the logic of desire), it represents the position of the marginalised Irish woman artist on the brink of modernity, between divine transgression and human reconciliation, between the gravity of canon law and the lightness of its absence, between Catholic guilt and inspiring betrayal, between sin and innocence. On the threshold of two different worlds, Troy's nun projects her desires from the enclosed world of the cloister she inhabits towards the free world of her familiar homestead, in a movement that goes from muted claustrophobia to a type of domophilia, that is from misdoubt and apprehension for cloistered or secluded life to an increasing passion for the dis-remembered reality of selfdom. [....]

Excerpts from Purgatory III, Sioban Piercy, Screenprint, 30 x 30cms

Although Una Troy's story is minor in size, it unearths a vast assortment of issues which have literary resonances from Kate O'Brien to Eiléan Ní Chuilleanáin. Yet, to show that it is not only a literary paradigm, but also an artistic one and, more importantly, perhaps a figure of women's lives, one may also read the story through visual art, by juxtaposing it with a sample of the work of a contemporary living artist, Siobán Piercy, who practices the art of printmaking. Piercy was born in Oakham (England) in 1957, but moved to Ireland in 1962. [....]

In the first part of Troy's story, the nun is presented in a state of some excitement before facing temptation, that is in the anticipation of seeing the sea and her old home again: "Are you very excited, child?" Mother Mary Aloysius blushed. "A little, Reverend Mother." Reverend Mother laughed. "You are not the only one! They're like a pack of babies inside" (p. 35). The vision of Paradise that in Piercy's screenprint is conveyed by the Edenic tree set against the blue sky is in 'The Apple' conveyed by the sea: "Forgotten the sea! Oh, but you couldn't! Even if you only saw it once in your life, you could never forget the sea. To-day, it was blue – pale, pale blue, with no horizon but a misty curve far off where it sloped up to meet the sloping sky. I can see it, flowing over the roses there by the wall and the gulls' crying is loud above the blackbird's song …". The nun is portrayed while walking in the convent garden in a state of innocence, of "simple, unsearching happiness", with some *fear of knowledge*: "She had never used her mind for thinking, only for recording the thoughts of others. She was happy . . . She was not afraid of being happy; she was used to it" (p. 35). [....]

Revealing, re-veiling, unveiling: the conceptual metaphor of the veil is as precarious and fluid as minor art, writing or painting, especially when produced by women. With its characteristic fluttering movement of hiding and revealing, the veil recalls that vellum or parchment for writing and erasure – the palimpsest. At the end of metaphysics, the palimpsest that includes new writing after erasure of the original writing is woman. She is the invisible text to reappear again in this historical space left empty by a full metaphysics, on the outposts of a new millennium, where apocalypse never comes – and yet there is an end of man's history. Piercy's work, like that of Troy, witnesses within itself the co-existence of the opposite movements of founding and breaking ground open, of destroying and recreating, closing and opening, veiling and unveiling – in Heideggerian terms, an *abgrund* of mortality, between production and death; in Kristevan terms, it is the abject (the enigmatic Mona Lisa's smile, on the brink of an abyss). Their configuration of femininity not only questions the canon from the trenches, but also radically upsets the experience of art in the affirmation of an ever-new beginning. [....]

Note
1   E. Connor (pseud. U. Troy) 1942. 'The Apple' in *The Bell*, (Oct.), pp. 35–41.

Catherine Kelly

Marina Carr's Plays

Abstract: Economic improvements in Ireland in the two decades preceding the millennium created the impression that the country was thriving. In her writing, Marina Carr challenges this idea by questioning the claim that success has permeated every aspect of Irish life. In particular, the three plays focused on in this article, *The Mai*, *Portia Coughlan* and *By the Bog of Cats*, examine the condition of women. The deaths of the protagonists raise questions about what success means. This is interrogated in the context of a society where values associated with the feminine seem to be undervalued. As a consequence, tragic personal histories are frequently repeated by successive generations.

from 'Breaking the Mould:
Three Plays by Marina Carr',
Volume 8, pp. 105-114

In the context of Irish theatre, the manner in which [Marina Carr] highlights the female position and, in particular, appears to assert the legitimacy of female emotions, is a step which manages to break new ground. Other Irish playwrights, both male and female, have already dealt with issues such as marriage and motherhood. However, the emphasis which Carr places on 'the politics of emotions', without overt reference to the broader party political picture, together with her use of myth in modern situations, appears to mark something of a departure in Irish theatre. In Carr's work the personal is integrally linked to the political. [....]

It is the plays which first brought Carr recognition in mainstream theatre that will be considered in this article: *The Mai* (1994), *Portia Coughlan* (1995) and *By the Bog of Cats* (1998). The plays display similarities in both theme and style. However, what particularly connects them from the outset is the fact that in all three the heroines commit suicide. Language and imagery may be deliberately bleak and obscure, but the message is in bold and underlined: despite appearances to the contrary, all is not well in Ireland regarding the state of women and the status of what might be regarded as feminine. Carr's shock tactics, her delving into the murky worlds of parricide and incest, serve as a jolt to those members of the audience snug in the belief that things are otherwise. [....]

The Mai is a woman who possesses both personal and financial resources. Yet from her point of view, the success which she has achieved in many areas of her life remains subservient to the one thing which matters most to her, her relationship with Robert. The overall structure of the play is built around the shifting fortune of their love. [....] Her suicide is directly linked to Robert, and Carr is certainly critical of the type of man he represents. He is able to exert control over the Mai by manipulating her emotions. He avoids communication about painful issues, which he does not want to address properly, through resorting to silence. [....]

Motherhood and the difficulty of breaking the cyclical nature of abuse, is at the centre of *Portia Coughlan*. Injured women abuse their children either emotionally, physically or both and they, in turn, behave in a similar manner towards their own offspring. [....] However, *Portia Coughlan* does in many respects uphold the significance of the role of the mother, although this is achieved in the negative. Carr suggests that maternal feelings do not necessarily occur naturally, but also shows the extremely influential role that mothers play in the formative years of childhood. She illustrates the price that families pay and, consequently, that society pays, when such nurturing does not take place, and promotes the idea of a cultural climate which is supportive towards mothers. There is a distinction to be made between this and one that simply encourages motherhood. The latter is more functional and based on the assumption that all will run smoothly because nature will take over. The former looks to a more holistic view of women, taking into account psychological as well as material needs. [....]

Many aspects of the first two plays re-emerge in *By the Bog of Cats*: the treacherous partner, the abandoned child and rancorous women engaged in bitter rivalry. The play makes use of Euripides' *Medea*, but has a peculiarly Irish stamp. Carr extends the themes in *Medea* by incorporating into the story a fundamental layer that exists beneath the male–female bond. It is Hester's relationship with the mother who left her which fuels her rage against Carthage when he attempts to do the same. It is this that motivates her to kill her young daughter; to break a cycle of damage which she anticipates will only be repeated. Again, Carr appears to stress the circularity involved in relationships; the mother–child relationship prefigures the adult sexual relationship, while a combination of both dictates the tone of the next mother–child unit. Thus, female/male interests are integrally linked. A society which loses sight of 'nurturing' in the broadest sense of the word, Carr seems to be suggesting, is courting disaster. [....]

At a symbolic level, rather than reading the suicide of the main characters in these plays in a pessimistic way, the deaths may perhaps be seen as an inverted assertion of the feminine in a society where the qualities associated with this are little valued. The deaths of these women may be viewed as protests. They have chosen death rather than the coldness of an impersonal, uncaring, loveless world. The deaths are portrayed in poetic terms, both verbally and visually, rather than in off-putting, gory descriptions which give graphic accounts of the extinction of life. The Mai dies to the sound of music and birds; Portia's death is marked by a stylised, careful choreography when her body is raised from the Belmont River; Hester and the 'Ghost-fancier' perform a dance of death. While Carr portrays the disappointments and disillusionments of romantic love, in an almost contradictory way, the lyricism of her work seems to celebrate the romantic. What is really mourned is the loss of the feminine, both within men and a culture that has been dominated by male values, and within women who have adopted masculine approaches.

Bernadette Fallon

SYLVIA PLATH

Abstract: This essay first challenges the widely held opinion that Sylvia Plath was concerned only with self destruction in her work. It proposes the notion that the driving force in her poetry and prose is an affirmative, recreative one which overcomes male dominance in life and literature. Since Plath's work is based almost exclusively on autobiography, it is vital to take a look at the circumstances of the life which shaped the work. Therefore, an outline of her life is presented, with an emphasis on my main theme in the chapter, *i.e.* the doubles and masks in Plath's life. The use of doubles in the life is next extended to her novel *The Bell Jar* and her last collection of poetry, *Ariel*, where the doubles are overcome and, ultimately, the positive voice emerges supreme over the negative.

from 'Sylvia Plath: The Double in the Woman and the Use of it in Her Work', *Volume 1*, pp. 117-122

Sylvia Plath is known to many only as a cult figure who achieved her status as a result of her suicide in February 1963. Looked at in this light it is inevitable that her poems are seen as self-destructive death wishes and the suicidal ravings of a woman determined to die. This is how *Ariel*, her last volume of poems, written in the months before she died, is usually seen. Critics have observed that the circumstances of her death have been the main contributing factor in seeing her life and work as being morbidly attracted to death.

It is true to say that some of the poems in this collection are quite depressing and death-related in themselves. Obviously, poems written in the weeks immediately preceding her death reflect her suicidal tendencies at the time. But the strength of the book and its main driving force comes from the 'October' poems. Written in October 1963, they are the product of early morning writing sessions after her separation from her husband, poet Ted Hughes.

These poems are positive affirmations of her new-found independence. She had overcome her depression at the initial break-up and had found a positive voice. They are poems of strength and rebirth. She was elated by them herself and although people do interpret them as destructive because of the references to death, it is not death as destruction that she is concerned with. Instead it is the death of the self, which is necessary to precede resurrection in a new recreated form. [….]

Although Plath had been writing both poetry and prose since she was very young, her earlier style is very artificial and shallow. She aimed towards a commercial market, publishing pieces in magazines for payment – therefore her style varied to suit each particular magazine. Only in later years did she find her authentic voice (acknowledged also by Ted Hughes in his introduction to her *Journals*). Hence, her appreciated work is not very extensive. Besides her collections of poetry she published a novel, *The Bell Jar*, in 1963, just before her death. The novel is famous for its detached, ironic account of her first breakdown and suicide attempt when she was twenty. Although written in a fictionalised form, almost all of the characters and incidents in it are real. [….]

In reading her journals, her poetry, her prose and various accounts of her life, it is easy to become bewildered by the array of personalities and conflicting doubles that one has to sift through to find the real Plath. There are so many different faces presented – the calm confident high achiever versus the scared berating voice of the journals; the Sylvia who loved life to the full versus the destructive suicidal case; the longing to be an ordinary housewife and mother versus longing to be committed only to her art. [….]

Sylvia Plath died by her own hand in February 1963. Finally, the conflicts became too much for her, the masks she had employed as supports failed her. But, as I have pointed out, she achieved freedom and rebirth in life while she lived. This is what we should remember her for, this is her legacy.

Nóirín Ní Riain

Female Musical Creativity

Abstract: This esay centres largely on a subjective, singer's analysis of Irish traditional women's songs of work, desire and prayer. A brief evaluation of other non-Irish female song forms is made on the level of musical performance, structure and style. The integral nature of singing and song creating in women's lives has not been widely acknowledged and this intuitive overview is an attempt to address that fact.

from 'Sound Women: An Irish Perspective on Female Musical Creativity in Song', *Volume 2*, pp. 95-109

[....] Gender studies in Irish music are almost non-existent as yet and the field of ethnomusicology – a relatively modern discipline, which includes a comparative study of the music of human peoples – has barely touched the surface of women's music. Therefore, the scope of this article will range broadly from the female song in the Irish tradition through diverse women's songs from various other traditions, cultures and ages. The purpose of this study is twofold: firstly, to define certain characteristics of the song composed by women and, secondly, to articulate to some degree the effect or power of re-creating or singing these songs in a contemporary context.

The Female Song in The Irish Tradition

It is necessary, in discussing feminine creativity in song, to confine observations to the subjective feminine song – the song composed by the woman rather than one composed about her. This former female song-type has far fewer survivals that the latter male-composed song. The reason why this is so is ambiguous, but certain features presented here in this song-type could well have contributed to this paucity of women's songs. Furthermore, the use of the terms 'masculine' and 'feminine' in this essay is essentially different from that used in the tradition of Western Art music, where they are conventional terms concerning cadential endings and technical theme labelling. Here the definitions are gender based. [....]

Songs of Work

[....] Female work songs fall easily into two categories. The first are those songs composed by the woman within the home and nearly always related to her role as mother and child-rearer. Two maternal song-types emerge. The first – the lullaby – tends to be soothing, hypnotic and tranquilising. The second – the dandling song – is metrical, vigorous and vivacious. The function or performance context of both types largely indicates their structure and movement; in the first case, the infant is lulled to sleep in the cradle; in the second, the child is awake and demanding attention through physical contact.

The second category of work songs are those composed and performed during such activities as spinning, weaving or herding. Spinning and weaving were social functions, and so the construction of these songs caters for group participation. This is illustrated by such songs as '*Im Bim Baboró*', '*S'Ambó Éara*' and '*Ailiú Éanaí*' where the first and last phrases of the three-phrase construction are sung communally while the middle phrase is sung, usually with improvised text, by one person. [....]

Songs of Desire

[....] Female love songs describing the beloved objectively or expressing fulfilment in love are rare. Tension, conflicts of desire and unrealised relationships were the essential inspiration for feminine creativity. An excessive obsession with oneself as opposed to the beloved is very evident, although this would appear to be the typically western response of the love-stricken woman. [....]

In the broadest sense, this song-type is exclusive of other people and this is immediately perceptible through the absence of a chorus which by its very nature implies group participation. [....] The solitary song appears to have a strong therapeutic function, providing an ameliorative effect of appeasing grief following its creation and re-creation. [....]

Fig. 2 *Fill fill a rún o*

(Return, return, my dear
Return my dear and don't leave me,
Return to me, my love and my treasure,
And the Queen of Glory will be waiting for you.

When I go to Mass on Sunday ... the young girls will say
'there goes the mother of the minister'
My curse forever on women, they stole from me my little priest...)

Songs of Prayer

Religious song in Irish comprises three strands: eighteenth-century religious poetry by known poets which was sung to popular airs of the time; poetry which was artificially wedded by collectors and editors to unrelated, secular folk tunes; and finally, authentic, anonymous spiritual songs where the text and tune are collected from one source. It is the latter genre which is relevant here because it represents the pure, oral folk tradition. [....]

Generally, female expression in those genres of songs presented here can be divided into two musical streams: a song-type which exhibits a social element in the broadest sense and a song-type which is essentially a solitary, almost narcissistic, exercise. The social song, whether it be work song, love song or religious song of praise, has certain strong musical features. The presence of textual or musical repetition indicates group participation – this repetition is sometimes in the form of a chorus, sometimes as a reiterated phrase. A clearly definable tempo or rhythm facilitates the transmission of a song to others and seems to indicate a less personal mode of expression.

The solitary song, on the other hand, excludes ensemble performance through the complexity and intricacy of the musical style. The free tempo added to the lack of musical repetition and emphasis on through-composition further heighten this separation or isolation within the performance situation. The corpus of women's songs in the Irish context, is significantly smaller than its male counterpart. It is suggested as a possible explanation that since singing for women was primarily viewed perhaps as a private medium for the release of deeply personal emotion, the fewer women's songs were therefore heard, transmitted or preserved. On the other hand, it is important to note that the oldest music to have survived in Ireland may have been largely created by our foremothers, many of whom lived at the time of Hildegard and before, sharing a similar feminine musical expression and creativity.

Jane O'Leary

Women Composers

Abstract: This essay reviews the situation of women composers in a profession traditionally dominated by men, where women's creativity has only recently begun to be recognised. This paper refers to the social pressures facing women composers in the past, and to the current situation in Ireland regarding performances of music by women composers. The facts indicate that women's music is still clearly outside the mainstream.

from 'Swimming Against the Stream: Women Composers Then and Now', *Volume 1*, pp. 79-85

Composition is a field which has been remarkably male dominated, so much so that it has been argued that women are actually *incapable* of writing music. The fact is that women have *always* written music, but it has been suppressed, ignored, stifled, even published under men's names. And if music is not heard and responded to by a receptive public, it soon ceases to exist.

Ethel Smyth, spirited campaigner for women's rights and a gifted writer of both prose and music, described the position of women composers in England in 1933 as "outside the pale of musical civilisation".[1] When confronted with his daughter's ambition to compose, her father remarked "I'd sooner see you under the sod".[2] Smyth perceptively noted that a woman composer is:

> swimming against the stream, which is the privilege of the female. One of the greatest spiritual difficulties we have to contend with, the responsibility for which lies mainly with the elementary condition of

musical culture in England, is the extreme isolation of the woman composer, an isolation none save those who have endured it can imagine.[3]

It is this isolation which has prevented women from making a mark on history. It has affected their attitude towards themselves and prevented them from aspiring to a professional career; it has in effect been a blindfold on creativity. Acting in isolation, a talented, brilliant woman like Clare Schumann considered her piano trio inferior: "it is only a woman's work, which is always lacking in force, and here and there in invention"[4] she wrote in her diary in 1846. It is true that there have been no female Beethovens, but from a base of how many thousands of competent male composers do the very few geniuses arise? Women, swimming against the stream, lacked role models and in isolation shared Clara Schumann's viewpoint: "a woman must not desire to compose, not one has been able to do it, and why should I expect to?"[5]

There *have* been individuals who swam against the stream – people like Elizabeth Maconchy, born in England in 1907 and brought up in Ireland. She had written music all her life, despite being told as a student at the Royal College of Music that she would not be awarded the prestigious Mendelssohn Prize (although she deserved it) because she "would only get married and never write another note".[6] In 1987 the British Government acknowledged her considerable achievements as a composer and made her a Dame: the only composer to previously receive this honour was Ethel Smyth in 1922.

But … were any of her works performed in this country, the land of her heritage, during the year of her 80th birthday … or after? While pieces were played by the chamber ensemble Concorde and the Irish Youth Wind Ensemble in 1987, Maconchy was magnificently ignored by all the professional musical organisations in the State: the RTESO, RTE String Quartet, ICO, Wexford Opera, Opera Theatre Company. But this is the normal state of affairs for women composers, perhaps a reflection of the attitude society (or at least decision-makers within society) has towards the abilities of women. Look at the views of George Upton, a Chicago music critic, an influential person in musical society: in 1880 he wrote, "it does not seem that woman will ever originate music in its fullest and grandest harmonic forms. She will always be the recipient and the interpreter, but there is little hope she will be creator".[7] His argument was that women are too emotional, unable to control their emotions and therefore only able to absorb music as performers. [....]

Finally, one must ask whether the relatively small number of performances of music by women indicates that women are incapable of writing music or that society has hindered them in their efforts to communicate. Assuming that they are indeed capable (and always have been), we must acknowledge the problems of the past. We can all help to rectify the situation for the future by seeking out women's music. It is not easy to programme the works of women, one has to search for manuscripts, one has to overcome the isolation that separates so many composers from the usual channels of communication. But it is rewarding, because much of the music speaks so personally. It deserves at least an equal chance to be heard, a chance to be brought within the pale of musical civilisation, if only as an encouragement to the Clara Schumanns and Fanny Mendelssohns of the future, that they may no longer have to swim against the stream!

Notes
1. Quotation from Carol Neuls-Bates (ed.), 1982. *Women in Music: An Anthology of Source Readings from the Middle Ages to the Present*, New York: Harper & Row.
2-7 *Ibid.*

Berni Divilly

WOMEN AND DANCE

Abstract: This article offers information and reflections on my work facilitating dance workshops. I wanted movement to be a part of my work in community education because I want a more embodied way to work with groups. Movement, I knew, could access powerful information in a very vital and immediate way that was different from working with a rational cognitive approach. I think that many people living under patriarchal conditioning are alienated from their physical bodies. They have lost the capacity to respond to life from a felt sense. Working with the intelligence of the physical body made sense to me. It felt like a wise way to proceed with being an active feminist. I asked the Women's Studies Centre (WSC) to support my early explorations with dance as a form of active research. In my workshops I use dance, music, voice, ritual and art to explore personal and political issues using creativity and groupwork. In this article I use feedback from women who have participated in workshops to illustrate the process. I also draw on theories of depth psychology and dance therapy, which have informed my work. The workshops referred to here took place in UCD between Spring 1993 and Summer 1996.

from 'Down to Earth: Meeting the Dancer Within: Women's Studies in Movement', *Volume 4*, pp. 157-166

[....] Groupwork is an important part of the dance experience. I sometimes adopt a structure that was created by Marian Chance, regarded as the founder of dance therapy. She worked with feelings in the context of group interaction and used a shared leadership format with her groups. Themes would emerge from the group and her dance therapy sessions would explore these. She used rhythm to support the dance of the individual and at the same time provide a sense of connection within a group. Dancing individual dances, but to a shared rhythm, gives a group security and strength – there is the bonding and yet the freedom to be separate. [....]

When I work with a group my attention is primarily with energy. I am using my own body as a sensor to pick up feedback from the movers. If I am feeling far off, I'll ask the group to focus on where they are conscious in their bodies now. It is not possible to know ahead of time what experiences are going to get mobilised by movement. What becomes significant is how to work with movement, so it can become part of self-expression and a feedback system to move about their own experience. Dance is likely to magnify our defence systems, by which I mean magnify movement patterns that we have developed to protect ourselves from being flooded by uncomfortable unconscious material. These movement patterns are connected to personality development in the formative years of childhood. [....] Learning about our bodies through following our breathing, coming to sense where we were uncomfortable or feel restricted, can give valuable information to us about ourselves. Sometimes I invite the movers to amplify defences. A common intervention of this kind would be to ask the group to do whatever they are doing to protect themselves from feeling shy or embarrassed with their bodies. I would generally support defence patterns by acknowledging them as creative aspects of the psyche's ability to defend itself. I work from the premise that learning about defences, by bringing the conflicts they create in body and mind out through dance, can be empowering. This ultimately can give dancers more choice. Habitual defence patterns that are no longer needed in the present hold us back from experiencing our lives more fully. So the dancer who runs away and is validated for running away, is also supported to return. Recognition and respect are key issues here. [....]

There are stories held in immobilised hips. The pain of unmet needs and rage may be locked in arms and shoulders. Dance can be used to gain experience about our physical bodies in a way that can empower the mover to integrate old stories and balance their energy. This is slow and powerful work. There is a need for containment. Themes of emotional, physical and sexual violence come up in dance groups regularly. [....]

Catherine Marshall

ART AND 'WOMEN'S WORK'

from "I'll spin you a yarn, I'll weave you a tale ...': Subverting Patriarchy Through Art and 'Women's Work'", *Volume 8*, pp. 87–90

[In 1985 the artist Pauline Cummins created] *Inis t'Oirr Aran Dance*, a series of images on slides, accompanied by a voice on a tape, that takes us on a journey that begins with ruminations about the patterns used in a knitted Aran sweater, then moves to the male body that will wear it, and ends with the sexual arousal of the wearer and the consequent pleasure of both wearer and knitter. Like Cummins' earlier works, *Nine Months and After* and *Celebration*, commissioned for the 100th anniversary of the founding of the National Maternity Hospital at Holles Street, *Inis t'Oirr Aran Dance* springs directly from the artist's own life experience.

Cummins had been struck by the sensuality of an Aran sweater on a tailor's dummy in the National Museum in Kildare Street. Years later, having worked as director of a craft training centre in Kenya, and co-founder of a ceramics studio at home in Ireland, she was well aware of the negativity with which craft traditions were greeted in fine art circles. By focusing on knitting, a craft identified with women, Cummins unequivocally locates her *Aran Dance* in the domestic sphere, but she also uses it as a challenge to the patriarchal values in art which have traditionally denigrated knitting as mere craft and denied recognition as 'artists' to the women who practised it. [....] But *Inis t'Oirr's* subversiveness only begins there. The viewer is guided unsuspectingly down a familiar route, only to discover that familiar associations are consistently being overturned. 'Man' is now associated with nature while it is 'woman' who is the creator of culture. The patterns in the sweater are linked, in turn, with the landscape and then with the man's body, and it is the woman's gaze that reveals the appropriateness of this to us. The knot stitch is likened to fruits and berries, then to nipples as the knitter/artist draws closer to the body, to sexual arousal, and to its resolution. [....]

Inis t'Oirr's only precedents, in terms of expressing female sexuality, were literary—Edna O'Brien's books, banned in Ireland for over twenty years and, more importantly, Kate Millet's writing, and Germaine Greer's frank discussion of the male body. Other liberating factors for Cummins were growing up in the iconoclastic Beatles culture of the

1960s and the example of a Canadian, feminist artist, Rochelle Rubenstein with whom she worked in Toronto in 1978–79. Within the frames of reference of visual art, Cummins' allies in deconstructing the language of patriarchy were American artist Susan Hiller and her friend and fellow Irish artist, Alanna O'Kelly, both of whom investigated the use of voice and new technology as alternatives to the 'male' practices of painting and sculpture. [....]

The title, *Inis t'Oirr Aran Dance*, conflates the name of the westernmost of the Aran Islands *Inis Oirr* with *Inis an t'oir* meaning 'the golden island'. The title might suggest other West of Ireland artwork – the paintings by Sean Keating and Paul Henry that became the visual exemplars of post-colonial Ireland. Keating's imagery of simple, traditionally clad Aran fishermen, priests and Gaelic sportsmen consciously harked back to an ancient Irish culture while Henry's idyllic Connemara landscapes evoked a world that appeared untouched by colonial urbanisation. Cummins subverts their gender models while simultaneously disavowing their association between the West and Irishness, laughingly proposing instead the link between the vulgar commercial marketing of Ireland and the Aran sweater. More seriously, though, she derives real satisfaction from the knowledge that similar knitting patterns have been found as far away as Crete. Universality is more important than parochialism, the periphery feeds the centre.

Sheila Dickinson

INTERVIEW WITH ALICE MAHER

Abstract: Alice Maher was born in Tipperary in 1956 and her country upbringing continues to influence her art. She received her art education in Cork, Belfast and San Francisco, but now lives and works in Dublin. Her work has been exhibited widely in Ireland and in 1996 she was elected to Aosdána. Her most recent exhibition, *The History of Tears*, was shown at the Butler Gallery in Kilkenny, the Green on Red Gallery, Dublin and Purdy Hicks Gallery in London. She also had a recent solo exhibition at the Nolan Eckman Gallery in New York. A Galway audience was delighted and inspired recently during her guest lecture in honour of the tenth anniversary of the Women's Studies Centre at NUI, Galway. Sheila Dickinson (SD): Interviewer/Alice Maher (AM): Interviewee

from 'Multiplicity in Art Practice:
Alice Maher in Conversation with Sheila Dickinson', *Volume 8*, pp. 53–70

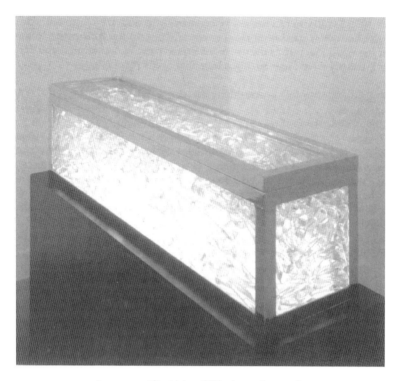

Lacrymatory, Alice Maher, 2001 – brass, chrome, glass

SD: In the late 1980s you stopped depending on painting as your main medium. Since then your paintings are always accompanied by sculptures or drawings. The interchange between various media feels fluid and seemingly effortless.

AM: I think that was the time when I began to look at painting as just another medium. I put away that great respect for painting that was taught to us in academia and in the art world, that painting was a very special act and only special people could do it. This idea was coming from the 80s and New Expressionism. If you could paint you were a great artist. But I began to examine that as a language and actually didn't believe in it anymore. I began to treat paint as another material, like charcoal or nettles or anything else. It was no longer a mysterious, religious language, which was the way people were talking about it in the twentieth century. In New Expressionism it was so self-self-self, so my-life-as-a-man was what it was about. The language [of Expressionist painting] didn't hold much for me even though I tried it out, of course, because that's what I learned in school. It was a conscious rejection, actually, of painting, as the right way.

SD: It seems like your older paintings were extravagant, beyond Expressionism.

AM: Well, angry too, they were full of anger. Expressionism is angry, it's about expressing yourself. It would have been an angry time. In the 80s in Ireland, women were walked on right, left and centre. This was before even talk of divorce, contraception was illegal, young girls dying having babies in fields, a woman dismissed from her job for having a baby with a man to whom she wasn't married. It was the most appalling carry-on you could imagine. It was actually an under siege thing. I was very anti-church at that time.

SD: It's a quality you share with other Irish women.

AM: And men, actually, there was an anti-church theme in their work too, though they might come from a different route.

SD: In an earlier interview, I read that a lot of your various interests converged in your painting of the swimmers, that it signalled a move away from using the tiny girl-child swimming in the vast space to using multiple women's heads half-way emerging out of the water.

AM: They break off into multiples. There's freedom in that too. For instance, in the outdoor sculptural swimmers, *Daughters of Uranus*, the piece I did in France, they are all from one mould. It's like one person who has split. [The piece was also exhibited on the canal next to Galway Cathedral during the 1998 Galway Arts Festival.]

SD: It's interesting that they are body-less.

AM: They are not displayed, they are covered, they only display a certain amount of themselves. If you think of the tradition within art history of images of Venus, she is right up out of the water so that you can see her. *The Daughters of Uranus* retain their integrity, festering underneath the water.

SD: The female figure doesn't appear very often in your art.

AM: But it's there all the time.

SD: Yes, she's under the water, under hair, under a bee dress.

AM: But she's also not allowing herself to be owned or appropriated by voyeurism. I'd be very aware of that within art language, obviously. Sometimes [the female body] is a hard thing to deal with in art. How do you do that? But you have to do that, because you're dealing with yourself. How do you do that without putting yourself on display or without allowing yourself to be owned?

SD: Another thing that happens in your art is this fluctuation of size. It reminds me of Medieval art where people are represented in different sizes according to rank or …

AM: … or whatever, they just fitted in, in maybe a corner. I particularly like manuscript work, the Bayoux tapestry or if you've seen the Book of Dorrow, if you look at the margins, it's most interesting. It is the margins that interest me. Say somebody's concentration slipped, so they just did a little doodle in the margins. That to me is more interesting than the main work. If there is a magnificent intertwining cross or something, I would be more interested in what happens around its edges. Marginality or the margins is of great significance to me, because in the margin lots of things can happen. In the centre the law operates, but in the margins you are between wild green forest and the manicured garden.

SD: Even the materials you've chosen to use in the past, the nettles, the briars, and things that can grow in the hedges.

AM: Things that push themselves out.

SD: People are always trying to cut them back.

AM: … and order them.

SD: As a woman creating, it seems that it is much harder to use the body.

AM: Perhaps, because of the way things happened over the centuries. Male artists may feel they own the imagery of the female body or the male body and they just use it right, left and centre. I think women artists are wary when using anything, because they know they take on the cultural history of the material. You don't just think 'boats, ok I'll use boats' without thinking about the multiple meanings of boats, and this is particularly so in the multiple language of the naked body. You have to think very hard about that before you just take it, own it, and use it for your art.

SD: Even though it would seem in a logical way that as a woman you should have all the resources, in the sense that you live within the female body. But it is so charged.

AM: Yes, it is very charged, in every way, not just in art or culturally, but in every, every way. I think it is an interesting place for women artists to be now, in trying to negotiate this. That is why women artists resort to multiple languages. First of all, it's because we think in a multiple fashion, but also as a way of negotiating the art language that has been passed down to us. How do you break that open? Certain people completely reject it and try to invent a new language altogether. There are other ways of breaking in, like little rivulets that go in.

SD: Like, as you say, start working in the margins.

AM: If you use a material like a nettle or something that hasn't been used before or is not normally used as an art language, that gives you a head start in a way, because the history of it isn't there in the art world, so they can't own it.

Luz Mar González Arias

A CONVERSATION WITH CARMEL BENSON

Abstract: Carmel Benson is an Irish artist, originally from Wexford but based in County Wicklow. Although she has explored the possibilities of sculpture, video and photography, Benson is mainly known for her prints and paintings. Her work has been shown in numerous group and solo exhibitions, both in Ireland and abroad, such as the Listowel Graphic Exhibition, *Art into Art* at the National Gallery of Ireland, the London Contemporary Print Fair, *Works on Paper* in New York, and several exhibitions, from 1986 onwards, at the Graphic Studio Gallery, in Dublin. She has won many awards for her prints and paintings, including Arts Council Materials Bursaries and Publications Assistance, 'Best Print' at the Claremorris Open (1986), First Prize at 'The Salmon' Competition (Galway, 1988) and First Prize at the 'Impressions' Print Exhibition (Galway, 1991). In the following interview Carmel Benson talks about her work and interests and addresses issues of gender, location and tradition. Luz Mar González Arias (LA):Interviewer; Carmel Benson (CB): Interviewee

from 'Beyond categorisations: A Conversation with Carmel Benson', *Volume 8*, pp 91-95

I first met Carmel Benson in the summer of 1998, when I was working on my PhD in Dublin. Her pagan iconography was extremely interesting for my studies on Celtic mythology, female corporeality and Irish culture. Since then I have had several conversations with the artist about her work and its relevance for contemporary Ireland.

LA: It is clear to me that from the 1980s onwards women in Ireland have started reacting very strongly against images of women inherited from a tradition of muses, passive in nature, very often asexual and invariably happy with their roles of mothers and wives. You are an Irish woman and I wonder if those two categories have affected you as an artist.

CB: Well, naturally I am the product of my gender and location as much as anyone and, of course, that has affected my work. The passive image of women in Ireland which you depict is mainly a product of the Catholic Church, in my view. And one of the formative events of my life was my rejection of the Catholic Church when I was quite young in boarding school. It caused all kinds of problems, but it did leave a vacuum and I have always been deeply interested in spiritual matters. I see the Catholic Church, despite its positive aspects, as authoritarian and patriarchal and I rejected it on an emotional level long before I understood that rejection from an intellectual perspective. I think that turning to 'art' as a means of expression filled some of the gaps left by this rejection, though I certainly didn't consciously do it for that reason. Some of my images have presented an aspect of the female which was denied or rejected by Catholicism.

LA: I suppose the recurrence of Sheela-na-gigs in your work has something to do with that. Also, the Irish pagan tradition is rich in goddesses and heroines characterised by their overt sexuality and their strength, very much the opposite of the asexual, chaste Mother Mary iconography. Would the Sheela-na-gigs, despite their medieval origin, help you to by-pass, so to speak, Christian models and connect you with other pre-colonial, less patriarchal ways of understanding the female?

CB: I'm not sure that I was in pursuit of a further understanding of the female when I drew the Sheela-na-gigs into my work. Initially, I worked on the theme of childhood. Those early images the *Outsider* series dealt with - the isolation, the secrecy, the struggle, the bonding with nature and animals, the essential primitiveness of childhood and its elemental spiritual nature. This led on to an interest in the carvings on the early Celtic High Crosses of the ninth to the eleventh centuries. I was enchanted by the clear, simple, childlike quality of these depictions of simple Bible stories from a time when instruction took a more visual form. I visited most of these at Moone, Clonmacnoise, Monasterboice, etc. and did a series of lithographs based on them: *Daniel and the Lions*, *Adam and Eve*, *Cain and Abel* Interestingly, my *Flight into Egypt* left both Joseph and the baby out of the picture, thereby initiating my series of women on horseback! Anyway, one of the High Crosses, Clonmacnoise, I think, has a tiny Sheela-type figure incorporated into its imagery. It has been the subject of some debate whether or not it is really a Sheela. But it led me off on a whole Sheela odyssey. I visited, with a friend, all the documented ones that I could get to in this country, numerous in County Tipperary, having to climb over barbed-wire fences and cross fields past 'Beware the Bull' signs. It was great fun. Naturally, I visited the poor Sheelas buried in the bowels of the National Museum at that time as though they had been interred for some awful offence. I wanted to 'liberate' these images in some way. Hence, the very bright colours of my own Sheelas. Since then I have researched and pursued early images of the 'goddess' notably the goddess temples in Malta. I don't know if the Sheelas helped me to by-pass Christian models of the female. I think I had left those images behind before I knew about the Sheelas, which I came to quite late. Actually, when I think of a prominently placed picture of the Virgin Mary in our living-room at home I remember that, as a child, I was very taken by the snakes wriggling about the crescent moon at her feet. I remember asking about these. Of course, we know now that those snakes represented the old goddess being crushed and replaced by the new, pure virgin female! Saint Patrick driving out the snakes has similar intent!

LA: You just mentioned that some of the images in your work present aspects of the female which were denied or rejected by Catholicism. I am again thinking of the Sheela series you did at the end of the 1980s. Because that decade was particularly problematic for women in Ireland, I suppose not everybody was happy with those lithographs? Where would the negative reactions have come from?

CB: Yes, there was some negative reaction at the time, mainly from older men. One newspaper critic (old, male) described them as being 'far too blatant'. Where does this negativity come from? Who can say for certain? Where does any negativity come from? Fear and ignorance? A fear of that overt sexual aspect of the female? A need to retain an image of the female that is passive and pleasing?

LA: Do you think that would also be the case now? I mean, do you think part of the audience, and I am talking about an Irish audience, would still consider that kind of work too explicit, even pornographic, and reject it on the basis of morality?

CB: I don't think reaction to this type of imagery has changed much. There is only a small, minority audience drawn to this imagery, probably for intellectual as much as visual reasons.

LA: As you said, your work is not only the product of gender, but also of place. What is your relationship with landscape and what importance do you attach to your trips abroad, which must have influenced your perception of space, colours etc.?

CB: I think my relationship with landscape, with place, had a very strong influence. From a very early age I can remember the feeling of being alone with nature, by a river, in a cornfield, with a tree, an animal, that feeling of connection. My travel has certainly influenced my work. The light and colour in North Africa, and Greece, the shrines, the juxtaposition of unlikely objects, sacred icons beside Coca-cola bottles etc. India hasn't surfaced yet. Sometimes it takes a long time for an influence to come through. [….]

Helen O'Donoghue and Catherine Marshall

ALTERNATIVE REPRESENTATIONS CREATE ALTERNATIVE POSSIBILITIES

from 'Alternative Representations create Alternative Possibilities', *Volume* 8, pp 97-104

The visual arts have faced many challenges over the last millennium, but few have had more far-reaching implications than those posed by women during the last decades of the twentieth century. Since the 1970s, women and other marginalised groups have turned that patriarchal stronghold upside down by calling art history, education and criticism into question. Most pertinently for our time they have also forced us to look again at meaning in visual art, and how and to whom it is communicated.

Silence is not a sign of passivity, but rather a position from which to wage war. This was certainly true of Anne Devlin in Pat Murphy's film of the same name, but there is another kind of silence – the silence that arises when marginalised voices are drowned out by mainstream clamour. To speak in such circumstances only further alienates and disenfranchises the speaker. Finding the mechanism to be heard is difficult, but empowering. The exhibition, *Once is Too Much*, at the Irish Museum of Modern Art (IMMA) and other venues between 1997 and 2002, set out to do just that.

Once is Too Much was a group initiative involving women from the Family Resource Centre, Saint Michael's Estate, Inchicore, Dublin and their friends, together with artists from Ireland and abroad, and the IMMA. It began as a response to the death as a result of violence in the home, of one of the women from the Resource Centre in 1991. Following on from a very successful art project that culminated in the *Unspoken Truths* exhibition in 1992—93, the women felt empowered to use art as a means to tackle their unresolved emotions and address an issue that was still all too prevalent in their own and the wider community. Between 1995 and 1997 the women, the artists and IMMA worked collectively to make art that would help them come to terms with the issue of violence against women. They worked on a variety of projects and in a variety of media and technologies to create eleven artworks that became the exhibition *Once is Too Much*.

In July 1995, eighteen local women and friends came together at IMMA in Dublin, to make the first piece of work for *Once Is Too Much*. They did not intend at that point to develop a major exhibition, but wished to channel their collective response in a private way to address their experience of losing a friend through domestic violence. Such was the response to the initial piece of work, a printed felt blanket, that they pledged to continue and went on to create the exhibition which, seven years later, has toured Ireland extensively, and has powerfully affected the lives of many who have experienced it, raising awareness of domestic violence.

Once is Too Much, 1996, photograph. Women working with Rochelle Rubenstein in the artists' studios at IMMA

The Irish Museum of Modern Art is committed to creating opportunities for artists and people to engage with art and to work together. For *Once Is Too Much*, the women worked with international artists both from the IMMA Exhibitions and Artists Work Programmes, and with artists resident in Ireland who work on an ongoing basis as part of IMMA's Education and Community Departments'Artists Team (see illustration).

Through the Artists Work Programme, Rochelle Rubenstein, a Canadian artist, came to Dublin in 1995 and 1996. Her work at that time was concerned with the situation of abused women and children. She and the women developed a series of fabric prints and created a blanket and a set of hand-made books under the generic title *Once Is Too Much* (see illustration). Another piece, *Quilt*, was made during her second residency and is a memorial to all of the women missing or found dead during the production period of this exhibition.

Scottish born, Dublin based artist, Rhona Henderson, has worked on various projects through IMMA's Artists Team. She responded to the invitation to be involved and worked intensively on the installation *Beauty & the Beast*. Of this she says, the group wanted to explore male power in a domestic setting and its effect on the family. *Beauty & the Beast* recreates tension surrounding meal-time as mother and children await the inevitable explosion. The result is a powerful and complex piece which required a sophisticated approach from the group and provoked hours of rigorous and challenging discussion. The series of 6 text and mixed media pieces, *He Told Me ... I Told Him,* grew out of this work and is about women reclaiming power. The artist/filmmaker, Joe Lee, was funded as part of the Arts Council's Artist in the Community scheme and the three video installations are the result of his involvement with the women. *Open Season,* (later purchased for the IMMA collection—see colour plate) is based on the experience of violence. It uses extracts from audio interviews with a cross-section of women to explore the pattern of violence in their lives. It combines slides and studio-based video work of Dublin streetscapes and inhabitants taken by the women.

He Loves Me, He Loves Me Not flips the familiar folk rhyme and disturbs the romantic association of its usual context. *Hear Nothing, See Nothing, Say Nothing* has been created to facilitate the telling of the real-life experiences of a number of women who have contributed their stories to this process. *And they tell me ...* is a work that sadly grows over time in that it represents each woman who has died or gone missing since December 1995. The piece is made up of clear perspex shelves which are inscribed with the dates on which women have either died or disappeared and on which a single fresh white lily is placed each day. The lilies act as a continual reminder of our role and responsibility to act on behalf of the 97 women who died, or were reported missing between December 1995 and January 2002. This artwork was realised in collaboration with the artist Ailbhe Murphy.

The quality of the exchange that has developed between artists and the women in this project was facilitated by the six-year relationship between the Education and Community Department at IMMA and the Family Resource Centre.This partnership began in early 1991, and it faciliated the introduction of local women, men, and children to many of IMMA's programmes and to artists visiting and working on site.The extended link to Women's Aid has also been facilitated through the Family Resource Centre and this has given the project a national significance.

These creative collaborations with artists have been central to the development of *Once Is Too Much*.The work on the exhibition evolved out of a dialogue between the women and each of the artists.Communication between artist and group had to undergo critical scrutiny on an ongoing basis to ensure that the integrity of meaning was retained in the final object.

Raising awareness and understanding of one's own life and social issues are central to the process of working creatively in any medium. Many contemporary artists are keenly aware of their role in and responsibility to society.Bringing the private, often intimate details of a person's life to a public forum is not an easy task.For most of us it is quite a daunting one.

The exhibition *Once Is Too Much* aims to throw public light on the plight of too many women in contemporary Irish society. The issue is raw, the reality is bleak, but the artworks can act as a metaphor for the lived experience.The exhibition acts as a catalyst through which the collective energy of the artists and seventeen women may engage a wider public, to address the issue of violence and its causes and effects, invoking action and changing attitudes so that violence against women will not be tolerated in the future. [....]

Catherine M. Boyle

Latin American Women Writers

Abstract: The concept of silence has been important in the criticism of women's writing in Latin America. It is problematic in that it is often an interpretation imposed from outside the writing, and in this paper, I look at what the idea of a silence 'peculiar to women' could be in the Latin Ameican context, aiming to show that it is only from the outside that the notion can be regarded as having validity, for from within there is a resonance of voices and a real sense of writing as being a centre of cultural and political sensitivity and action.

from 'The Creative Force in Marginality – Women in Latin American Writing: Through the Body and Word into the Centre', *Volume 1*, pp. 107–116

[….] The notion, the experience of silence is at the centre of one of the great debates about women's writing in Latin America. How could it not be, when its antithesis is the use of a voice, of a pen, of the word? Writing is an ante-chamber to being heard. [….] Silence is important to the Latin American writer, because it is a real, concrete experience, not an abstract literary notion. [….]

Women's writing in Latin America should be brought into the spotlight and studied because it has been ignored, and because there are writers who have contributed a huge amount to the cultural and literary wealth of Latin America who also happen to be women. In order to study this we need a criticism that is born from within the work itself, and not imposed from without, from the perspective of studying difference, a criticism that recognises the roots of the experience of writing, beautifully expressed. [….] Latin American writers ask us to read, to listen to what the writer, conscious of her own roots, is saying, to look at how the writer places herself in society. [….]

Gender, in Latin America, undoubtedly plays a dictating role in determining life experience. The ubiquitous *machismo* is part of a 'knowledge' that the westerner has about Latin societies. And yet, while there has been less of a tendency to separate gender from other social and political circumstances, paradoxically, gender plays a far greater role in relation to social action than it generally does in Europe. [….]

The Ruse of the Weak

[....] The ruse of the weak is not specifically female, weakness is not. The 'weak', the defeated, invent the means by which to subvert from within the space available. This is also a political necessity. From within the dictatorships of the Southern Cone, women have done this brilliantly. [....]

Once, as critics, we can understand the relation of the word to the individual (body) and then to society, to the power and the impotence of the word in society, we can really look at women's writing in Latin America as the writers themselves want it to be regarded, as born from the roots of society, not as the comfortably and conveniently absent voice of the 'other.' Is there a theory? One possibility is looking at the key notions of control, space and time, through them we look at language, themes and structures, never losing sight of the multiple 'centres', the roots and driving force. We let the writing speak for itself. First we dig, then we tell the story. [....]

Francesca Counihan

MARGUERITE YOURCENAR

Abstract: This paper sets out to investigate whether or to what extent Marguerite Yourcenar may be considered as a 'woman writer'. Although the portrayal of women characters in her novels is limited, stereotypical and sometimes borders on the misogynistic, her male characters, and to some extent her way of writing, reveal certain feminine characteristics, so that her writing, although certainly not 'feminist' may perhaps (and despite itself) be described as 'feminine'.

from 'At Last a Woman in the Academy?: Marguerite Yourcenar as Woman Writer', *Volume 2*, pp. 111-124

In 1981, Marguerite Yourcenar (1903–1987) became the first woman ever to be elected to the Académie Française. As this is the highest official honour available to French writers, her election was hailed by many as a victory for her sex, and as evidence that the literary establishment was finally beginning to acknowledge the worth of women writers.

However, closer examination of the literary work for which this signal honour was awarded leads one to suspect that, in choosing this particular candidate, the establishment was allowing its presuppositions to be challenged less than would initially appear to be the case; that, in fact, the members of the Académie chose the woman writer who was perhaps least likely to disrupt certain conservative ideas, particularly in relation to women themselves.

This is particularly true in terms of the way in which women characters are represented in Yourcenar's work. At a time when, following on the women's movements of the 1970s, women writers in France were concentrating on giving a voice to women's experience and to women's points of view, and on creating a specific medium of expression for this 'women-centred' content, Yourcenar wrote, as she had always written, in a somewhat traditional and distinctly un-feminist mode.

[....] Women in Yourcenar's work are defined in terms of passivity, irrationality, passion, earthiness, and purity; the list would hardly be surprising, coming from a French male writer of the time. However, coming from a woman, and particularly from a woman who herself showed such personal and intellectual independence and such rational and analytic powers as did Marguerite Yourcenar, the list is, to say the least, disquieting. [....]

It is apparent [....] that, in terms of characterisation at least, Yourcenar's writing is very far indeed from being 'woman-centred'. However, whereas comments such as these indicate a considerable distance between Yourcenar and her female characters, the same cannot be said of her attitude to the male characters who dominate her work, and it is here, perhaps, that we should look for a further understanding of her work. What I would like to suggest here is that, in her treatment of her male characters, Yourcenar is in fact writing as a woman, and that aspects of her femininity become apparent not so much through the material she presents as through the way in which it is presented.

One of the key points in this regard is the concept of identity. It has been suggested by recent psychoanalytical theory (for example by Nancy Chodorow) that women and men differ in their sense of personal identity; whereas men experience themselves as strongly defined and individuated beings, women have a less distinct sense of self and experience themselves as more 'connected to the world' to use Chodorow's phrase. [....] These theories throw light on an intriguing aspect of Yourcenar's work; both she and her characters repeatedly question the concept of identity as something fixed and clearly defined.

[....] Just as she rejects the 'self' as a separate and distinct entity, she questions in other ways the limits by which categories of things and people are distinguished from one another and, thus, defined. In several instances in her work, and particularly in descriptive passages, boundaries and limits are blurred, one category merges into the next, so that reality (or at least, the character's experience of that reality) is fluid and continuous rather than structured and compartmentalised.

Marguerite Yourcenar revisits her childhood home, 1980

We may conclude [....] that certain aspects of Yourcenar's work (the question of identity, the individual's experience of reality as fluid rather than fixed) indicate a strongly feminine quality in her writing; however, this remains at odds with the limited way in which she chooses to portray women. Indeed, it is apparent from a study of representations of women in Yourcenar's work that their place is, to say the least, a minor one. In a body of work dominated by strong male characters, women are specifically excluded both from central roles and from such positively valued qualities as lucidity and reason. And yet, within this work, another current is present, which seems to question the basis of reason itself, to dissolve the solid building blocks on which it rests, and to suggest instead a world of fluid forms and merging shapes, where reality is closer to a continuum than to a set of separate and fixed categories. It would be overstating the case to suggest that this current is the dominant one in Yourcenar's work; however, its presence can be felt, leading the reader to discover in this work hidden aspects which invite further exploration.

Christine O'Dowd-Smyth

ALGERIAN WOMEN WRITERS

Abstract: This article is an analysis of the twin themes of silence and exile in the works of Nina Bouraoui, Soraya Nini and Malika Mokeddem, who are three women writers of Algerian nationality or origin, living in France and writing in French. These three writers are part of a literary movement, North African Francophone Literature, which is one of a plurality of literatures written in the French language.

from 'Silence and Exile in the Works of Three Algerian Women Writers: Nina Bouraoui, Soraya Nini and Malaki Mokeddem', *Volume* 6, pp. 61-67

In France, from the middle of the 1980s and onwards, there has been a very significant increase in Francophone literature, North African Francophone literature in particular, with writers such as the Moroccan novelist and intellectual, Tahar Ben Jelloun, winning the prestigious French literary prize, *Le Prix Goncourt,* in 1987 for *La Nuit Sacree (The Sacred Night)*[1] and the young writer of Algerian origin, Nina Bouraoui, who won the *Prix Inter* in 1991 for *La Voyeuse Interdite (The Forbidden Peeping Jane)*. This rise in popularity of 'exotic literature' coincides with what many perceive as the decline of the French novel and its waning influence on literary trends.

In Algeria, Morocco and Tunisia (the three countries of the Maghreb, or former French North Africa), writing in French has paradoxically increased after independence from France. In these countries, French remains the language of the educated and powerful, in spite of governmental policies of promoting Arabic in schools and universities. [....]

Many writers from the Maghreb see their role as being that of spokespersons for their society, as speaking out, or 'breaking the silence' in an international lingua franca, for an international audience, against the perceived injustices and tyranny of a patriarchal society.

Perhaps the most important group writing in the French language today within the confines of this 'emerging literature' that of Algerian women writers, living in exile in France and often in hiding for fear of fundamentalist reprisals. Their subject matter is essentially an outspoken critique of traditional Islamic culture where women are reduced to silence in the name of Allah and his Prophet. In fact, the central theme of this literature would seem to be the silencology, or collection of silences, that inability to communicate which lies at the heart of their culture, the silence between men and women, segregated and unequal before Islamic law, the silence between the all-powerful father and his submissive children, and the silence between the mother, banished to the kitchen, fearful of being repudiated, and her unwanted, status-less daughters. The North African Francophone author has a vocation, then, to break these silences, and at the same time, to destroy them. [....]

When we consider these writers, we must also include the young generation of writers born in France of North African immigrant parents, often referred to as the 'Beurs', which is French *verlan* or 'backslang' for *Arabe* or Arab, an insulting and derogatory term which has unfortunately 'stuck' and is still in common use, as a more acceptable alternative remains to be found or coined. Writers such as Soraya Nini write about what it is like to be considered as neither French nor Algerian, as being "lost between the two shores of the Mediterranean".[3]

Nina Bouraoui's novel, *La Voyeuse Interdite* (*The Forbidden Observer* or *The Forbidden Peeping Jane*), is a violent critique of the position held by women in Algerian society. It is written from the viewpoint of a young girl who is the omniscient narrator of the story. [....]

The young observer has distanced herself from her surroundings and from her own feelings, in order to convey as clear a picture as possible of what it is like for a young girl to live in a fundamentalist Islamic society, deprived of all rights, walled up and veiled. In Nina Bouraoui's novel, silence is omnipresent, as a metaphor, as a leitmotif, as a description of the young girl's environment, as she looks down onto a noisy street where men are everywhere: "Madmen kept apart forever from women by the Muslim religion."[4] [....]

Soraya Nini, a young writer of Algerian parentage, grew up in Toulon, a city in the South of France and a stronghold of the extreme right-wing political party, the National Front. Nini's father was a good

Muslim who believed in veiling and shutting away his wife and daughters from the temptations of a 'decadent' and secular French society. Her first novel, which is highly autobiographical, deals with the problematic status associated with the ethnicity of immigrant families, and the fate of a young woman from an immigrant family who finds her quest for personal independence blocked by the traditional Islamic values of her parents. [....]

Soraya Nini originally wished to call her novel *L'Entre-Leux (Between Two Cultures)*, but her publisher wanted it to be called *La Beurette (The Young 'Beur' Girl)* in order to increase sales. Nini refused to accept an alien label imposed on her from the dominant French population. This reservation remains apparent in the compromise title *Ils disent que je suis une Beurette (They call me a young 'Beur' Girl)*. [....]

One writer who refuses to be placed in a "Third World Writers' Ghetto"[5] is the Algerian writer Malika Mokeddem, whose novels are published by the major French publishing house Grasset, and not the smaller, more obscure publishers often associated with Francophone writers. Perhaps with no other Algerian woman writer can we see as clearly the twin themes of silence and exile as in Mokeddem's two novels *L'Interdite (The Forbidden Woman)* and *Des Rêves et des Assassins (Dreams and Assassins)*. [....]

For Algerian women, education would seem to be the key to freedom, and if exile is preferable to slavery in their own country, then breaking the silence around the taboos that surround Islamic culture is an imperative.

For Nina Bouraoui and Soraya Nini, the French language has been their link to the wider world outside the immigrant ghetto in which the traditional ways and values still flourish. For Malika Mokeddem, it was much more:

> French is my written language, it is through French that I had access to the world in my little corner of the desert. I am only happy when I am between the two languages, the two worlds. I write from my particular perspective, that of a woman who has lived in Algeria. I have a foot on both shores of the Mediterranean.[6]

Malika Mokeddem, no doubt, speaks for all Algerian women writers, living in France, writing in French, raising their voices passionately against their condition, demanding that their message be heard, when she justifies her reason for writing, for 'breaking the silence', for calling attention to herself and in so doing, receiving a death threat under which she still lives, when she says:

Western Heads of State and intellectuals sometimes take action on behalf of oppressed minorities all over the world... but never for women! Woman is not deemed to be a part of Man's future, but remains a shameful silence in a world that is supposedly progressive.[7]

Notes
1. All titles and quotations are translated by the author of this article.
2. Jean-Louis Joubert 1994. *Anthologie des Litteratures Francophones du Monde Arabe*, Paris: Nathan, p. 11.
3. Nina Bouraoui 1991. *La Voyeuse Interdite*, Paris: Folio, p. 22
4. Christiane Chaulet-Achour, interview with Malike Mokeddem, 19 Dec. 1994, in "place d'une Litterature migrante en France" in Charles Bonn, (dir.) 1995. *Litteratures des Immigrations No 2: Exils croises*, Paris: L'Harmattan.
5. Christiane Chaulet-Achour, *op. cit.*
6. Malika Mokeddem 1995. *Des Reves et des Assassins*, Paris: Grasset.

Ana P.L.N. Nunes

GAYL JONES'S CORREGIDORA

Abstract: This essay will explore the ways in which African-American history conditions the identities of twentieth-century Black American females. For that purpose, an analysis of Gayl Jones's first novel, *Corregidora* (1975) illustrates how the dynamics of sexual abuse continue beyond the abolition of slavery, for two former slaves and their descendants. Caught in a definition of the self based on biological determinism, the Corregidora women remain the possession of their master. Excluded from a written history and access to literacy, Great Gram and her daughter believe that the transmission of their memories can only be accomplished via the spoken word. They want their descendants to 'make generations' in order to keep their story alive. These characters bequeath to their daughters an emotional imperative which perpetuates the master/slave discourse. Ursa, the fourth generation of the Corregidora women, fights to free herself from the bondage set by her ancestors by embarking on a journey, the successful completion of which implies a redefinition of her identity and sexuality.

from 'Marked at Birth: History and Identity in Gayl Jones's *Corregidora*', Volume 6, pp. 69-85

[....] Gayl Jones's first novel, *Corregidora*, published in 1975, explores the ways in which history, revealed in an absolute truth-telling form, can entrap individuals in its webs and take control of their lives. Jones emphasises the necessity of defining boundaries between private and collective history. She explores these two spheres almost to their limits in order to illustrate how African-Americans are susceptible to being swallowed up by a history that has the potential to endanger their lives. In an interview with Charles H. Rowell, Jones states:

> History and personality are interests there [in *Corregidora*] – the relationship between history and personality – personal and collective history – history as a motivating force in personality... Michael Harper – my advisor and teacher at Brown – asked me a question: What is the relationship between autobiography and history? So, much of the answer for it became part of the creative process of writing that book.[1]

In this sense, *Corregidora* invites the reader to enter a fictional realm in which history and personal life are closely braided, often entangled, but if Jones's highly crafted narrative voice guides the reader in such a way that she or he will not confuse one with the other, it continually exposes the ways in which history influences and conditions the lives of her characters.

Front cover of Gayl Jones's *Corregidora*, published by Camden Press, with photo of the author (inset)

Ursa Corregidora, the protagonist of the novel and its narrator, starts her autobiography, to use Jones's terminology, in a rather unusual way. There is no mention of her name, her place of birth, or any other basic factual information about her origins such as would usually open autobiographical narratives. Rather, she commences her story by exposing the two main tensions in her life: her art, and her love for a man who does not understand how her songs are as much part of her life as he is:

> It was 1947 when Mutt and I was married. I was singing in Happy's café around on Delaware Street. He didn't like for me to sing after we were married because he said that's why he married me so he could support me. I said that I didn't just sing to be supported. I said I sang because there was something that I had to do, but he never would understand that. We were married in December 1947 and it was in April 1948 that Mutt came to Happy's drunk and said that if I didn't get off stage he was going to take me off. I didn't move ...[2] [....]

Notes
1. Charles H Rowell 1982. 'An Interview with Gayl Jones', *Callaloo: A Journal of African-American Arts and Letters*, Baltimore MD, p. 45.
2. Gayl Jones 1988. *Corregidora*, London: Camden Press, p. 3.

Áine O'Healy

ITALIAN FEMINIST FILMMAKERS

Abstract: Though critically overlooked and rarely screened, the documentary and experimental films produced by Italian feminists during the 1970s provide compelling traces of the discourses articulated by the women's movement in its most productive phase. Focusing on the documentaries and super-8 films created by prominent activists in Rome and Naples during the 1970s, this essay discusses the film production of Italian feminists within the broader context of the struggle for legislative reform being carried out simultaneously by women throughout all regions of Italy. [....]

from "Nemesis and her Sisters: Feminist Filmmakers in Naples and Rome", *Volume* 6, 1999, pp 123-138

Italian feminism constituted one of the most vigorous, politically effective, and heterogeneous women's movements that flourished in the West during the years that followed the explosion of liberationist activism in the late 1960s. Throughout the 1970s thousands of women all over Italy were mobilised in demonstrations, political rallies and consciousness-raising activities that ultimately led to important changes in legislation on issues specifically affecting women's lives. Simultaneously, feminist writers, philosophers and artists set out to formulate new, historically contingent terms for a politics of the psychosymbolic. In the English-speaking world the accomplishments of Italian feminism have been eclipsed by the rival claims of American, British and French feminisms. Even now, as the theoretical texts produced by Italian feminist philosophers have begun to appear in English translation,[1] most of the cultural production that emanated from the women's movement in Italy during the 1970s and 1980s remains unknown abroad. Yet, at the high point of the movement, Italian women created a vibrant body of literary and theatrical work. During the same period in several Italian cities feminists also produced a variety of documentary, experimental, and avant-garde films. Unlike the experimental filmmaking carried out by women in Britain, the United States, and Germany at the time, the films produced within the context of the Italian women's movement have almost completely escaped scholarly attention. [....]

In focusing on the practical circumstances of women's lives and the need for social change, many of the earliest films produced by Italian feminists during the 1970s reflect the concerns of the initial, activist phase of the movement. Some of the films of this period were hastily assembled, agit-prop productions, directly related to issues being argued at rallies or other political venues. A small number of low-budget films, however, were produced by activists with some previous experience in filmmaking. Among the best known documentaries of the period was the controversial *Aborto: parlano Ie donne/Women speak about abortion,* made in 1976 by the well-known writer and activist Dada Maraini who had directed her first and only commercial feature film *L'amore coniugale/Conjugal Love* in 1969. Shot in 16 mm, *Aborto: parlano Ie donne* was inspired by Maraini's participation in the campaign to legalize abortion and her desire to raise the level of public consciousness regarding the real conditions of women's lives. In preparing the film she interviewed dozens of women of different ages in lower-income neighbourhoods, all of whom had undergone the risky experience of illegal abortion. One of the most striking aspects of *Aborto: parlano Ie donne* is the prominence it accords to the women themselves as speaking subjects. [....]

A similar preoccupation with the hardships endured by economically underprivileged women is found in a film made around the same time by Maraini's one-time collaborator, Maricla Boggio. Entitled *Marisa della Magliana* (1976), this 16 mm film, which was made for television, took a critical look at the material conditions of a working-class woman living in the Magliana district on the outskirts of Rome. Like *Aborto: parlano le donne,* Boggio's film was conceived as a consciousness-raising exercise, and resonates with the debates simultaneously articulated on the streets, in women's groups, and at political demonstrations throughout the mid-1970s.

Anna Miscuglio, the principal figure in a loosely defined group of activist filmmakers active in Rome during this period, made a small number of controversial films and videos in collaboration with Rony Daopoulo and several other women. One of the most widely discussed of these was the dramatized reconstruction of a rape trial *Processo per stupor/Trial for Rape* (1978). Produced in 16mm format, the film articulates a critique of dominant patriarchal culture and its intrinsic violence towards women. Miscuglio's next film, *AAA offresi/AAA Services Offered* (1979), a documentary on prostitution, proved even more controversial. Shot with a hidden video camera, it candidly recorded the activities of a prostitute at work with her clients. [....]

The three super-8 films made by Maraini in the late 1970s – *Mio padre amore mio/My Father, Love of Mine* (1976/1979),[2] *La bella addormentata nel bosco/Sleeping Beauty* (1978) and *Giochi di latte/Milk Games* (1979) – were shot as silent films, with a musical track added at the post-production stage. *Mio padre amore mio,* visually the most complex of the three, is an autobiographically inspired meditation on a woman's phantasmatic relationship with her father, alternatively resented and adored. The narrative is framed in the dressing room of a theatre where a young actress, seated before the mirror, is applying a clown's face. [....]

Giochi di latte, by contrast, explores the relationship between a mother and her daughter in a magical-realist key, using the recurring image of a vast river of milk. This film thus explicitly attempts to find new ways to smybolise the mother-daughter relationship, responding to a directive issued by the women's movement at the time. Luce Irigaray's critique of the unsymbolized nature of the mother-daughter relationship was taken up by Italian feminist artists and theorists in the late 1970s and early 1980s. According to Irigaray, a woman has 'too few figurations, images, or representations by which to represent herself',[3] meaning that there is a lack of iconic, mythical, or other cultural representations of women that are not already inflected by the patriarchal symbolic system. In other words, there is no sense of a maternal genealogy. This awareness has led a number of feminists to reformulate the mother-daughter relationship, and to propose an alternative symbolic system predicated not on the phallus but on the power of the maternal figure. In Italy, the work of Luisa Muraro and Adriana Cavarero has been particularly important in this regard. According to Muraro, author of *L'ordine simbolico della madre*, although feminist discourse has produced a convincing critique of patriarchy and the cultural systems supporting its dominance over women, the legacy of this critique will disappear in a matter of years if women do not create a movement to affirm the power that is held in woman's relationship with the mother.[4] [....]

Even before Maraini began to produce her experimental films in Rome, a group of women activists known as Le Nemesiache had become involved in feminist filmmaking in Naples. Here, the effort to address in cinematic terms the problematics of the body and the possibilities of psychosymbolic transformation was carried out in a different way. The group was founded in the early 1970s by Lina Mangiacapre, also known as Nemesis (after the ancient Greek figure of retribution and transformation), who set about reconstituting the concept of *autocoscienza* in performative terms. Rejecting the predominantly verbal form of consciousness-raising propagated by feminists elsewhere, Le Nemesiache ('followers of Nemesis') gave prominence to music, bodily movement, and gesture in their psychosymbolic project. For Le Nemesiache, *autocoscienza* [self-awareness] involved not only the spoken word, but also dance, mime, music and song. The group used the term *'psicofavola'* (psychofable) to describe their distinctive performative project, and their staged performances often involved revisionist interpretations of well-known patriarchal narratives. [....]

The engagement of Mangiacapre and her colleagues with the myths of the Neapolitan region is especially evident in two of their super-8 films *Il mare* ci *ha chiamate/The Sea Has Called Us* (1978) and *Le Sibille/The Sibyls* (1979). These films evoke female figures associated with the Bay of Naples while directly alluding to the necessity to save the environment from its current state of degradation. Part ritual, part narrative, part documentary exploration, the films evoke an ambivalent time frame, shifting between the present and the mythical past. The oneiric effect of this temporal indeterminacy is heightened by the haunting music of Lina Mangiacapre.

One of the most interesting projects undertaken by La Nemesiache was *Follia come Poesia/Madness as Poetry* (1980), a 60-minute documentary film on the group's visits to the women's section of the Frullone psychiatric hospital in Naples. The interest of Mangiacapre and her colleagues in the hospital grew out of their support for the movement initiated by radical psychiatrists, which called for a restructuring of psychiatric health care and a reform of the practice of lifelong hospitalisation. The group thus attempted to open a dialogue with the hospitalized women by having them watch the film version of *Ceneralla psicofavola femminista*. *Follia come Poesia*, which was shot on videotape over a period of weeks, was at first intended simply to document these visits to the hospital. The voice-over introduction to the finished film suggests that the filmmakers' objective was neither to examine the material conditions of the women's incarceration, nor to denounce the social pressures that might have led to their illnesses, but to explore the 'madness' as a phenomenon with specific expressive power. [....]

Notes

1 see, for example, Paola Bono and Sandra Kemp, *Italian Feminist Thought: A Reader*, Blackwell, 1991
2 Maraini first made *Mio padre amore mio* in 1976.the film was later lost by a processing company, and was reshot by the filmmaker in 1979.
3 Luce Irigaray, *Speculum of the Other Woman*, trans Gill, Cornell UP, 1985.
4 Luisa Muraro, *L'ordine simbolico della madre*, Riuniti, 1991

Christiane Schönfeld

THE *FEMME FATALE* ON FILM

Abstract: This paper focuses on the cinematic representation of the most powerful female archetype – the *femme fatale* – while exploring generally the role women have played in film since its very early stages. Hollywood, as the dominant mainstream cinema producer, has influenced women's self-image as much as it has dictated varying ideals of beauty and deportment. Its presentation of the deadly woman, however, has changed little from its earliest depictions by Marlene Dietrich and Louise Brooks to contemporary archetypes personified by Sharon Stone or Liv Tyler. What has, then, been the impact of feminist film theory on cinema of the last thirty years? I will concentrate here on images rather than their creators, for it is the cascade of stereotypes on screen that shapes us and our interpretations. American mainstream cinema has had the most dominating influence on global visual culture and, therefore, most films discussed in this essay with regard to their stereotypical representation of women, are Hollywood productions. Josef von Sternberg's *Der blaue Engel/The Blue Angel* (1930) is introduced here as the basis for the representational confinement of women in film—for it was the star of this picture, Marlene Dietrich, who moved from Berlin to Hollywood to firmly establish the image of the dangerous sexual woman on global screens.

from 'Women on Screen: A Short History of the *Femme Fatale*', *Volume 8*, pp. 29-46

When we think of women in film, an endless stream of images comes to mind: archetypes of power from Louise Brooks as the epitome of the *femme fatale* in G.W. Pabst's *Pandora's Box* (1929) to Sigourney Weaver as the worthy opponent of slimy alien creatures in a series of *Alien* pictures (1979, 1986, 1992, 1997). Yet images of woman's defeat are similarly universal in film production, and countless films of the last century from around the globe depict women as victims. They are destroyed on screen by man, by society, by the will of God, but most of all, by their own destructive nature. In fact, it would be easy to read films merely as direct representations of the role of women since the invention of the medium more than one hundred years ago. However, rather than dwelling on Alfred Hitchcock's close-up of Janet Leigh's imaginary blood swirling down the shower drain in *Psycho* (1960), the following essay would like to contemplate more ambivalent and at least potentially emancipatory representations.

Women's rights issues, for instance, have clearly influenced the depiction of women on screen and this is reflected by revenge narratives like Ana Carolina Teixera Soares's *Mar de rosas* (1977), Shekhar Kapur's *The Bandit Queen* (1994), or even the recently released Michael Apted film *Enough* (2002, starring pop queen Jennifer Lopez as the abused wife who decides to kill her tormentor). But how should we read these images and personae? As Carol Clover's analysis of US American rape-revenge films suggests in *Men, Women and Chain Saws* (1992), the appeal of these films lies less in an interest in women's liberation than in a broadly based public enjoyment of images of unwarranted violence. 'Vengeance may very well be the mainspring of American popular culture,' she writes, 'from western and *Dirty Harry* to teen comedies and courtroom dramas. Nor is the rape-revenge drama exclusive to "low" genres; the success of such mainstream films as *Lipstick, The Accused, Straw Dogs, Extremities,* [and] *Sudden Impact* … suggests that the appeal of rape-revenge stories is in fact broadly based.' In this context it is interesting to note that although women in films of this genre are depicted as fighting back, their liberation more often than not remains doubtful. When women are beaten, raped, humiliated, their revenge is nowadays usually depicted as justified, but at the same time violent women can rarely function as heroes and earn salvation. Female violence usually lacks the cathartic element that not only offers validation but peace. *Thelma and Louise* (1991) learn to fight back but find liberation only in death or possibly during those seconds right before shooting over the edge of the canyon in their convertible. Revenge narratives rarely end happily. [….]

Lola Lola on stage (courtesy of the Deutsche Kinemathek, Berlin)

In contrast to the supposed change of women's status in society and the amount of books and articles on feminist film theory challenging stereotypical images of women, dominant cinema and its mainstream cinematic representations of women have changed little. The violent woman remains an attractive commodity in an industry that appreciates her violence as a successful technique of persuasion and social control. The power of the archetype is its identification of an essence, a core characteristic that consequently remains unchanged. As archetypes signify an essence, are we therefore to believe that violence is an activity that pertains to woman's fundamental nature? One could argue that female violence is reactive, but the most common stereotype is not the Amazon who uses violence solely defensively, but rather the vamp or *femme fatale* who embodies violence as means to an end with no clear motive.

This becomes problematic when we consider the consequences. Within the realm of traditional morality, the *femme fatale* deserves to be penalised for her ruinous behaviour. Punishment often concludes fatal women narratives on screen, beginning with Lulu who eventually falls prey to Jack the Ripper in Pabst's *Pandora's Box*. And even if the *femme fatale* survives, the mass audience is certain to feel her threat and desire her elimination. Mounting evidence suggests that the way women are portrayed in the media influences the way we are treated in society. While the mainstream *femme fatale* movie usually has little in common with hard-core pornography or sadistic video games like *Duke Nukem*, which awards points to players who kill prostitutes, it time and again suggests female sexuality as threatening and potentially deadly, and therefore perpetuates the patriarchal call for its containment.

Chris Head

Creativity Workshop

from Volume 8, pp. 121-123

I know
that creativity is the natural order of life,
that if I overcome the self will that refuses creativity

I can work with, and not against, my true nature.
I know
that creativity is not just about producing poems, paintings, plays, sculptures or children,
that creativity is about bringing a state of truth into being.
Am I ready for that? Are you?

Try this: write a letter to your self, the self that we sometimes refer to as the 'me' that we are aware of, don't have time for, but won't go away. Give her a big 'hello'. Tell her everything that is going on with you right now. Write to her freely. Don't censor yourself. Don't re-read what you write. Put the pages in a self-addressed envelope, stamp it and give it to a friend for safe keeping. Ask your friend to post it in three weeks time. Better still, get your friend to try this too and you can be postie for each other, maybe even get together and share your responses on reading your letter.

I know
that I was taught to love success
and not what I was doing,
that I can undo what I was taught,
that this is the alchemy that leads me to my own set of keys.
I know
that belief separates you from me,
separates you from your self, and me from my self,
that loyalty to petrified opinion
never broke a chain or freed a human soul.

Try this: gather up a pile of magazines/colour supplements (8 to 10 should be enough). Allow your self an interruption free hour/hour and a half. No TV, no radio, some music is good. Flick through the magazines and, as you do, focus on the feeling 'my heart is'. Collect images, colours, textures, pieces of text that you feel drawn to when you say to your self 'my heart is'. Don't analyse or censor your choices. Allow your self to respond intuitively. When you feel you have exhausted this process, start to play with your selection, arranging them on a large piece of card. When the arrangement feels right, paste the pieces down. Add other materials, colours, if it feels appropriate. Put your work up somewhere where you can see it and watch it occasionally.

I want to know
what it feels like to be seamless,
to resonate with what is
and not with what went before,
not with what might be.

I know
that to live anonymously
is liberating,
that to seek recognition
is not,
that there is no special virtue
in doing things the way they have always been done.

Try this: watch a spider for a week. Watch it at work, how it uses its legs to check the quality of its construction, to sense change. See it sit forever without moving. Watch it capture and wrap up a meal and carry it to the 'dining' area. See it make repairs to its web. If you can, watch a web being created from scratch.

Sometimes in early morning light, when first dew shines and shimmers on endless acres of webs cast on the grass, caught in the bushes, captured in the gates, I feel the whole world is snagged together.

I know
that to emerge fully,
I must loosen every pebble in my wall
gently, silently,
that to occupy the presence of life
is to move from the known to the unknown,
the greatest work of all.
I know
that if I follow you, and you follow me
we corrupt each other,
that power,
without wisdom and love is dangerous,
that wisdom,
without power and love is academic,
that love,
without power and wisdom, is weak.
I know
that this knowledge is not available in books.

Consider this: either to your self, or over coffee with others, 'Am I the author of my story, the weaver of my tapestry, the maker of my movie'? This has nothing to do with being in charge of your life. It does have a lot to do with who and what gives it shape, rhythm, colour and meaning. It is, after all, your greatest work!

Mary Dempsey

After Twenty Years

from Volume 8, p. 128

She has come back to plant a garden,
scatter seeds that grow like wild flowers:
cabbage, broccoli, sage, broad beans.
She kneels in front of miniature drills
fingers young shoots, clears the weeds.
Her two children circle the house in a toy tractor
as she talks to a neighbour, leans on the fence.

I visit my eco-friendly, rural sister.
Over lentil soup she lets her hair down,
talks twenty to the dozen: how she left there
and came here to plant a half acre.
Sometimes her thoughts wander to traffic-jams,
taking the children to the mountains at weekends.
In the next field two horses nod and whinney.

Jessie Lendennie

REFUGEES

from Volume 2, p. 85

They lean out from the pages of a discarded magazine;
leering men casually posing around a skinny, naked boy
before they set his dark skin on fire.
A recorded instant of triumph. History.

And me? I'm a sometimes vegetarian
with a share of middle-class guilt.
My outrage has a muted sound.
I know there are all kinds of deaths.

My son is tall. Thin, but blond and bright.
How can he be a refugee, an outcast
lost in pain, in darkness ..
murdered through a mischance of hatred ..
without me.

Joan McBreen

Woman Watching the Door

from Volume 2, p. 88

I am walking in an orchard with my mother.
She is naming the apple-trees as we pass;
'Cox Pippin' and 'Beauty of Bath'.

She stoops to fasten the strap of my sandal,
sunlight the colour of leaves in her hair.

We made our way from one year to another,
to my children around her
in an over-heated room, her eyes dim, puzzled.

Someone carries a tea-tray towards her
as the winter light fades outside.

She neither eats nor weeps
but steadily watches the door
as a woman in a dry field watches
for any beast to give her passage beyond.

From the Personal to the Political

Liz Stanley

'Experience' in Recent Feminist Thought

Abstract: In this paper I look at the 'speaking positions' that contend within different styles of feminist thought, in which feminist researchers and writers speak 'for the...' research subjects, or speak 'as a...' member of such a group themselves. In recent work, some feminists have criticised what is seen as an 'essentialist' reliance on personal experience as the basis of a theoretically and politically informed feminist speaking position. I take issue with these and related criticisms. I start with the murders of women students in Canada in 1989 for the 'frame' of my argument, to begin with 'an experience' in such a way as to recognise the role of such emotions in apparently bloodless phrases about women's position in society. I then critically discuss feminist criticisms of the uses of personal experience, rejecting the idea that epistemology can be grounded in anything other than ontology. This is followed by looking at a personal experience of dealing with death, that of my mother, and the everyday theorising that arose from it. Asking questions about who speaks, where they are located, and the consequences of this 'politics of location', enables a different kind of epistemological project to be assembled, one which is concerned with the explication and analysis of the category experience. The discussion concludes by returning to the topic of death, outlining the particular epistemological interest that the human experience of death has, and its ontological problematics which have epistemological consequentiality, and arguing that criticisms of the use of 'experience' mis/represent this position by erecting a new binary, between those who use experience and those who falsely claim not to.

from "Speaking 'As A...', Speaking 'For The...' On the Mis/Use of the Category 'Experience' in Recent Feminist Thought", *Volume 3*, pp. 19-28

The problematic 'As A...'

The two terms in the title of my paper, speaking 'as a...' and speaking 'for the...', are a re–working from a different use of them in Nancy Miller's (1991) *Getting Personal*. Miller's excellent book is concerned with feminist performances on academic feminist occasions, at conferences, seminars, colloquia and so on, and so these terms are appropriately used regarding another feminist performance – mine – in the two seminars in which this 'paper' was given orally,[1] and now in this other academic performance which is a published journal article.

The problematic 'as a...' stands for the recognition that there are a number of feminist criticisms of speaking/writing, and in particular theorising, out of experience, out of one's own experience in particular.

What I see as the even more problematic 'for the...' is the recognition that speaking 'for the...' occurs on behalf of persons who are representative of a category by someone whose knowledge-claim and expertise is founded on standing outside this category. I regard it as even more problematic than speaking 'as a...' because 'for the...' dissembles: there is no standing outside of a category-based speaking position: speaking 'for the...' always inevitably means speaking 'as a...' member of some other category-membership; in this sense there is no objectivity and detachment, only competing subjectivities and involvements. Regarding feminist criticisms of the problematic 'as a...', it is clear that there are a number of different, and sometimes competing, arguments involved, and I briefly outline five of these and my objections to them.

Firstly, there is the argument that the political and intellectual justification for feminism lies in its role in theorising experience, which is assumed to be unseamed, amorphous and entirely untheorised. Speaking 'as a...' is seen here to speak out of, indeed to remain immersed within, subjectivity: women experience, feminists theorise, is the essence of this argument. This seems to me the shakiest and least defensible criticism of speaking 'as a...', for 'experience' is better understood in social science terms as inter-subjectivity which depends upon categorisation of its components, which are thereby *a priori* theorised: the social world is apprehended in theoretical terms, through typifications tied to concrete instances, of persons, behaviours, situations. In addition, of course, it presupposes a breath-takingly elitist view of the relationship between the categories 'women' and 'feminism'.

Secondly, there is an argument that the crisis of representivity that characterises contemporary intellectual life, most often associated with post modernist and deconstructionist positions, demonstrates that the recognition of 'difference' dissolves the ability to speak in terms of categories, 'as a...' particular category-member, for doing so is dependent upon the articulation of false generalisations. However, within this formulation 'difference' is seen in highly individualistic terms, personalised as multiplicities of fragmentations, as a universal category of particularities. Apart from noting the massive contradiction here, it also needs to be emphasised that 'difference' is not mere difference, but also involves difference *from*: some people are different, other people are that which they are different from; women, black people, lesbians and gay men, for instance, are different in category-terms and such categories exist in a subordinate hierarchical relationship to that to which they are 'other'. [....]

Thirdly, there is the argument that 'identity politics' and the knowledge-claims which arise from this are premised to the idea that there can be 'separatist knowledges', whereas knowledge and truth are single. That is, this is a basically foundationalist position, that when there is true knowledge any distinction between speaking 'as a…' and 'for the…' is collapsed, *and* that true knowledge is better able to be generated, not by those who are immersed and involved but those who are dispassionate because removed. Thus the distinction is both removed, and a hierarchy between the two speaking positions insisted upon. This argument is an extremely familiar one, for it represents the point at which feminism entered the academy, entered insisting that there are in life only situated knowledges, but that most of these situated knowledges become subjugated by a voice presented as objective and removed but actually articulating a highly particular, and situated, and local speaking, position which has come to be treated as '*the* truth'. [....]

Fourthly, there is the related argument that embedded within the speaking 'as a…' position is a claim to inverse the traditional hierarchy, in which speaking 'as a woman' becomes *a priori* superordinate over any knowledge-claims men might make. This is seen as both separatist and essentialist and as untenable solipsism. However, there is in fact neither any necessary recourse to essentialism in such a position, for differences between men and women are more typically understood as socially constructed and mutable, nor anything separatist in arguing that such socially constructed difference is epistemologically consequential. [....]

Fifthly, there is the argument, common among mainstream epistemologists and increasingly frequently expressed in feminist theory (with a capital 'T'), that epistemology cannot be founded on an ontological basis. Within these arguments, 'experience', 'identity' and related terms are frequently used the Humpty Dumpty way, to mean what the critic wants them to mean. The underlying notion of 'experience' in particular is treated as limited and merely descriptive, as a litany of 'political correctness' markers, both as self-affirmed but also as applied to people belonging to the 'other' categories (and see here the fourth criticism above). [....]

Each of these criticisms assumes that it is possible not to 'use experience' in the production of knowledge, that there is an alternative in which, to reiterate the last of these criticisms, there can be an epistemology which is not ontologically based. I cannot agree. Actions and statements about experience, be they never so epistemological, require a thinking and feeling subject. Relatedly, in spite of the claims of scientism there is no means or method for escaping the subjecthood of the inquiring agent – and this includes those who inquire and reflect as much as those whose lives are inquired about and reflected upon. Moreover, at basis there is a good deal more in common between everyday and formalised theorising about the social world than there are differences. [....]

Note
1. Different versions of this paper have been given as oral presentations at the Women's Studies Centre Seminar at UCG, and at the Women's Studies Network Seminar at the University of Manchester, both in December 1993. [....]

Sylvia Walby

Citizenship

Abstract Citizenship is a concept which is useful for conceptualising key issues in gender relations, even though many of the classic texts have neglected to address issues relevant to women. When we take seriously questions of diversity and gender, not only in relation to class and ethnicity, but also in relation to nations and states, there can be more than one construction of the public and of citizenship. In this paper, a comparative perspective is applied to the exploration of citizenship, not only civil and political, but more especially social citizenship. The Republic of Ireland is considered in relation to other member states of the European Union, in particular the UK and Denmark. The rate of change in the gender regime in Ireland from domestic to public is rapidly changing the different routes to citizenship available to Irish women.

from 'Women and Citizenship: Towards a Comparative Analysis', *Volume 4*, pp. 41–58

[....] Citizenship is an important concept for contemporary social analysis because of its engagement with notions of social cohesion and social exclusion in societies with competitive and inegalitarian economies. It reaches discussion of rights as well as duties, and notions of justice and fairness, not as abstract concepts, but in the context of grounded and material analyses.

However, the gender dimension is neglected in many of these discussions. There is a question as to whether citizenship is gendered or whether it is a more universally valid concept. Is it a concept which can be applied equally for women and men and mean the same thing in different countries, or is it always affected by deeply rooted social diversions of gender, class and nationality? The intellectual focus of British social debate on the topic has often been quite narrowly concerned with the extent to which class restricts effective access to citizenship, as in the debates around T. H. Marshall's work, although there is some interest in the relationship of citizenship more generally to social cohesion. [....]

When we take seriously questions of diversity and gender, not only in relation to class and ethnicity, but also in relation to nations and states, there can be more than one construction of the public and of citizenship. [....]

National Diversity

Recent feminist theory has emphasised the need to understand and theorise diversity among women. Many discussions of difference between women have focused on ethnicity and class. My focus here is on differences derived from nation, state, and nation-state. Nira Yuval-Davis and Floya Anthias have argued that national projects are gendered, but in diverse rather than simple ways. They can be reproducers of members of collectivities; reproducers of the boundaries of these groups; central to the ideological reproduction of the collectivity and transmitters of its culture; signifiers of differences between national projects; as participants in national struggles. For our purposes, the most important issues here are whether the Irish national project has a different gender project from that of Britain, and the significance of this as a signifier of national difference.

There are two ways to think about comparisons for women and citizenship. One is to compare the extent to which women have achieved citizenship using the conventional route of women moving into the public sphere, in a manner similar to men. The second is to ask whether there are routes to citizenship for women which draw positively on women's differences from men, in particular ones which find ways of providing citizenship to women who engage in caring in domestic settings. [....]

The question of citizenship belongs not only to classic debates about the balancing of liberal freedom with the demands of a capitalist economy, of the relationship between the labour market and the state, of class and capitalism; it is also about the major structuring principles of gender. When half of the population might be denied effective citizenship because of gender, then gender matters to citizenship.

In most western societies access to the full range of citizenship rights increasingly depends upon participation in full-time employment, since this is increasingly the basis of sufficient income necessary for social citizenship. As the population ages, pensions become more important; as employment becomes more insecure, unemployment benefits become more important; as marriages cease to last for life (through death or divorce), dependence on a husband becomes an insecure substitute for one's own direct access to benefits and income. Those women who spend time out of employment in order to care are disadvantaged under such conditions. Is it possible for a society to support women who care, so that employment is not the only route to full citizenship? The traditional answer to this in some countries was for women to marry for life. In many western countries today women are increasingly entering employment, and becoming less dependent on husbands. This entry to employment is occurring in Ireland also, indeed more rapidly than in many other countries, giving rise to major differences between women according to age. The rate of change in the form of gender regime in Ireland is faster than in many other western European countries. Young women in Ireland are seeking a different route to full citizenship than that of their mothers, one more like that of their brothers. [....]

Karen Offen

NATIONAL SPECIFICITIES IN EUROPEAN FEMINISMS

Abstract: This article addresses problems and opportunities in defining feminism cross-culturally, pointing to the importance of relational argumentation in the European past. It argues against imposing the relatively recent 'equality versus difference' dichotomy on the more distant past and proposes an alternative vocabulary for understanding feminism both historically and in the present. The author then outlines the specificities of the French case, which has always been extremely influential and has interacted with Anglo-American versions of feminism, but is all too often universalised, especially in French scholarship.

from 'Reflections on National Specificities in Continental European Feminisms', *Volume 3*, pp. 53-61

The Problem of Definition

We must begin at the beginning, that is to say, with the matter of definition. In order to write a history of feminism, one must first establish the object of interrogation. The question of definition is the motor that drives all the rest. Our understanding of historically-situated feminisms, feminisms in the plural, is necessarily based on how we understand the term 'feminism'. The same goes for the term 'movement', moreover. [....]

At the level of general ideas (that is, at a theoretical or philosophical level), there is unquestionably a phenomenon that we can call 'feminism', well before 1890, when the word 'féminisme' began to cross the borders of France and to become common currency throughout the rest of the world. I have already published my findings on that subject and I now feel justified in using this term, even retrospectively, as the basis for my book on the history of feminism.

It should be emphasised that in the various countries of Europe – and throughout 'the West', if you will – criticisms of the subordination of women – (the critique which had no name before the 1890s) – all had common roots, roots plunged into the fertile loam of Roman Catholic Christianity, of Humanism, of the controversies of the Protestant Reformation, and especially these criticisms drew on the critical vocabulary of the Enlightenment of the seventeenth and eighteenth centuries, and on the subsequent very radical and very secular political vocabulary of the French Revolution. Why did France play such a preponderant role in the development of this critique? [....]

Evidently in France, as elsewhere, the history of feminism, like that of the debate on the 'woman question', is also closely tied to the development of national political cultures and the institutions of the early state. Since the sixteenth century, for example, the French monarchy – alone in Europe – deliberately excluded women from succession to the throne. This decision had very serious consequences; moreover, as the research of my colleague Sarah Hanley demonstrates, the French state privileged the development of an implicit accord between heads of family and the state which attempted – effectively – to submit married women more and more to the legal and economic control of their husbands. During this entire century, one finds remonstrances, beginning with Marie de Gournay's *Grief des Dames* (1622), criticising the multiple aspects of this control. The criticism of women's subordinate and inferior position in marriage, in education, in economic, and property terms, and in respect to governance, which developed in France during the eighteenth century, is without parallel, except in England, where the civil status of married women was without question the worst in Western Europe. And if one compares the critique elaborated by Mary Wollstonecraft in England with that of her contemporaries in France at the outset of the French Revolution, there is no doubt which is the more radical. Why should that be?

What seems to me to be original in France, in comparison with other countries in Europe at the time, is precisely this:

First, the open (or public) and constantly repeated attribution of an extraordinary 'influence' or 'power' to women even as they are deliberately excluded (from 1590 on) from wielding royal authority. I think this exclusion should be taken very seriously; it is not simply a question, in my opinion, of gallantry with little meaning. No, the effort to exclude women from all positions of authority is directly linked to this attributed influence, and both to the explicit recognition by men in France of the sexual power of women. The element of fear is too manifest in the men's texts, even as the celebration of influence by precisely these means can be found in some of the women's texts. One does not find either this fear or this celebration expressed in such an overt manner in the other national cultures that I have sampled. Why? We must analyse and explain this masculine resistance to the power and influence of the women, along with its particular character in the French context.

Secondly, I am impressed by the enormous strategic and political importance of bio-medical thinking in France in the secular effort to dethrone theological thinking. I find that attempts to rethink, reconfigure, and rejustify hierarchical relations between the sexes, the discourse based on bio-medical knowledge seems to play a far more important and decisive role in France than elsewhere. Why? We must analyse its effect, we must explain also the reasons for its manifest success, especially during the counter-revolutionary reaction, or 'backlash' of the nineteenth century.

Thirdly, what is also striking is the insistence on maternity and the maternal element, including its socio-political possibilities, and the fact that this accompanied a falling birthrate, throughout the nineteenth century and up until 1950. Would feminism in France have taken the same form, would it have encountered the same difficulties in the absence of a grand debate over the fall in the birthrate? Evidently no! 'Maternalism' is a particular form of the relational feminist argument, no doubt, but a form which became particularly powerful and effective for feminists in France in the nineteenth and twentieth centuries. We must analyse and comprehend its political effectiveness in this complex of circumstances. We must understand how these feminists understood their socio-political roles.

Finally there is a peculiar, even bizarre character of French republican nationalism, stemming from the French Revolution, but particularly from 1848 on, with the introduction of universal *manhood* suffrage, which lasted until the First World War and even afterward. Alone in a world of monarchies, the French republican nation was manifestly and deliberately constructed 'masculine', even as its male leaders enshrined a 'feminine' goddess of Liberty. As a nation, France was very divided – but virtually every competing sector – religious, secular, political social medical – manifested its desire to control women, whether by law or by education or through money. This was perhaps the sole issue on which all the contesting parties were agreed! Why? What did this mean? [....]

What we must do, I believe, is to recognise and to study feminism and historical feminisms as a sort of spectrum of possibilities, of articulations present during specific epochs and at various levels – European, Western, even global. We must explore not only those feminisms we might prefer, or those which seem to provide attractive models at present, or even those that seem to be precursors of the present, but also those that failed, those that have been neglected until now. We must evaluate the conditions for success or lack of success of each, but also we must look for what they had in common. We must study the utopian projects, but also the pragmatic articulations, and all these in the particularities of their historical and cultural contexts.

The history of feminism, a history that is truly contextual, comparative and comprehensive, at once political and intellectual, social, economic, and cultural is only beginning. There is much to be done. Let us begin!

Ronit Lentin

Feminist Research Methodologies

Abstract: This paper has three central aims. One, it argues, by examining the basic tenets of feminist research methodologies – their commitment to making visible women's lived experiences, to gender and gender relations as socially constructed and historically specific, to reflexivity and the inclusion of the researcher and the research process as researchable topics, and to the emancipation of women – that feminist research methodologies are a separate paradigm. Two, through describing the methodological choices made for my study of Israeli daughters of Shoah survivors, it examines the discontents of feminist research methodologies and asks how feminist researchers can address them. Three, it asks why as yet only few published studies by Irish feminist scholars dare 'name' feminism in their methodology sections.

from 'Explicitly Feminist? Feminist Research Methodologies Re-visited', *Volume 3*, pp. 1-18

Introduction[1]

While working on the preliminary stages of my Ph.D. study of personal narratives of Israeli writers and film makers who are daughters of Shoah survivors, I have decided that my methodological path would be qualitative, feminist and reflexive. Feminist research methodologies, based on women's lived experiences, both researched and researcher's, on gender and gender relations as socially constructed and historically specific, on reflexibility (the analytic attention to the researcher's role, and the inclusion of research itself as a researchable topic), and on a political commitment to the emancipation of women, seem to be the most appropriate to my study. The decision to first look at data and only then select an appropriate methodology may seem a simplification of the research process. 'Theory', in the sense of formulating ideas which attempt to explain something, always comes before methodology. Since all research is above all pragmatic, a series of concurrent decisions as to data and the choice of methodology was involved, of course.

Women's Studies in Ireland and work by Irish feminist scholars have done a lot to provide knowledge to a growing number of women, to open the door to degree and non-degree students, to align politically with the Irish Women's Movement and to put Irish womanhood firmly on the political agenda. This paper asks why, despite this, feminist research methodology, in its multiplicity of methods, has up until now not been explicitly 'named' in much published Irish feminist scholarship and why feminist research methodologies themselves have not been sufficiently debated in the Irish context. In particular, this paper asks why there have been only a few published feminist studies which have made visible the lived experiences of Irish women or which have included the researcher's lived experience and reflexibility as part of the research process and findings. [....]

Conclusion: Irish feminist research

As can be seen from this very partial survey, the feminist methodology debate is alive and kicking, although not much of it has found its way into published research by Irish feminist social scientists and Women's Studies scholars. The answer to the question as to whether one can be a good feminist researcher without using feminist methodologies has to be yes. There are, however, two important points in relation to Irish feminist scholarship. Firstly, adhering to the feminist tenets of unveiling women's lived experiences, in their own words, and reflexively positioning researchers within accessible research texts, must narrow the gap between academic feminists and Irish women who they seek to empower. Secondly, the danger is that if, as Evelyn Mahon argues, "aspects attributable to a feminist methodology may be implicit rather than explicit",[2] feminist scholars may be giving in to a pragmatism which dictates caution in the face of an increasingly patriarchal academic establishment.

Women's Studies has made a major impact on the agenda of Irish women in the 1990s, through its input into the *Report of the Second Commission on the Status of Women.* The Coalition's Programme for Partnership in Government stated, as part of its Affirmative Action Programme, its "support for the promotion of Women's Studies in third-level education".[3]

Irish Women's Studies staff and graduate students, employing a variety of study methods, from textual analysis, through quantitative surveys, to qualitative studies, have done research in diverse areas: social issues – control over female fertility and women's bodies, violence against women, childcare and care for the elderly, lone mothers, the feminisation of poverty; experiences of women in childbirth; women and work – the disadvantaged proportion of women in the Irish labour market, the absence of women from 'non-traditional' jobs and the lack of flexibility at work; the low level of representation of women in political life; rural women; feminist literature and critique; spirituality; gender and education, amongst other topics.

Eileen Drew argues that feminist research will continue to have a role in understanding and changing current social practices and that Women's Studies has a key role in promoting gender awareness and access to women by: making women and gender part of the Irish political agenda; by publishing and disseminating research; by promoting women in the arts; and by making demands for law reform and for greater representation in politics and on boards.

Anne Byrne, in her survey of academic Women's Studies in the Republic of Ireland, argues, however, that the providers of Women's Studies courses "in the ivy", sometimes "lose sight of objectives, spending little time interrogating the relationship between our feminist activities on campus and social and political change for women".[4]

Ailbhe Smyth[5] is pessimistic about shifting the academic balance of power. Women's Studies, despite its vitality and dynamism which threatens Irish academic institutions, has had an enormous impact on ... Women's Studies, she writes. I share Smyth's concern about Irish Women's Studies losing sight of the material and political realities of women's lives and agree with her that 'integrating the disciplines' may go a long way towards solving the problem. However, I also believe it is crucial to 'name' feminism in feminist research texts and adhere more rigorously to feminist research methodologies, in particular through positioning women's lived experiences centre-stage and reflexively reporting both the researcher's experience and the research process. This will shorten the gap between academic and non-academic women, and bring closer the ultimate dual aims of 'outing' the material realities of Irish women's lives and strengthening the position of Irish feminist academics. [....]

There are three important reasons why reflexivity is a feminist issue. Firstly, for academic feminists, 'research' and 'life' cannot be compartmentalised using separate intellectual tools. Privileging lived experiences, rigorously and reflexively, may, I believe, be as 'scientific' as an unchallenged claim to a universal objectivity. In other words, push 'reflexivity' and it becomes 'objectivity'. Secondly, if according to post-modernism, all meta-narratives are dead and we are in danger of being left with no causal explanations of the subordination of women and are, therefore, 'in chaos', then we must return to our material lives and the lives of other women, as sites of possible explanations in the context of sexist oppression. Thirdly, we are witnessing recently, side by side with postmodern deconstruction of all categories, including gender, a return to positivist-funded research justifying the 'institutions of ruling' which today, increasingly, carries the tag 'Europe'. This, necessarily, relies more heavily on quantitative studies, and on so-called 'objective' scientism. The 'personal' , according to one of the better-known slogans of second wave feminism, is 'political' , but it is also 'theoretical'. In the face of the advent of the so-called 'post-feminist' era, I for one, shall be a post-feminist only in post-patriarchy.

The feminist methodology debate seems to still be in its infancy in Ireland. The more Irish feminist social scientists incorporate feminist methodologies *explicitly* into their research projects, the more we shall contribute to a greater visibility not only of Irish women and therefore assist emancipation and narrow the gap between feminist academics and the women we research, but also of feminist academics within Ireland's patriarchal academic institutions.

Notes

1   Thanks to Dr Barbara Bradby and Mary McDermott of Trinity College Dublin, and Richard Giulianotti of the University of Aberdeen for their comments and references.
2   Evelyn Mahon 1994. 'Feminist Research: A Reply to Lentin', *Irish Journal of Sociology,* 4,p. 168.
3   Eileen Drew 1993. 'Country Case Study: Women's Studies in the Republic of Ireland', paper presented to the UNESCO-KEGME seminar *Gender Studies Towards the Year 2000,* Athens, 2–5 June, 1993. [....]
4   Anne Byrne 1992. 'Academic Women's Studies in the Republic of Ireland', *Women's Studies Quarterly,*3 & 4,pp. 15–27.
5   Ailbhe Symth 1992. 'Women's Studies and "the disciplines",' *Women's Studies International Forum,* 11:1, pp. 21–27.

Anne Byrne

Single Women in Ireland

Abstract: This paper argues that single women are stigmatised in contemporary Irish society and that this is particularly evident in people's everyday interactions with single women. Stigmatising interactions are apparent in relation to singleness itself, marital status, the bearing of children and sexuality, indicating the pervasiveness of heterosexual, familistic ideologies in Irish society. The paper describes a set of stigma management strategies deployed by women in response to single stigma. Within these responses, emerging forms of resistance to dominant ideologies of womanhood are evident in women's explanations of 'why I am single'.

from 'Singular Identities: Managing Stigma, Resisting Voices', *Volume* 7, pp. 13–34

Introduction

To be single remains an unacceptable and discreditable social identity in contemporary Irish society.[1] This is not a viewpoint which remains hidden, but is present in others' routine interactions with single women. Single women are aware that singleness is a discreditable status and work to manage interaction in this context. The discreditable aspects of singleness are concerned with marital status, reproductive behaviour and sexuality, core attributes of female gender identity in a familistic society.[2] This paper examines a set of stigma management strategies deployed by women in response to single stigma. [....]

The Right Man

Nearly every woman, whether speaking in general about other women or more specifically about themselves, say they just have not met the right man. 'Mr Right' clearly encompasses the ideal characteristics and personality of the perfect person with whom they could consider having a relationship. As an explanation, not having met Mr Right serves very well, though charges of being 'too choosy' can also follow. This explanation has much potential as an identity account as being too choosy can also be read as 'not willing to settle for less'. Together with educational and career ambition, it calls up the necessity of scrutinising the concept of choice to understand the pathway to singleness in greater depth. Being particular about the personality and disposition of a potential partner can be indicative of the extent and attachment to the single status, as women speak about marrying, but only if their explicit conditions in relationship can be met.

Broken Romance

Almost all of the women had a story about a man in the past whom they might have married, were on the point of marrying, were engaged to or were involved with for a considerable period of time. But, as the explanation reveals, the relationship ended, but the woman herself is not to blame. The man either left abruptly when the engagement/marriage plans became public, or when the woman's family strongly disapproved of the woman's partner, or the man is discovered to be violent, mentally-ill, alcoholic, already married or engaged to another woman. The experience of the broken romance left many women doubtful about involving themselves in future relationships, angry at the investment of time in a relationship that had no future and the lengthy time period occupied with recovering from a broken romance. Celie said, for example:

For years I was just broken up ... even if some man would come looking at me or touch me I would cringe ... what kind of eejit was I? ... I wasted all those years (Celie, Career Woman, age 36)

On the other hand, women themselves ended relationships, broke engagements, knowing that this is not 'Mr Right' and that they are not really prepared to marry after all. The broken romance explanation again can be interpreted as stigma management and part of an identity account. As a stigma management strategy, it informs others that the woman is heterosexual, that she has attempted to form a partnership with another and that she is presenting herself as an adult, pursing adult-type relationships. The fact that the attempt has failed has little relevance to others, but could be interpreted as crucial to negotiating the maintenance of single self-identities in a stigmatised setting. [....]

Concluding Comment

Single stigma operates on a deep level in contemporary Irish culture: it is evident in the routine interactions between single women and their friends, families, acquaintances and strangers, all of whom focus critical comment on women's marital status, childlessness and sexuality. It is evident from women's accounts of interactions with others that a gendered, stigmatised social identity continues to inform and intrude into social interactions with single women, underpinning a conception of womanhood tied to heterosexuality, marriage and motherhood. In response, single women utilise a repertoire of stigma management strategies: these are effective in managing face-to-face interactions. Stigma management strategies are not generally regarded as having the potential to fundamentally challenge conceptions of how to be a woman, for example. Despite this, evidence of the valuing of single self-identity and resistance to dominant woman identities are clearly evident in the narrative accounts women use to explain 'why I am single'. It is in these resisting voices that the possibilities for expanding women's identities in contemporary Ireland lie.

Notes
1 Considering the centrality of the family to Irish culture, there has been little contemporary sociological research on single people. [....]
2 The term familism is used by Michelle Barret and Mary McIntosh. 1982. *The Anti-Social Family*. Verso: UK, as "the propagation of politically pro-family ideas", while familisation refers to the "strengthening of families themselves" (Barret and Macintosh, p.26). [....]

Christina Quinlan

A Journey into the Women's Prison

Abstract: This paper details my volunteer relationship with the women's prison at Mountjoy Prison in Dublin and with women imprisoned there. It charts my experiences with the women documenting my voluntary activities from my initial 'befriending' experiences in the old female prison at St. Patrick's Institution to my move in 1999 with the women to the new female prison at Mountjoy, The Dochas Centre, to my ultimate immersion in the Irish female prison through my PhD research. The photographs in the work are part of the visual element of my PhD research, an exploration of women's experiences of prison space. In order to contextualise the paper, I begin with a description of Ireland's female prisons and I briefly detail the numbers of women imprisoned in Ireland and their offences.

from 'A Journey into the Women's Prison', Volume 9, pp. 59–78

The Irish Female Prison: Some Facts and Figures

[....] Currently, Ireland has two women's prisons among its 16 prisons. The main female prison is The Dochas Centre, the new purpose-built female prison within the Mountjoy Prison complex. The Dochas Centre holds 79 women at capacity. The second female prison is Limerick Prison, which is the oldest prison in the country, and though predominantly a male prison, can hold up to 20 women. Women from the prison system are also accommodated in the Central Mental Hospital, in practice no more than three at a time. There are generally about 100 women in prison in Ireland on any day and about 3,000 men.

Some of the most striking aspects of female imprisonment in Ireland are the rates of imprisonment, the recidivism rates among imprisoned women, and the crimes for which women are imprisoned. While historically huge numbers of women were imprisoned in Ireland, in the 1800s, for example, up to 50% of 60,000 people imprisoned annually were women[1] — throughout the twentieth century, the numbers of women imprisoned here dropped. While in 1950 there were on average only 100 women held daily in Ireland's prisons, this number was down to 20 by 1960, and down to 14 by 1970.[2] In addition to the striking rates of imprisonment, the annual Prison Reports of the twentieth century constantly recorded massive recidivism rates among the women who were imprisoned, and, in more recent years, figures published by the Irish Penal Reform Trust estimate current recidivism rates to be in excess of 70% among Ireland's imprisoned women.[3]

A Woman's Cell: Limerick Prison 2002

[....] No more than three or four women were in prison in Ireland in any year from 1930 to the present day for the crimes of murder or manslaughter. Drug related offences feature in the recorded offences from 1985. Vagrancy and begging accounted for substantial numbers of imprisoned women until the 1970s. In recent years, begging has again become a feature in the imprisonment of women in Ireland, most notably through the imprisonment of East European women immigrants.[5]

In the year 2001, 751 women were committed to Mountjoy women's prison. Of these, 64% were Irish nationals and 36% were foreign nationals. Substantial numbers of the Irish nationals were committed for offences such as breach of the peace, drunk and disorderly, danger to self. 58 women were imprisoned for offences against the Road Traffic Act, 16 for casual or illegal trading, 11 for begging and 6 for vagrancy. Four women were imprisoned for domestic violence charges and four on charges of soliciting and prostitution. Two were imprisoned for not having a bus ticket while travelling on a bus, one for not wearing a seat belt, one for not having a TV licence, and one for failing to send a child to school. Over that same year, two women were imprisoned on murder charges, while the numbers for assault were relatively small. Larceny, stealing and robbery were the most commonly occurring offences, and while my analysis of the records of offences does not evidence the nature of these offences, the record of the sentences passed on the women does. Over half of the women were being held on remand, almost one quarter of the population had been sentenced to days in the prison, with or without fines, 14% had been sentenced to imprisonment for periods of one to twelve months. Only 3% of the committals to the prison had been sentenced to periods of one year or over.

[....] foreign national women committed to the prison in 2001 were mostly European, almost 200 of them. There were 62 women from Eastern Europe, more than 50 from Africa, 43 from Asia and 23 from South America. Many of these women were aliens in prison awaiting deportation. The remaining women were in prison charged with a variety of offences from vagrancy and begging to money laundering and drug trafficking. In all, 68 women were imprisoned that year on charges of possession, importing or supplying drugs. In recent years international drug couriers have represented up to between 20–25% of Ireland's imprisoned women and most of them come from South Africa. Drug trafficking for the couriers is neither terribly lucrative nor profitable, but among the traffickers it is the couriers who are the most visible and perhaps because of this visibility, the women's criminal activities are easily prosecuted. Their crimes are constructed as serious, their trials are public and visible, and their prison sentences, when they are sentenced, are long. [....]

Notes
1   See T. Carey 2000. *Mountjoy: The Story of a Prison*, Collins Press, p.139.
2   Source: *Annual Prison Reports*, Dublin, Government Publications, for relevant years.
3   See I.P.R.T. 2001. Position Paper on Women in Prison.

Siobhán Kilfeather

ENTERING THE FIELD DAY

from 'Editing the *Field Day Anthology*', *Volume 8*, pp 47-52

I began work on *The Field Day Anthology of Irish Writing,* Volumes IV & V 1 in 1992, the year I moved from teaching at Columbia University in New York to Sussex University in England. I made that move because of my parents' declining health. My father died in 1996 and my mother came to live with me. She died in 1998. Many of my decisions about the shape and contents of my sections in the anthology were formed in conversations with my parents, conversations that had been going on all my life, and which have continued in some ways after their deaths, because my chief inheritance from them was a library of many tens of thousands of books, mainly Irish books collected by my father from about 1940 onwards.

My parents' lives were devoted to reading. They had jobs, of course, and families, and political commitments and friends, but these were all subservient to their passion for books. Apart from periods in World War II when my mother was evacuated to Culleybackey and my father spent time with his family in Fermanagh, and short spells after the war when my mother worked in an office in Dublin and my father for the Northern Ireland Civil Service in Antrim, they lived all their lives in Belfast. At first most of their books came from Smithfield Market in Belfast, and later from Jim Lyttle's shop on the corner of Bradbury Place and Sandy Row. My mother was passionately interested in nineteenth and early twentieth-century French fiction (in translation); my father was keen on German Romanticism, modernism, American writing, and all things Irish. Neither of them had been to university. My mother left school at fourteen to work in a dry cleaners, and my father, although not poorly educated for a Catholic of his generation, worked in his father's grocery shop from the age of seventeen and later went into the library service and later still into the Civil Service. Most of my father's American books were published by New Directions; not long after the war he wrote to the publisher, the poet James Laughlin, about his interest in a particular author and from then on Laughlin regularly sent him packages of new books. When he was 40 my father started learning Irish at extra-mural classes at Queen's University, Belfast. From that point he began to weed out some of his books in English to replace them with hundreds of books in Irish, mostly bought in the 1970s from Seán Anderson's book shop in Andersonstown.

Reading and writing happen in a material world, however much they sometimes seem to offer an escape from that world. My parents lived in an imaginative world that was at once extremely parochial and completely cosmopolitan. I remember once a visit from our new parish priest, Fr Magee, when he jumped to the conclusion that a framed photograph of Vladimir Nabokov in the living room must be a picture of my father butterfly hunting. In my early years I was sometimes confused myself. For many years I supposed that Gorky would, like my Canadian uncles, come home on a visit some day. Given the intensity of their involvement in world literature, why was everything Irish so deeply interesting to them? The simple answer would be partition, I suppose. They lived in a world framed by unresolved conflict and they lived from day to day in a state of dissent and critique. Private life was not a separate sphere from the world of politics. Their income, housing, educational opportunities, health provision and even their erotic and family lives were overshadowed by political tension. My mother was raised as a Protestant but, at the age of 23, she collapsed with a brain tumour and was taken to the nearest hospital, which happened to be the Mater. She made a deathbed conversion to Catholicism (probably not uninfluenced by her friendship with my father) and then nonplussed her family by recovering and marrying my father. It was, I suspect, this alienated existence that made my father an advocate of equal rights for women and for lesbian and gay people, and a lover of the poor and dispossessed everywhere. It was from my father that I first heard the word 'feminism'. My mother lived out many of the frustrations of women before feminism. As a child she had been punished for reading too much. She had been kept at home to look after babies while her younger brother was educated. She broke her health on sewing and cleaning and night shifts in hospital. She was a remarkably brilliant woman, but completely lacking in self-confidence. My mother and father were interested in all my academic projects, but the anthology was special because it reached out to anyone interested in reading about Ireland and because they felt confident about their own knowledge and judgements. [....]

Since the Table of Contents for the anthology appeared on the Cork University Press web site in April 2002, I've realised that for many people the most controversial decision we took was one made very early on and that—to the best of my recollection—caused us no difficulty at all, that is the decision that we wouldn't restrict ourselves to producing an anthology of writings *by* women, but would feel free to draw material from any sources that contributed to an understanding of women's history, culture and traditions. As far as I remember this decision came about because Máirín Ní Dhonnchadha and Angela Bourke pointed out that they would be contributing a very high proportion of anonymously or collectively authored texts. Virginia Woolf claimed that 'anonymous is a woman', but whatever its metaphorical resonance, in the literal sense this is nonsense. Most anonymous texts were written by men, but they do operate in a different way to texts which foreground the identity of a male author. 'Anon.' is anonymous for different reasons in the medieval period than in the oral tradition, but the realisation that we weren't going to think of our project as being only about rescuing women writers, but about explaining the contexts for women's cultural production meant that we could produce a much richer narrative. It also meant that we could present powerful statements by women enfolded into narratives by men—for example the lament of Peig Nic Seafrardh in Amhlaoibh Uí Shúileabháin's diary, the evidence of Mrs. Murphy when her husband James was prosecuted 'for cruelly assaulting, imprisoning, and starving his wife' at the Dublin sessions in 1803, or the violent early life of the Countess of Blessington as told to R. R. Madden.

One huge advantage I gained from my mother and father's library and from their memories and conversation, was the opportunity to approach editing my section of the anthology as a reader and browser. It's very difficult to browse in major research libraries with their closed stacks. Many Irish women writers who appeared to some critical acclaim may have been neglected by academic critics, but as readers my parents still remembered and valued figures such as Charlotte Riddell, Anne Crone, Patricia O'Connor, Kathleen Fitzpatrick, Norah Hoult, Helen Waddell, Kathleen Coyle and Frances Browne, and they had kept their books. They had also kept runs of periodicals including *The Bell*, *New Irish Writing*, *The Honest Ulsterman* and *Kavanagh's Weekly*. My mother had written stories and poems all her life and a few of these had been published in *Kavanagh's Weekly* and *The Irish Press*. It seemed clear to me that the obstacles to women's writing and publication might mean that many potentially interesting careers might have been stalled at the level of small press or periodical publication and that it was important not to reproduce the prejudices of literary establishments which, particularly in the twentieth century, might have dismissed or misjudged certain kinds of women's writing. [....]

Freda Donoghue

WOMEN AND VOLUNTEERING

Abstract: This paper presents data on women volunteers in Ireland and poses questions about the role they play and the societal contribution they make. It explores some of the associations between stereotypes of volunteers and women, and notes that these are worth critically examining in greater detail. It raises questions about definitions of volunteering and about the need for further research on women as particular kinds of volunteers.

from 'Women and Volunteering: A Feminised Space?', *Volume 9*, pp. 1–14

Introduction

Volunteering has been defined in the Irish context in a number of ways. At a policy-making level, for example, the White Paper, *Supporting*

Voluntary Activity, has suggested that volunteering entails "the commitment of time and energy for the benefit of society, local communities, individuals outside the immediate family, the environment or other causes. Volunteering activities are undertaken of a person's own free will, without payment (except for the reimbursement of out-of-pocket expenses)".[1] The more recent report of the National Committee on Volunteering (NCV) notes that several definitions can be found, however, which have relevance for varying historical and socio-economic understandings within a particular societal context. Thus, in Germany some categories of volunteering qualify for social security entitlements, and in Canada some volunteering occurs in compulsory programmes.[2] The NCV report recognises that activism or social action is an important part of volunteering and that the motivation of the individual gives rise to an activity which involves relationships with various other groups and individuals in society. Volunteering can be understood as one way of providing meaning to an individual's life or existence but, as relational, voluntary activity can also be viewed as an important contribution to social capital and to the social and societal fabric. The NCV report also indicates that a distinction is made, in international as well as Irish work, between formal and informal volunteering; the former occurs through or with an organisation, whereas informal volunteering takes place outside that domain. [....]

Volunteers in Ireland

In 1997/98 one-third of the population was estimated to be engaged in voluntary activity, whether through an organisation (formal volunteering) or on their own (informal volunteering). More women than men were likely to volunteer. 40% of women, compared with 28% of men stated that they were involved in voluntary work during the survey months. In the volunteer pool, therefore, women outnumbered men by two to one.

Those most likely to volunteer lived in towns, rather than in cities or in rural areas. Almost 43% of those living in towns, compared with one-third of those living in urban or rural areas were engaged in voluntary work. Amongst women, however, the differences between town, urban and rural dwellers were even greater. Just over half (51%) of townswomen, compared with approximately 38% of country and urban women volunteered (38.2% and 37.2%, respectively). [....]

In summary, therefore, volunteers in Ireland have a greater tendency to be women, aged in their middle years and drawn from the middle classes. They are highly educated and there are more volunteers living in towns than in urban or rural areas. It is interesting to note, in this regard, that among survey respondents, town dwellers were the least numerous, so their over-representation among volunteers is probably worthy of some note. [....]

First of all, there is a far higher proportion of women, like all volunteers, in the South-East of the country (Carlow, Kilkenny, Waterford and Wexford). Secondly, in the North-East (Cavan, Louth, Meath and Monaghan) all volunteers, including women volunteers, are the most poorly represented. Third, the western regions (Mid-West, North-West and West) show the greatest disparity between women volunteers and the total volunteer pool. What this indicates is that men in those areas are volunteering at far lower rates than women. By comparison, the data from the South-East indicate that there is little difference between women's and men's volunteering levels (and between women and the total volunteering pool). The difference, nationally, between women and men's volunteering levels in 1997–98 was 12 percentage points (28% of men volunteered in comparison with 40% of women). In the Mid-West and North-West, the difference between women and men's volunteering rates was in the order of over 20 percentage points, while in the South-East there was only a difference of one percentage point. [....]

Motivations for and Rewards of Volunteering

Several themes can be identified among the reasons for individuals choosing to volunteer. First of all, respondents identified believing in a cause as the most important factor for their engagement. This was followed by several other reasons, which could be loosely termed as related or contributing to social networks. A desire to be neighbourly, knowing the individuals already involved, and being asked to help emerged as very important reasons for choosing to volunteer. [....] Amongst women, themselves, there were some differences between these responses, however. Women aged between 30 and 39 were most likely of all women to emphasise the reward of volunteering as 'seeing results', while women aged 60 and over were the least likely (by a ratio of two to one). Satisfaction at doing good was most appealing for women aged between 18 and 29 (71% of whom cited this, compared with only 44% of women aged in their thirties). Finally, it is noteworthy that being appreciated was far more important for women aged under 30 than for other women.

No discussion of the cited rewards of engaging in voluntary activity is complete without considering the societal and economic benefits that can accrue. [....] Ruddle and Mulvihill have indicated that the top three beneficiaries of volunteering within an organisation were sports and recreation (32% of all time), social services (24% of all time) and religion (11% of all time).[3] Women volunteers, however, tended to be predominant in the social services where they gave more than half of all volunteering time and they were over-represented in the time given to caring for the sick, visiting and caring for older people (both formal and informal volunteering). As can be construed, therefore, there is an economic contribution accrued through voluntary activity and a societal contribution from the input of women's volunteering in the social services. [....]

Volunteering and Feminised Space

[....] As volunteers, women are more associated with caring activities. On the formal side (that is, volunteering with an organisation) the main area of women's activity was in social services. In the arena of informal volunteering women were also concentrating in visiting and caring duties. This occupation of certain kinds of spaces within volunteering is interesting to explore further. In Ireland, a tendency has been noted to associate the voluntary sector with social service provision and also what Donnelly-Cox and Jaffro have referred to as the "myth of goodness".[4] It could be argued that women's volunteering may be emphasising the stereotype of women as carers, and there are a number of points to explore arising from this observation. [....] Given the predominance of women volunteers in caring duties, overlain by social stereotypes of women as carers, are women filling gaps in social service provision, and has the burden of care fallen disproportionately on the shoulders of women volunteers? These questions could also be related to notions about the voluntary sector itself, which might be stereotyped as the 'heart' of society. It may be suggested, and it is certainly worth exploring in future research, that there is an association between women volunteers and an image of the sector as caring. A study on women and political participation in Northern Ireland, for example, has indicated that while there were few gender differences in the tendency to be 'politically' active, women were more likely to be associated with voluntary activity than men.[5] Voluntary activity may not be perceived as 'political' as party political activity, and it is interesting to speculate about the associations between volunteering and notions of feminised space. Health and social services are large components of the Irish voluntary sector. Are these seen as 'women's work' even if women in those areas are not in decision-making positions? [....]

Notes

1 Department of Social, Community and Family Affairs 2000. Supporting Voluntary Activity, Dublin: Stationery Office, p.83.
2 National Committee on Volunteering 2002. *Tipping the Balance*, Dublin: National Committee on Volunteering.
3 Helen Ruddle and Ray Mulvihill 1999. R*eaching Out: Charitable Giving and Volunteering in the Republic of Ireland. The 1997/1998 Survey*, Dublin: Policy Research Centre, National College of Ireland, *op. cit.*
4 Gemma Donnelly-Cox and Gwen Jaffro 1999. *The Voluntary Sector in the Republic of Ireland,* Belfast: Association for Voluntary Action Research in Ireland.
5 A broad definition of 'political' was taken to encompass more than just party political activity. See Robert Miller, Rick Wilford and Freda Donoghue 1996. *Women and Political Participation in Northern Ireland*, Aldershot: Avebury.

Maggie Ronayne

AN INTERVIEW WITH PHOEBE JONES, GLOBAL WOMEN'S STRIKE

Abstract: Phoebe Jones is East Coast co-ordinator of the Global Women's Strike (GWS) in the US whose theme is 'Women Say No War: Invest in Caring Not Killing'. She has three times been invited to Venezuela as a representative of the GWS, including to the April 2003 and April 2004 anniversary of the popular uprising that saved the peaceful and democratic revolution, its government and constitution from the US-backed coup, which briefly ousted President Chavez. Phoebe did some of the filming of interviews of grassroots Venezuelans for the GWS's latest film, *Venezuela: Talking of Power.* The GWS has been supporting women and spreading the achievements of the revolution and has written an Open Letter to AFL-CIO President Sweeney opposing its support for the coup and the corrupt trade union which backed it. Phoebe has been involved in the women's, anti-war and justice movements largely through the International Wages for Housework Campaign for over 30 years. She was a spokesperson for the July 4th Mobilisation against War at Home and Abroad. Phoebe is an author of *The Milk of Human Kindness: Defending Breastfeeding from the Global Market and AIDS Industry*, published by Crossroads books in 2002. She is a Quaker, a mother and a runner with a PhD in Physical Education. She works out of the Crossroads Women's Center in Philadelphia which is a base for a growing grassroots 'opt out' campaign to 'opt' the military 'out' of our schools and communities.
Maggie Ronayne (MR): Interviewer/ Phoebe Jones (PJ): Interviewee

from 'Invest in Caring Not Killing: An Interview with Phoebe Jones, Global Women's Strike, Philadelphia', *Volume 9*, pp. 175-186

Phoebe Jones (in white jacket) speaking at the 8 March 2003 Global Women's Strike march and rally in Philadelphia.

MR: Phoebe, on our weekly Galway picket against the occupation of Iraq we regularly give the news about the enormous anti-war movement in the US because we've heard about it from you and others. A lot of people here in Ireland, because of media censorship, don't know that it's so huge and that so many sectors of grassroots people are involved. Can you say what your experience is of this movement?

PJ: I think that, in addition to media censorship, one reason a lot of people don't know about the anti-war movement in the US is because they don't know how bad most people in the US have it, how much of a price people here have had to pay for war, and therefore how much of a fight against the war and the military budget is going on. The US has the worst poverty rate of all industrialised countries. 34.6 million people live in poverty, one third of them children. 44 million people have no health insurance. Schools are in crisis everywhere. The state of Oregon had to cut off the school year five weeks early because of state budget cuts, and achievement levels are flat or declining. And whatever the statistics are for the population in general, they are double that for people who are Black or Hispanic. And women are the poorest of the poor in all communities. The US is not the land of milk and honey for most people.

So the anti-war movement is also a movement against poverty and cutbacks in wages and social services to pay for war.

As a movement in the street against the war itself, it was extraordinary. Before and during the war, people who had never marched or demonstrated before were out on the street. Philadelphia had the largest anti-war rallies since the Vietnam War. Philadelphia doesn't have a big history of protests like San Francisco or New York or DC, so the numbers were smaller. But there were 10,000 people at one rally and no one remembers a rally of that size ever before in Philadelphia.

In addition, the anti-war sentiment was everywhere. I did not know one person who was for the war, none of my friends or family – and they're not in any way left wing, none of the people in the park where I walk my dogs, no one who pumped my gas or delivered my mail or waited at my table in a restaurant. No one standing in the line at the grocery store with me. No one. The most 'support' you ever heard was, 'Oh God, please let it be over with quickly.' That's support? And now you have family members of the troops openly opposing the war, calling for their loved ones to come home, defiantly confronting the military brass. There was one meeting of an army general with wives of service men, and he had to be escorted from the room for his own protection, the women were so angry about their loved ones (mainly partners) being kept in Iraq and in danger. I don't remember that even from the movement against the Vietnam War which is the point of reference for all movements against war in the US since then. That movement stopped the war. And this one will too.

Obviously the war happened, so the movement didn't stop it from happening. That's a big lesson for all of us – they're entirely out of control. Well, not entirely: it messed up their plans and it continues to mess up their plans. They are making noise about Iran and Syria but they were intending to bomb by now. And they are having to scramble to get out before all hell breaks loose. And it must be said that the attacks on the US soldiers there, as dreadful as they are, are also putting tremendous pressure on the government to get out.

The movement has not gone away. True there may not be the numbers in the street but everyone knows that something fundamental has shifted. First of all the connection was abundantly clear between the resources being drained from our communities to pay for war. One protest we held in Philadelphia on July 4th, which is the place and day that the Declaration of Independence from the British empire was made in 1776, was called Stop the War at Home and Abroad, putting together the often white middle class peace movement with the movements against poverty, homelessness, prisons, and so on which is more grassroots, and people of colour. There was a lot more that could have been done to bring those movements together, but acknowledging that there is a war going on at home was an important step. The demand of stopping war at home and abroad has to be the standard because it is the two sides of the military-industrial coin.

It also begins to indicate that what is at stake is not just stopping this war and going home, but changing everything. Everyone knows on some level that really the whole thing is at stake. Stopping this war means stopping Bush's endless war, which means stopping the war machine, the military-industrial complex, the arms industry, globalisation, the global market, the multinationals, all of it, and stopping the racism that keeps Black people the poorest, and the sexism that keeps women – beginning with Black women, the poorest. And this is all a rather tall order. I got criticised by a few people when I spoke in Ireland about the US anti-war movement. Why couldn't it have done better? Why wasn't it bigger? Why didn't it win? I can understand the frustration. But that kind of question doesn't appreciate how much needs changing to stop the war. It's not a one-issue campaign. It's an all-out war of another kind. Non-violent maybe, but they're bound to come out shooting to defend their right, their power, to make war when they decide to. That's the war we're taking on, and must win globally.

And really, who has control over their government? If people in Ireland don't have control over everything your government does, which seems to have a very cosy relationship with the US, you can imagine how difficult it is to gain control over the government in the US, the belly of the beast.

For more information see www.globalwomenstrike.net

Stephen Mannix

Feminist Moral Psychology

Abstract: This paper addresses the concept of 'moral voice' and a claim made by certain developmental psychologists that women and men tend to speak in different moral voices because of early childhood experiences. Particular attention is given to the work of Carol Gilligan who first introduced the concept of moral voice into mainstream developmental psychology. The critical response which this work has received from various disciplines is examined. It is argued that much of the criticism in relation to the association of women's experiences with the 'care voice' and men's experiences with the 'justice voice' is misplaced. Moreover, the point is made that when the medium through which psychological experiences are expressed is stories about real-life moral conflict, then it behoves researchers and others interested in women's development alike to *listen* to what women are saying about their lives. [....]

from 'Women, Stories and Feminist Moral Psychology:
Listening to the Voices of Experience', *Volume 4*, pp. 141–156

Moral Voices, Moral Selves

Carol Gilligan[1] was the first researcher in the field of moral development to bring a narrative methodology for understanding the nature of moral decision-making into mainstream developmental psychology. Gilligan's approach differed significantly from the major theoretical perspective in developmental psychology at that time – the cognitive developmental tradition – in that she asked *women* to speak about their real-life moral conflicts and how they dealt with them. She also moved away from the categorisation of moral statements as reflections of deep structures of cognitive organisation (which is a main characteristic of the cognitive developmental paradigm) toward a more hermeneutical understanding of the narrative 'text' provided by women who spoke about their experiences of moral conflict.

In contrast to Gilligan, the dominant figures in the cognitive developmental tradition such as Piaget,[2] Kohlberg,[3] and Perry[4] had derived their theories from all-male samples. On the basis of her initial research with women who were considering abortions, after the Roe v. Wade landmark case on the right to abortion in the 1970s, Gilligan claimed that Kohlberg's theory represented a masculinist tradition in moral thinking and was biased in portraying human moral thinking as primarily justice oriented. Instead, Gilligan claimed that there is another moral orientation, that of care and response, which is characteristic of women's thinking. Successive studies by Gilligan and her associates, which have included both male and female participants, but in recent years have focused primarily on women's and young adolescent girls' thinking, have shown that different groups of people understand and speak about their moral experiences in different moral voices. Most controversy surrounds her classification of 'care voice' and 'justice voice'.

When speaking of 'voice', Gilligan is referring to a particular understanding of the medium through which people give account of their experiences to one another:

> Voice is central to our way of working – our channel of connection, a pathway that brings the inner psychic world of feelings and thoughts out into the open air of relationship where it can be heard by oneself and other people... Voice, because it is embodied, connects rather than separates psyche and body; because voice is in language, it also joins psyche and culture. Voice is inherently relational – one does not require a mirror to hear oneself – yet the sounds of one's voice change in resonance depending on the relational acoustics: whether one is heard or not heard, how one is responded to (by oneself and other people).[5]

In light of this concept of voice, Gilligan views psychology as a relational practice; that is, the voice of both the participant and the researcher interact with each other and notions of truth and objectivity become obsolete: the dialogue between researcher and participant becomes paramount. The reason for this is that the assumption underlying the claim to objectivity is that voice is disembodied, exists apart from relationship, and is not influenced by culture or gender. Instead, a psychology which strives to be aware of its own prejudices and biases, and its responsibility to both the individuals and the groups which it studies, emerges.

Research by Gilligan and her associates, guided by this concept of voice, has consistently found, in American culture, that there are two recurrent moral voices in the narratives of moral conflict provided by both women and men. The 'care voice' speaks of concerns about staying in relationship – focusing on the reciprocal nature of loving, listening and responding to the perceived needs of another. This ideal of relationship is seen as undermined by disconnection, lack of attentiveness to one's or others' needs, withdrawal from emotional commitment, and not being listened to. [....]

The 'justice voice' is one which expresses concerns about fairness, equality and reciprocity between people. A moral conflict arises when the person speaking in this voice has personal experience of or perceives others being treated unequally, unfairly or being oppressed or dominated by another person, group or institution. [....]

There is a tremendous need to recognise the moral voice of a person. As demonstrated in Brown and Gilligan's most recent work on American teenage girls, the transition from childhood to adolescence signals a watershed in their practice of relationship with others. The lively, open and intense relationships which many girls enjoy in childhood is replaced with confusion and loss of confidence in adolescence. Brown and Gilligan argue that the journey from childhood through adolescence is one of silence and disconnection for many girls, when they feel pressurised into maintaining relationships for the sake of relationship and being perceived as nice by others. Brown and Gilligan characterise their methodology as allowing the young adolescent girl to voice resistance to the pressures which she feels push her toward silence and disconnection. On this level then, Brown and Gilligan's method can indeed be characterised as a feminist and politically aware method because it makes:

> it easier for girls and women's voices to be heard and engaged openly in relationship – to encourage the open trouble of political resistance, the insistence on knowing what one knows and the willingness to be outspoken, rather than to collude in the silencing and avoidance of conflict that fosters the corrosive suffering of psychological resistance: the reluctance to know what one knows and the fear that one's experience, if spoken, will endanger relationships and threaten survival.[6]

In summary, I have tried to show that the study of women's experiences of moral conflict through a focus on narrative have led to a significant reappraisal of the moral domain in developmental psychology. The work of Carol Gilligan has been instrumental in this approach, and the rapid development of a psychology based on narrative is leading to new and exciting alternatives to the traditional rationalist and empirical paradigms.

Notes
1. Carol Gilligan 1982. *In a Different Voice: Psychological Theory and Women's Development*. Harvard UP.
2. J Piaget 1965 [1932]. *The Moral Judgement of the Child*. Free Press.
3. L Kohlberg 1963. 'The Development of Children's Orientations Towards a Moral Order: 1. Sequence to the Development of Moral Thought', *Vita Humana*. 6. 11–33.
4. W. G. Perry 1968. *Forms of Intellectual and Ethical Development During the College Years: A Scheme*. Holt, Rinehart and Winston.
5. L. M. Brown and C, Gilligan 1992. *Meeting at the Crossroads*. Ballantine. p. 20.
6. *Ibid*, p. 41.

Jane Tynan

FEMINIST IDENTITIES IN THE IRISH CONTEXT

Abstract This paper enquires into issues of difference in relation to national identity. Looking particularly at Ireland and feminist theorising of the nation, theoretical connections made between feminist theory and postcolonial theory frame a discussion about the politics of location for Irish women. I intend to take an aspect of the project which analyses the dynamics of oppression which have shaped the republican feminist agenda. Representing an aspect of Irish feminism, this resistance movement grows out of particular women's experiences of sexism, classism and sectarianism. A global perspective on women's oppression, introducing the crucial analysis of difference into feminist thought, has particular implications for Irish feminism, where issues of class, race, religion and nationalism have challenged and conditioned Irish feminism's evolution and development. This contemporary cultural analysis works with the conditions which shape a feminist politics in a postcolonial State, providing the opportunity to question any notion of homogeneity of Irish women in their negotiation of national identity. I want to highlight the importance of a feminist analysis which takes account of the way women's oppression is structured in different socio-economic contexts. In setting out a framework to discuss the interactions of feminist concerns and national concerns, theoretical connections have to be made between the post-colonial and the feminist.

from 'Redefining Boundaries: Feminism, Women and Nationalism in Ireland', *Volume 4*, pp. 21-30

In its analysis of the construction of the subject under colonisation, post-colonial theory locates the ways in which identities are constructed within systems of meaning. Particular social meanings inscribed onto people within the colonising process serve the self-representations of the coloniser. The violence of colonisation, underpinned by a cultural consensus, stabilises a subject people in a subordinate position within a hierarchy of meaning. A patriarchal system of definition works similarly, where women are inscribed with meanings which construct them as 'other' to men. The objectification of a colonised people under imperialist domination privileges the prerogatives of the coloniser. The objectification of women within a patriarchal organisation of meaning provides a similar notion of mastery and self-representation for a dominating group of men.

In post-colonial Ireland, the identity politics of the coloniser were replicated by utilising women as the territory over which the postcolonial subject (man) would gain power. Man's self-representation, dependent upon the subordination of an 'other' category, would guarantee his right to self-determination. In the Republic of Ireland post-colonial nationalist ideology relegates women to the private sphere, to service men. This subordination encourages the invisibility of women. The 1937 constitution, with subsequent amendments, maps out a limited space for women in Ireland, to act as a territory and guard the race.

Where the nation has been conceived in patriarchal terms, there has been a difficulty in presenting issues of nationality as a feminist concern. However feminism and nationalism have particular areas for dialogue. A feminist politics engages with the everyday realities of women, implying a history, a local knowledge and a politics of location. Noting the engagement of women in national liberation struggles necessitated by partition and British occupation of Northern Ireland, I hope to problematise the notion of feminism as internationalist. In the Irish context, feminism is challenged by the conditions of partition, the post-colonial, sectarian conflict and class structures. [....]

Mary Mangan

AUNT KATY

from 'Woman of the House',
work in progress, *Volume* 7, pp. 148-150

A recent lecture with the above title made me recall my memories of my Aunt's life and experiences, and to compare them with mine forty years later. 'Woman of the House' fitted Aunt Katy to a tee. She lived in a two bedroom cottage in the Wicklow countryside. We were sent there as children in ones and twos for our 'holidays'. Aunt Katy ruled over her domain with a rod of iron. Her adult son and daughter lived at home. One son 'took the king's shilling' and joined the British army. He was never mentioned. Her daughter cycled sixty miles to work on Sunday and the same distance home again on Friday. Her son was a forester who never married, he courted a few ladies, but I don't think anyone would have been brave enough to share a kitchen with Katy, that being the norm at the time. Katy rose at six-thirty in order to get her son off to work. The big kettle would be filled from the spring well jug on the dresser and hung on the already blazing fire to boil. A basin was filled from the bucket outside the door which contained stream water for washing. Beside this was put her son's razor and a big chipped mug along with soap, and left ready for the morning shave. The soapy water was used again to wash yesterday's socks. Afterwards she would sit on the form and comb her long gray hair with a big comb and twist it into a chignon.

Her first task was straining the milk, which stood hot and steaming on the dresser. It was strained using a series of jugs and some muslin. It was then separated and the cream from the top used to make butter or as buttermilk. Some was added to the mash for the calf and hens. The transistor resided on the mantle and was only used for the Angelus and Sunday football. Mornings were spent cleaning the kitchen. The plain concrete floor was brushed and scrubbed using a bucket and carbolic soap. All the wooden furniture was scrubbed white, starting with the kitchen table then the benches by the fire and the settle bed. Lamps were trimmed and filled with oil and hung on the wall. The toilet facilities were outside in the cow shed; each day she would fork human and animal waste onto the manure heap. Cattle and hens were fed and eggs collected.

Cooking was done over a big fire in the cast iron pot suspended from hooks in the chimney. Each day she baked big cakes of soda bread, currant cake or apple dumplings, and baked them in the covered griddle which hung on one of the highest hooks. Her fridge was a shopping bag hung on a hook on the wall. Out of this was taken a piece of smoked bacon and a bit cut off and set to boil along with a pot of potatoes. After the drudgery of the day she would sit down to darn or knit. Before retiring she brought in the chamber pots and filled the earthenware jars for the beds. After a mug of cocoa it was bed for all by ten o'clock. [....]

Sharon Murphy

MAMA

from Volume 6, p 96

I am just a kid,
I've walked through Hell's doors,
Mama, why leave me there, alone?

They tell me they're my masters now,
'Do what we say!'
You gave them that power,
And I must obey.

My home is St. Joseph's school,
Lots of kids around.
What happened, Mama,
Did you try, or just walk out?

It's not easy, Mama,
To be lost in the crowd.
They say I must be grateful,
I got food in my mouth.

Where are you, Mama?
Was it hard to go your way?
Do you still remember me?
Or have I faded away?

Mary O'Donoghue

Dauernarkose

from Volume 8, p. 135

She has been asleep for three
days, a liquid length of time
closed over her head
like a sheet of lake-water.
They think they have
her dreams cached away
in their clutterbook
of explanations, and see no
flicker-hint from behind
eyelids fern-stitched
with blue veins.

But she is navigating
equations, pointed fir
jungles of isosceles triangles,
the screams of chalk and nails
like seagull voice, dust
of chalk a scurf on her cuffs.

She walks past the bossy
signposts of sine and tan,
and her map begins to make
sense, when the curved
two-legged travel stool
of pi is pulled from under
her and she is splashed awake.

She leaves infinity, her last
mark, a slender eight sleeping
with its face to the wall.

'Dauernarkose was an experimental treatment for schizophrenics, involving prolonged sleep under the influence of drugs. Also called 'the continuous sleep cure'.

From the Local to the International

Mary Owens

Rural Women in Ireland

Abstract: Pressure is growing on rural Ireland to restructure and adapt to changes occurring at national and international level. European Community and Irish rural development policies are intended to help the most vulnerable rural areas cope with peripherality, marginality and disadvantage. However, in doing so, they overlook the gender dimension to rural development – the peripherality, marginality and disadvantage which is peculiar to women. If these policies are to genuinely improve the lives and opportunities of rural women, they will have to be accompanied by deliberate measures to rectify women's inequality in the home, on the farm and at work by improving their access to a wide range of facilities, organisations and policy-making institutions. [....]

from 'Women in Rural Development:
A Hit or Miss Affair?', *Volume 1*, pp. 15-19

The Gender Dimension

There is another dimension to 'peripherality', 'marginality' and 'disadvantage' which is peculiar to rural women and which is not adequately addressed by rural development policies at either the national or European level. This gender dimension needs to be tackled hand in hand with developments of an infrastructural and institutional nature if the latter are to genuinely change rural women's lives and opportunities. For in order to take that course, set up that business, keep that job or chair that committee, rural women also need better access to cheap and reliable child-care and transport facilities. They require improved access to land, credit, training, adult and continuing education and advisory services. The vast majority of Irish women are not in the paid workforce and there are many attitudinal and institutional obstacles to their taking up a full-time job or making a long-term commitment to a project. That is not to say that rural women are not robust development agents. But their contribution, which is largely in the form of domestic, farm, voluntary and community work, remains unpaid, undervalued and unrecognised.

Moreover, women are acutely under-represented at key decision-making levels in organisations which claim to represent their interests, e.g. farming organisations, community councils and local development organisations, trade unions, local authorities, health boards and vocational education committees. As a result, their voice is still unlikely to be heard in new institutional arrangements which take a 'bottom-up' or integrated approach to rural development.

Against this background, women must ensure that opportunities for development which arise from diversification, small rural businesses or industries, reward their contributions and respect their rights. Rural tourism, organic farming, manufacturing and crafts etc. can provide jobs for women and could offer them the prospect of an independent and a secure income. For some women, however, farm diversification could entail an extra work burden with no extra income, e.g. more unpaid work keeping accounts, tending livestock or poultry, picking and harvesting farm produce, looking after tourists. Other women who take up part-time jobs picking fruit or vegetables, working in a hotel/restaurant/shop/hairdresser's or looking after children will usually do so with no security, no statutory rights, low pay and during atypical or anti-social hours. Women already 'crowd out' sectors of the economy which offer these conditions to their workers and so it should come as no surprise to us if the pattern is perpetuated with the opening up of job and business opportunities in rural areas.

Training, education and employment generating agencies play a key role in ensuring that women are not ignored in rural development programmes. In practice however, local training and job creation initiatives rarely challenge the traditional sexual division of labour in rural areas or lead to a more equitable sharing of resources and responsibilities within households.

Conclusion

If rural development is not to be a hit-or-miss affair for Irish women, it will have to be accompanied by measures on a much broader front to provide the following:

(i) training which challenges sex-stereotyping and opens doors for women irrespective of their marital status, age, fertility, class, or location.

(ii) assistance for women looking for greater control over resources, e.g. to buy land, sell their own produce or crafts, own their own businesses, set up co-operatives.

(iii) rural infrastructures other than roads and bridges, such as childcare, public transport, flexible and appropriate education and training services.

(iv) a bigger say for women in farming and other professional organisations, trade unions, community development associations, credit institutions, state agencies, local authorities, government departments, and European institutions alike.

There is a great need for more and better information on the realities of rural women's lives, their similarities and differences and their development needs and aspirations, so as to inform policy makers. These issues have not been a priority for research institutions in the past, although the situation appears to be improving. Rural women too need to break out of their isolation and take action at domestic, local, national and European level to secure their rights and rewards. There are encouraging signs that this is already happening throughout Europe with the growing number of women's networks, lobbies and organisations operating on a broad front to fight for equality, opportunity and development for all. [....]

Anne Byrne

Rural Women in Ireland

Abstract: This paper looks at the available statistical information which describes certain characteristics of women's lives. While the statistics are often gender blind and time limited, they contain much useful demographic information, including labour force trends, social welfare uptake, and a description of the health status of the population. The paper takes a brief look at these sources and raises issues in relation to rural women.

from 'Statistics – What do they tell us about women?',
Volume 1, pp. 1-13

Introduction

There are many annual published statistical sources of information which are used by a variety of agencies, organisations, community groups and individuals in the course of their work. Reflecting the growing interest in gender issues, these statistics have been much criticised for the lack of attention to the particular position of women (Blackwell, 1987). It has been stated by many commentators that women are under counted in the official statistics, so for example we have no clear idea how many women are unemployed, as many working in the home are not eligible to 'sign on' the official unemployment register (Daly, 1989). But what do the statistics tell us? If we direct our attention to women in the countryside, what type of picture emerges from the published sources? [....]

So what do the published statistics tell us? Perhaps they confirm what we already know. Because of the inadequacy of the statistics it is very difficult to evaluate the position of women in the countryside. But there is no doubt that rural women are deprived in relation to essential services and employment opportunities. The lack of support services such as marriage counselling and family planning services for women on low incomes living within the traditional family unit have consequences for rural women who want to make changes and benefit from the services that are available to urban-based women.

But the consequences for rural women who are living outside the norm and on the poverty line, such as single parents or women who have been deserted are even greater. Lack of child-care facilities, expensive public transport, few employment opportunities or educational facilities contribute to maintaining the silence and invisibility of women who are poor in rural Ireland. This lack of access to resources needs to be documented and enumerated to a far greater extent than is currently provided by research or by the official statistics, so that the female voices in rural Ireland can be heard. [....]

Terri Conroy

ORAL RESEARCH IN BALLYCONNEELY

Abstract: The subject of this article is a reflection on the personal experience of conducting oral research in a small rural village in Connemara. The problems I encountered and overcame (such as being aware of the necessity for good time management and finding willing participants), are examined; and the positive and beneficial aspects of this type of research are also discussed. As well as addressing my personal experiences, this article also considers differing views on the methodology of conducting oral research and it acknowledges the necessity to recognise that there is a gender issue involved in the technique of interviewing.

from 'Oral Research in Ballyconneely', *Volume* 7, pp. 35–39

My thesis for my Master's degree was about the lives of women in Ballyconneely, Connemara c. 1900–1950. I used oral research as a major part of my thesis because I felt it was very important to hear what the Ballyconneely women had to say about themselves and their lives. I wanted to give them a platform – so to speak – before traditional experiences such as theirs were lost to history, and therefore, lost to us, forever. After all, Ballyconneely society as a whole barely makes it into the footnotes of history, never mind the women as an individual and distinct group. I believe that the subjects of a history have a right to be heard as they can speak of personal experience and observations. They can explain things which written records cannot always do and their voices bring the past to life.

When I embarked upon my research I had hundreds of questions. I wanted to know everything about every facet of life and it was a problem to narrow the focus to the extent that I had to. In the end though, having a narrower focus meant that I could concentrate very specifically on particular aspects of life, ending up with a genuine insight into the women's experiences, rather than with a mish-mash of lots of little details but no overall picture.

Finding the subjects to interview proved problematic because no-one responded to the advertisements I had placed in local shops and on the local community radio. The first two women I personally approached declined to talk to me. They did not want to look back to 'the bad old days', to hard times, because there were events in their past which would upset them to talk about. These set-backs made me very aware of the time issue. I had not realised the amount of time needed to negotiate for, set up and conduct the interviews, not to mention the time needed for analysis of the material. Eventually, after approaching other women in the locality I managed to interview six women in all.

It was important to pose a question that would elicit some kind of narrative and not just a yes or no. For example, if I had asked 'Did you make your children's clothes?' some of the women would have said yes, others no. But when I asked 'How did you clothe your children?' I discovered that they spun wool, dyed wool, knitted and sewed, and received clothes from relatives in America. [....]

My experience at the first interview that I conducted reflects Minister's view [that the traditional oral research method (questions and answers) is a form of male communication and that female narrators are, consequently, disadvantaged].[1] I questioned the lady in a very dogmatic (masculine) way, interviewing like a garda might a prime suspect, intent on obtaining a confession. I was nervous, she was nervous and I did not want to miss out any of my questions! As a result, I was not really listening to her carefully enough to acknowledge the possibility that there was more information to be gathered. I was also thrown when she answered two or three questions in one short sentence. I realised afterwards that I had not allowed her to communicate as a female, in a woman-to-woman fashion.

With my subsequent interviews I did not make the same mistake. I [....] talked to the interviewees the way that we women do talk to one another, on a personal, chatty level. If you decide to give the women the floor in an interview, allowing them to reminisce and ramble, they feel relaxed – as if they are talking to a friend – and this method proffers much more information than formal questioning does. Learning and appreciating this factor made the other interviews I conducted much more interesting, informative, entertaining and rewarding. [....]

I researched, I interviewed and then I sometimes discovered from the interviewees that I still needed to know more about a particular aspect of their experiences; perhaps on a national rather than local level. An example of the way this situation can arise is as follows. I knew from my general research that the income generated from the sale of eggs belonged to the *bean a' tighe* herself and there are references to this tradition in folklore and literature. There is a country saying: "Tis many the girl made her fortune from the egg money"[2] and I had presumed from such sources, and from advertisements in the *Connacht Tribune* placed by English buyers for eggs, that women in Ballyconneely must have also made some income from the sale of eggs. The narratives from the interviews conducted proved otherwise. Unlike other parts of Connemara, such as Letterfrack and indeed other parts of rural Ireland, women in Ballyconneely tended not to sell eggs, and if they did, it was a rare occurrence. The point I am making here is that despite a general trend in rural Ireland for the *bean a' tighe* to sell eggs, and despite numerous sources acknowledging this practice, oral research revealed that Ballyconneely women were exceptions to the rule. One should always allow for individual experience, experience which can only be determined through oral research.

Oral research is important when recording women's history and so especially enlightening when it is a local study. Arensberg's 1930s anthropological study of a rural village in Clare touched on women's lives – the domestic and the cultural – and one could be forgiven for presuming that the experiences he recorded were probably the same for all women at the time. I now know, thanks to oral research, that the lives of women in Ballyconneely were considerably dissimilar. They laughed at the idea of 'the match', eating after their men-folk and walking a discreet distance behind them.[3] Without oral research I would never have known of these differences because there are no written records which attest to the Ballyconneely experience.

It should be borne in mind that some people who are interviewed might embellish a personal history or omit details of their lives which they feel are too personal and private to share. One can even suggest that some interviewees may unintentionally be telling the story that they think the interviewer wants to hear. However, any doubts about the validity of oral narratives as historical source material can be levelled at all sources of research material. Careful analysis of narratives, when considered alongside other sources, can result in a greater appreciation and understanding of the lives of the past.

Notes
1 Kristina Minister 1991. 'A Feminist Frame for Oral History Interview' in S. Gluck and D. Patai (eds). *Womens' Words: The Feminist Practice of Oral History,* Routledge, 32.
2 C. O'Danachair 1985. 'Marriage in Irish Folk Tradition' in A. Cosgrave (ed.), *Marriage in Ireland,* College Press, p. 110.
3 C. Arensberg 1968. *The Irish Countryman,* American Museum Science Books.

Victor Luftig

POETRY, PRESIDENTS AND THE CENTRE

Abstract: One source of Mary Robinson's appeal – and one strategy she uses in making her appeal – has been her invocation of literature: in references to Yeats, Joyce, Heaney and Boland in her inaugural address, in comments on her interest in poetry on occasions like the opening of the Women's Studies Centre at University College, Galway, in praise for modem Irish writers in interviews at home and speeches abroad, etc. That strategy may oddly disarm criticism, by appropriating writers as Robinson's own appointed critics of the status quo (her own authority as President included) and by removing literature from the domains in which scholars are accustomed to applying their critical skills. Comparing Mary Robinson's remarks at the opening of the Women's Studies Centre at UCG to John F. Kennedy's remarks at the opening of the Robert Frost Memorial at Amherst in 1963, this paper argues for the need for a critical approach to those politicians whose appeals to literature may place them unhelpfully outside a certain range of (literary) criticism.

from 'Power All the Way:
Poetry, Presidents and the Centre', *Volume 3,* pp. 141-149

Mary Robinson's words at the official opening of the University College Galway Women's Studies Centre delighted me, just as, I imagine, they did most others who were present; so I now feel a bit curmudgeonly as I try to use the Centre's own publication to second-guess part of Her Excellency's dedicatory remarks. But what delighted me on the day of the opening – a politician's thoughtful, apparently extemporaneous embrace of poetic language as her own and her people's – now seems to me more disturbing, and I think the likely readers of this journal are uniquely qualified to determine whether my unease is reasonable. President Robinson suggested that day that her interest in poetry might be 'relevant to the Centre' [....] I have in mind the moment when President Robinson, after her speech, was offered five books of poetry. [....] She responded as follows:

> [....] I think it's becoming increasingly known there is nothing I like better than books, and on top of that nothing more special than a book of poetry... The reason that I am particularly pleased is probably just worth mentioning, because I think it's relevant to the Centre. I find my whole background [....] is as a lawyer, all about the definite language, the small print, the legislation, getting the words right in that sense. And now I'm in an office where I have to find a different kind of words, because a lot of what I'm doing is at the level of values; it's creative thinking on behalf of the people of Ireland. And I find that increasingly I'm looking to the poets and the writers to give me the words that will really communicate. And it is enormously important to me – and indeed a great resource – [....] when you want to put something into words, to be able to draw upon the writers. So it's a special delight to have another reason to do more reading; and I now have a very good resource from Galway to bring with me to rely upon when I'm back in the city.

[....] When the President's words, drawing readily on a prestigious set of ostensibly autonomous voices, speak ceremonially on behalf of the whole of the Irish people, how may literature be reserved any kind of dissenting role?

I hope to give emphasis to the question by noting another occasion at which a President, at an event like the UCG Women's Studies Centre dedication, made comparable claims about poetry's relation to politics. I have in mind John F. Kennedy's address at the opening of the Robert Frost Library at Amherst College on October 27, 1963. The speech represented the last moment in Kennedy's sustained engagement with Frost and his poetry. Frost had, famously, read at Kennedy's inauguration, visited him at the White House, and corresponded with him regularly. Their relationship had cooled after Frost's officially sanctioned visit to the Soviet Union, because the President had resented the poet's words, ascribed by Frost to Nikita Kruschev, saying that the U.S. was 'too liberal to fight'. [....]

A moment comparable to Kennedy's invocation of 'Acquainted with the Night' may be found in President Robinson's inaugural address. In a speech that also quoted phrases from Yeats, Joyce, and Heaney, Robinson relied on a phrase from Eavan Boland to make her case about the disenfranchised and under-represented: 'I want my presidency to promote the telling of stories', said Robinson, 'for women who have been outside history to be written back into history, in the words of Eavan Boland ... ' The invocation of that phrase 'outside history' amounted to a particularly striking kind of assimilation. In Boland's eponymous book and poem, the words 'outside history' are fraught with various ironies: historical loss is symbolised by the prehistorical stars "whose light happened/thousands of years before/our pain did: they are, they have always been/outside history"; the stars stand as reminders that "there are outsiders always", that those 'outside history' may perhaps never be included in it; the poem concludes by asserting that "we are always too late" in any attempt to draw near to such outsiders by an act of imaginative historical recovery.[1] [....] In the context of Boland's work, 'outside history' names a place where Boland and the women, on behalf of whom Robinson was speaking, have either never exactly been or may never be brought back from.

Women so subtly situated are not available for sudden political rescue. The ironies in Boland's phrase are inimical to the energies of the President's speech, and not only because an inaugural address hardly seems the place for fine nuances. Even less typical of such an address would be the acknowledgement that the ins and outs of history may be impossible to chronicle, let alone to correct. The politician who wants the disenfranchised to be 'written in' always, of course, hopes to count on their support. "We can really communicate as a people", said Robinson in [an] Arts Show interview;[2] there could be no more effective means, she suggested, than 'communicating through culture', through arts such as poetry. Yet 'we are always too late', says the poem from which Robinson quotes. And if "poetry never stood a chance/of standing outside history", then the act of writing women back into history must always mean introducing them into the arena where poetry complicates and challenges that act of political re-writing. Robinson's 'resource' is effectively double-edged. Perhaps poetic dissent always begins with rejection of the terms that call it into voice. [....]

In the absence of such critical commentary, some of the President's most interesting and sophisticated allusions might not get their due – might go unnoted or might get read only as ornament. I've been trying to show that the Presidents' literarily inflected remarks are worthy of scrutiny as much as of applause. I've meant to suggest too that academics might represent an important counter-force to a very strong pairing, when politicians call poets to their sides. At Kennedy's inauguration, Frost encouraged the new leader with the following words: 'Be more Irish than Harvard. Poetry and power is the formula for another Augustan Age. Don't be afraid of power'. The President sent a typed thank-you letter marked with a hand-written note that might serve now as a kind of warning, or at least as a solicitation for critical attention: it read, simply, 'Power All the Way'. [....]

Notes
1. Eavan Boland 1990. 'Outside History' in *Outside History: Selected Poems 1980–1990*. New York: Norton, p.50.
2. Arts Show interview (Mike Murphy/President Robinson), 31 Dec. 1992. RTE Radio 1.

Mary Quinn

WOMEN AND EMPLOYMENT

Abstract: This paper examines aspects of women's employment in the Republic of Ireland and Norway. The legal framework surrounding women's participation in the labour force in the two countries is described and compared. Workforce participation rates of women are then examined, and reference is made to women's 'second shift' in parenting and domestic work. Vertical and horizontal segregation of the labour forces, and the differential between pay rates of women and men in the two countries is then examined. The conclusion focuses on the similarity of the situations for women in the workforce in the two countries.

from 'Women and Employment – Norway and the Republic of Ireland', *Volume 4*, pp. 59–76

Introduction

The objective of this paper is to identify and compare aspects of women's employment in Norway and the Republic of Ireland. The legal framework influencing women's participation in the labour force in the two countries is first described. These are Norway's Equal Status Act,

1978, governing gender equality in Norwegian life in general, including employment, and, in Ireland, the Anti Discrimination (Pay) Act, 1974 and the Employment Equality Act, 1977. The structure of the labour force in the two countries is then examined with particular reference to gender roles and gender differences. [....]

Perhaps the most surprising result emerging from the comparison between the two countries is the similarities between them. The legislation shares the same conceptual approach, although there are important differences. The Norwegian law explicitly targets itself at the inferior position of women whereas Irish law is explicitly targeted at equality between the sexes. As a result, Norwegian law allows for positive discrimination in certain circumstances whereas Irish law does not. The Norwegian system does not provide for ordering either compensation or job award as redress for discrimination whereas the Irish system does. Apart from these administrative differences, women in the two countries share the problems of combining motherhood with employment, given the scarcity of state childminding facilities and the pattern of women taking most of the responsibility for parenting and housekeeping in both countries. Structural features of the labour market in the two countries are also similar with marked horizontal and vertical segregation. There is evidence of some change in the vertical segregation in both countries, apparently more so in Norway than in Ireland. However, this change, while welcome, by its nature will tend to affect only a limited number of women. There is little evidence of change in patterns of horizontal segregation. Lower pay for women for similar work is also a feature of the labour market in both countries. [....]

Mary C. Pruitt

NORTH AMERICAN INDIGENOUS WOMEN

Abstract Four points of view of women's history bring into focus the complexities of women's daily lives. The work of contemporary indigenous women in North America will illuminate each point of view – on topics concerning I. Health and Survival in the Nuclear Age; II. Economics: the Fish-ins; III. Politics: On the Docks, At the Legislature, and Kitchen Table by Kitchen Table: and IV. Ideology, or Core Values 'Our Future, Our Responsibility'.

from 'At the Center of Resistance', *Volume 3*, pp. 167–176

[....] When I led a lecture/discussion with the Diploma class in Women's Studies at University College, Galway in 1994, Irish women scholars immediately connected with the thesis that indigenous women have to be everywhere and have to concern themselves with everything about their people's fight for sovereignty. This article expands our intercultural communication with a review of contemporary American indigenous women's activism. [....]

1. *Health and Survival in the Nuclear Age*

The nuclear bomb and the Cold War have provided only the latest excuses to exploit indigenous lands. In the late 1800s it was the gold rush. In the mid-1900s it was the uranium rush in the Upper Midwest lands of the Great Sioux Nation. Ironically, we know that rich mineral deposits underlay the arid lands to which Lakota were banished a hundred years ago. These deposits have drawn the exploitation that indigenous women must fight today. In 1962 a massive spill of uranium tailings alarmed Lakota women. Recognising that uranium poisoning portended genocide, Lakota women Lorelei Decora, Madonna Gilbert and other health workers founded Women of All Red Nations (WARN).[3] Indigenous women viewed WARN as a 'sister' society to the male focused American Indian Movement (AIM), as their own space in a political movement where the men were influenced by the dominant mind set of colonisation. [....] Under the cover of health work for women and babies, WARN trained reservation women to conduct water quality studies and to monitor problem pregnancies, miscarriages, birth defects and other forms of nuclear age genocide. The nuclear industry had been denying women's experience of the health crisis, but WARN's research called the industry a liar and proved it. [....] The Akwesasne Mother's Milk Project upholds the standard set by WARN. Akwesasne are also called Haudenosaunee and, in English, Mohawk. The Akwesasne live along the St. Lawrence River on the boundary between New York state and the province of Ontario. A century of pollution from paper mills and engine foundaries deposited so much of the poisons called PCBs that the levels in the fish, deer and waterfowl there registered as the most contaminated in the whole Great Lakes Basin. [....] Akwesasne women enlisted the aid of the New York State Department of Environmental Conservation, the New York Department of Health and the National Institute of Environmental Health Sciences. The women collected basic data which proved convincingly and with scientific soundness that their breastmilk contained PCBs. The scientists then collaborated in widening the breastmilk study.

Some of the women and children who attended the Indigenous Women's Network Conference on sustainable communities at White Earth, Minnesota, in September 1994

The study trained indigenous mothers to monitor their breast milk for PCBs and, later, to eat less fish during pregnancy and nursing. To avoid traditional foods was a compromise when the women would have preferred safe, traditional food. But the trend that alarmed Cook – mothers afraid to feed their children their own breast milk – has been reversed through the change in diet. Although the U.S. infant mortality in the first year of life remains twice as high for indigenous as for white children, women are fighting back by pioneering hundreds of practical health projects in indigenous communities. [....]

Rosaleen O'Neill

East German Women

Abstract: German unification has had a devastating impact on the economy and society of the former German Democratic Republic. This paper looks at the lives of GDR women before and after unification. It outlines and critically examines the measures which enabled GDR women to combine motherhood with employment. Today two-thirds of the female work-force are unemployed. One of the results of this is a sharp decline in the birthrate.

from 'An End to Privilege? East German Women and German Unification', *Volume* 2, pp. 33-39

In the spring and summer of 1990, as the details of the German Unification Treaty were being worked out, there was much talk from West Germany's ruling Christian Democrats about the fact that the women of East Germany would have to give up the 'privileges' which they had enjoyed in their state, the German Democratic Republic. Many GDR women reacted with anger to the suggestion that they had been in any sense 'privileged' within their society. But the report by the GDR government to the United Nations on the UN Women's Decade (1976–1985) did in fact specifically refer to 'privileges':

> In view of women's social function in the reproduction of society, the socialist state grants them a number of privileges facilitating the combination of their careers with the duties of motherhood.[1]

In official documents, Party Congress reports, GDR information brochures etc., one repeatedly finds the state 'granting', 'offering', 'allowing' women certain 'supportive measures' to enable them 'to perform their roles as citizens, working women and mothers', or to live up to 'the requirements made on them as citizens of our state in their roles as working people and as mothers'.

The first Constitution of the GDR (1949) stated that men and women are equal, and it guaranteed the right to work and to equal pay for equal work to all citizens. The participation of women in the workforce was seen as an essential precondition of their economic independence and their consequent emancipation. As the right to work gradually became the duty to work, in what was known as the 'Workers' and Farmers' State', difficulties arose in relation to women's 'other' role, that of bearing and caring for the children without whom a socialist society could not be built. The significantly named *Maternal and Child Care and Rights of Women Act* of 1950 was the first of many laws aimed at making it easier for women to combine their dual functions, to wear, so to speak, both the mother's bonnet and the steelworker's helmet. But by the mid-1960s the birthrate was declining, and it was clear that more comprehensive measures would have to be introduced to keep women in the workforce where they were needed, while ensuring 'demographic stability'. The measures introduced in 1972 and developed and strengthened during the seventies and eighties, constitute the 'privileges' referred to in the aforementioned report to the UN.

These measures fundamentally changed the lives of women in the GDR, and made it "the state with possibly the most advanced women's rights legislation in history".[2] These were essentially working mothers' rights, but by the late 1980s over 92% of GDR women were mothers, and over 91% of mothers had jobs outside the home, were in vocational training, or were students. While the institution of marriage was honoured and financially promoted by the state, there were few moral or social foundations for discrimination against single mothers. In the 1980s children born to single mothers accounted for roughly a third of all births. [....] In 1990, Ursula Lehr, Minister for Women's Affairs in the Christian Democrat government, had said:

> For the first time in 40 years, GDR women have the right to limit, interrupt or give up their employment for the sake of their family duties.

They are now experiencing the right to be unemployed. This has had the most severe effects on women over 40 who will never see employment again, and on single mothers. While East Germany has managed to hold on to many of its childcare facilities, these are now in most cases expensive and will soon lose what subsidies remain. All other measures for working mothers have been brought in line with West Germany's laws or simply dropped. (Germany's new abortion ruling is a compromise between the old GDR legislation and the much more restrictive Western law, and it remains uncertain whether permitted abortions will be paid for under health insurance. There will probably have to be some test cases before this is clarified.)

The women of the former GDR have responded to their new economic and social situation in the only way they feel is left to them: they have stopped having children. The birthrate has sunk dramatically throughout East Germany, falling by over 50% in the past two years, by 70% in some regions. In this cataclysmic century, only the First World War brought about such a decline in Germany. Reasons given for this range from the new freedom enjoyed by women to their refusal to have a child 'for this Germany'. The marriage rate has fallen by 65%, the divorce rate by 81%.[3] With the traumatic transformation of their society, the disappearance of all that was familiar, people are clinging for security to what is left of the old ways. But the old ways belonged to a society in which there was full employment and in which women had learned to see themselves as mothers and workers. Their 'birth-strike' is surely their way of saying 'no work-no children'. Even if, as is expected, this trend will be reversed in the next century, an entire generation will be missing.[4]

If the trend is reversed, will our image of the strong, economically independent GDR woman have to give way to Helmut Kohl's picture of the German mother? In an interview in *Bild der Frau* he said,

> My highest respect is for our [German] mothers who spent their lives doing their duty without protesting, who never went on demonstrations and wouldn't even know how to.[5]

Notes
1. *Women in the GDR* 1985. Report by the GDR government to the Secretary-General of the United Nations, Berlin, p. 24.
2. Barbara Schaeffer-Hegel 1992. 'Makers and Victims of Unification: German Women and the Two Germanies', *Women's Studies International Forum*, 15:1, p. 103.
3. Wilhelm Bittorf1993. 'Das Glitzern in der Wüste', *Der Spiegel*, 39 (27 Sept.).
4. *Der Spiegel* 1993. 38 (20 Sept.).
5. Quoted in Viola Roggenkamp 1990. 'Der Neue Klassenfeind', *Für Dich*, 42, p. 37.

Rose Tuelo Brock

GLOBAL EXPLOITATION

Abstract: Through the colonial period, continuing to the present, the powerful, the privileged, the greedy etc. have used, against and about others, language and labels which have denigrated and derided the other. The use of such labels has been so common and so unquestioned that the labels have now become part of everyday language despite their detrimental origins and hidden meanings. [....] The aim of this paper is to stimulate some thought, some consideration as we go about our day-to-day doings, so that we begin to question ourselves as to why we assume that what is unfamiliar, different, perhaps strange, must be wrong and despicable and deserves to be exploited and destroyed. Why does a small part of the world continue to justify its plundering of the rest of the world and yet take no responsibility for making things right? I argue that these labels and the language used, serve to justify unfair market practices. [....]

from 'Labelling to Exploit: One Woman's Views of Global Market Exploitation', *Volume* 6, pp. 103-114

The words 'civilise' and 'civilisation' are relative or subjective terms which have come to be synonymous with westernisation and industrialisation. Sometimes the word 'Christianity' is juxtaposed with 'Westernisation'. As we know, these civilised Christians, sometimes doubling as missionaries, dared to go into foreign countries, proceeded to label the indigenous people with derogatory names, and insisted that the latter take up foreign names in order to show that they were Christian. On top of all that, some took the land and some of the property of the indigenous people. Anyway, how does usurping somebody else's culture make one a Christian? [....] So, we have the case where indigenous Americans, who were then being slaughtered with guns by the exploiters called explorers and settlers, were referred to as 'savages'.

Then you wonder: who really is 'savage' here? Who is doing the stealing and the killing and the usurping of the land? Are you savage only when you defend yourself with hand-to-hand combat, or bows and arrows, or assegais or knobkerries? You may kill millions of indigenous people and steal their land and their property, but, so long as you use gunpowder and poison and the bible etc., you are civilised, and your victims are savage, and presumably you are then justified in stealing from them and killing them?

As a result of the slavery industry and colonisation, people were transported from their parent countries to Europe and the Americas to do manual work and dirty jobs. People being people, most of them married and bore children who, in turn, bore children, and so on. Culturally, these children would be European if they are born and bred in Europe. However, although they are culturally European, on the basis of their colour they are given the labels of 'migrants' and 'immigrants'. That is fine if we use the same terms for those of European descent who have taken residence in other countries. Yet the same thing does not happen. For example, people of European descent in the United States claim to be the Americans, whilst the indigenous Americans are called 'Indians'. They even go further, and invite and welcome workers from European countries, such as Ireland, to go to the USA to make a living there, and offer them Green cards, whilst at the same time working hard to exclude Americans from the neighbouring countries. Any day on a flight to South Africa, you will find it full of people from Europe openly going to find work in South Africa, and expecting to get it, and not finding anything wrong with doing that. Yet people from Africa and Asia and other places of the developing world are not expected to come to Europe or other developed parts to look for jobs and to make a living. Why is this so? Why is the world free for the Europeans, the Canadians, people from the United States and from Japan? How is it that they can make a living wherever they choose to? How is it that when they choose to do so they are referred to as 'expatriates', and Asians and Africans working in Europe, paying their taxes etc., are called 'migrants'? How come the minority community of European descent in South Africa are not referred to as 'Ethnic Minorities' or even 'Migrants'? These double standards are confusing and discriminatory. [....] So, positively, what is needed?

> Thinking of other people, whether different in appearance or in culture, as people and valuing them as people.
>
> Being prepared to learn from other cultures and not assuming that the Western world is all knowledgeable about all things.

Accepting that there are different ways of living and that they all have negative and positive aspects, and that condemning them for their difference is irresponsible.

Working for justice in the world, and removing injustices and exploitations in trade and industry, no matter what part of the world they are in.

Taking responsibility for the environment. This involves not only the physical earth environment but also the creatures, including people, which inhabit it.

Realising that the earth has plenty and almost everybody could live well if there were no discriminatory, exploiting practices.

Informing ourselves about what is going on around us in our names as citizens of the world and shareholders and making our voices heard where we feel uncomfortable about the methods adopted to make profits for us.

I am saying that the world does not have to be the way it is. That people in the Western world vote by their shares and as consumers, and they have the power to influence policy so that beneficial practices are adopted world-wide.

Lorna Shaughnessy

NICARAGUAN WOMEN'S MOVEMENT

Abstract: The growth of a dynamic and assertive constituency of women in Nicaragua is inseparable from the most recent phase of 'Sandinismo' in Nicaraguan history. An examination of the complex and ever-changing relationship between the Frente Sandinista and the women's movement is therefore a key element of this article. The accelerated rate at which Nicaraguan women assumed a central place in national politics in the period from 1970-80 has much to do with their participation as combatants in the guerrilla insurgency of the 1970s, and the radicalisation of motherhood brought about by a combination of political, economic and cultural features of Nicaraguan society at this time. This paper seeks to provide some clues as to why the joint icons of mother and *guerrillera* have been so powerful in Nicaraguan society, and to examine why, since 1991, the women's movement has broken ranks with the Frente Sandinista, and now operates as an autonomous network of organisations.

from 'Military Participation and Moral Authority: Women's Political Participation in Nicaragua, 1975-95', *Volume 3*, pp. 151-165

Two of the political roles assumed by Nicaraguan women in the insurrectional period, which became icons of the revolution itself, both at home and abroad, were that of militant mother *(las madres combatientes)* and resistance fighter *(guerrillera)*. In the *barrios* of many Latin American cities, community-based groups of women have emerged as tireless campaigners on welfare issues such as food-prices, housing and health care. Managua's *madres combatientes* emerged from the ruins of the 1972 earthquake, and organised an informal relief network to tend to the sick, and distribute what little food and water were available. When vast amounts of international aid to earthquake victims were misappropriated by the Somoza family, the mothers' welfare-based action took a decidedly political direction, and many became involved in the anti-Somoza resistance.

Mother and child at meeting of young co-operativists, Waswalito, Jinotega, 1984

The presence of *guerrilleras* in the anti-Somoza campaign raised expectations that women would play a substantive, rather than peripheral role in the Revolution's Programme for National Reconstruction (1979–84). Most women who took up arms did so after 1975, when anti-Government guerrilla activity was at its peak. The FSLN (Sandinista Front for National Liberation) forces attracted women from many social sectors: middle-class intellectuals, landless rural *campesinas*, university students and the urban poor. Where women had traditionally lent support to the guerrilla forces by providing safe houses, acting as messengers, and providing crucial support-structures, they now began to assume the roles of combatants and commanders of small units and whole battalions. In the battle for Leon, for example, four of the seven Field Commanders were women (Reif, 1986, p. 159).

Statistics vary as to the actual number of women who took up arms in the 1975–79 period: Chinchilla claims that in the final FSLN operations, up to 30% of their forces were women (Chinchilla, 1983, p. 423), whereas Vilas estimates an overall membership in the campaign as representing only 7% (Vilas, 1987, p. 168). The discrepancy is interesting in its own right, as it highlights the relative insignificance of scale when measuring the psychological impact of mould-breaking political action.

> The revolutionary process brings about a fundamental change in concepts. Women are a case in point. They have participated in the revolution, not in the kitchen, but as combatants and as political leaders. This creates a new framework entirely.[1] [....]

The way out of prolonged sacrifice in Nicaragua is through negotiation by interested groups in both the parliamentary and popular sectors. To date, the only transition that the political classes have managed is from shared sacrifice to its opposite – greed. Only the women's movement and a few other community-based groups have managed to make a transition from conflict to negotiation, and it is their continuing commitment to grassroots support that bestows the very moral authority and answerability lacking in the executive and legislature. The criticism made most consistently in Nicaragua since 1992, of all political parties, is that they have lost touch with their constituency, the *base*.[2] After twenty years of struggle to establish a political system that would uphold the moral authority granted by electoral support, it is worth noting that morality and political participation in Nicaragua are more likely to meet outside of Government, and that the women's movement is one of the few arenas where the ideals espoused by the Revolution itself are still practised. If indeed, as Dora María Téllez upholds, "the revolution is a phenomenon of consciousness, and not of the state", the state could learn from the example of gender consciousness, one of the last preserves of meaningful solidarity and activism in Nicaragua today.

Notes

1   Margaret Randall 1984. ... *y tambien digo mujer. Testimonios de la mujer nicaraguense hoy.* Santo Domingo: Populares Feministas. Quotation translated by Lorna Shaughnessy.
2   1995. "One gets the feeling that two countries exist. One is hard and real and daily, in which the population suffers the stabilisation and adjustment measures even to the point of starvation. The other is imaginary, racked with politicking, in which the various actors in the political class engage in verbal duels, oblivious to the needs of the people. The citizenry, politically active up to 1992, has not lost interest in politics; the politicians have lost interest in the citizenry's concerns and needs", *Envio*, 14:167 (June) pp. 8–9.

Nóirín Clancy

BEIJING 1995

Abstract: The Fourth UN World Conference on Women was held in Beijing in September 1995. This paper presents an overview of the NGO Forum, describing the myriad of events that took place – the workshops, marches, celebrations and the endless networking. Workshops and plenaries discussed a range of issues from the conservatism and globalisation to planning alternative strategies to combat inequalities. The Irish government made many promises on a wide range of issues concerning women. The real challenge now is for NGOs and women's groups to ensure that the necessary resources are allocated to implement the actions and to monitor progress. [....]

from "Experiences of Beijing",
Volume 4, pp. 125-132

[....] The Fourth UN World Conference on Women was attended by over 30,000 women from 187 nations. China played host to 2 conferences running simultaneously, the NGO Forum for representatives of non-governmental organisations and the official conference for government representatives. The NGO Forum built on the three previous UN Conferences that marked the Decade for Women – Mexico in 1975, Copenhagen in 1980 and Nairobi in 1985. The NGO Forum was held in Huairou, a town 60km from Beijing. Its main objectives were to review progress on women's issues over the last decade, to network and celebrate and to influence the 'Platform for Action'. This document had to be agreed at the government conference and focused on 12 critical areas which included health, violence against women, education, armed conflict, the rights of the girl child, power and decision-making, economic structures and policies, human rights, media, poverty and the environment. [....]

'Look at the World Through Women's Eyes' was the theme of the more than 5,000 events held within the 42 acre site at the Forum. The events covered a wide spectrum from small workshops to panels, tribunals and plenaries with thousands of participants. The cultural programme consisted of outdoor performances, training seminars, collaborative art projects, a video festival, sculptures and cultural evenings presenting artists from the different continents. Over the 10 days, like a global arts festival, the Forum presented a wonderful display of colour, music, dance, song and celebration. [....]

The world was divided into 5 regions – Africa, Asia and the Pacific, Western Asia, Latin America and the Caribbean, North America and Europe. Each region had its own tent where information and exhibits could be displayed and meetings could be held. There were also 'diversity' tents focusing on specific groups such as older women, youth, refugees, indigenous women, women with disabilities, lesbian women, and grassroots organisations. When the going got tough there was even a 'healing tent' where you could go for massage and relaxation. [....]

Not all women at the Conference enjoyed equal rights. Women with disabilities experienced difficulty in gaining access to events. Tibetan women who tried to publicise the injustices in their country as a result of Chinese occupation received much harassment. Lesbian women were also targeted by both the press and the Chinese who confiscated information they had translated into Chinese. Unfortunately much of the media attention focused on the harassment experienced by some groups, on the bad weather, organisational problems and the visit of Hilary Clinton. The debates going on at the workshops and plenaries did not hit the headlines. Not surprisingly, the majority of the 5000 men who attended the Forum represented the world's media. China's record of human rights abuses also came in for much coverage, with, for example, attention drawn to their draconian birth control policies. [....]

Apart from networking with women from different corners of the globe, Beijing was also about making links with Irish women and learning about projects at home. One such project is an intergenerational tapestry which was on display in the Older Women's tent. This was created by the Boyle Active Group and VTOS (Vocational Training Opportunities Scheme). The tapestry was part of a project 'Women Weaving the World Together for Beijing'. [....]

Beijing was also about learning the skills of lobbying and negotiating from the more experienced UN conference-goers, such as politicians and civil servants. Meetings were arranged with Ministers Mervyn Taylor and Niamh Breathnach which gave the Irish group an opportunity to raise issues with regard to the 'Platform for Action'. [....]

Protest by Korean women. "Take Legally Responsible Measures for Sexual Slavery by Japan: Korean Council for the Women Drafted for Military Sexual Slavery by Japan".

As at many UN Conferences, at the final stages when the pressure is on to reach consensus, wording gets watered down and reservations are lodged. For groups lobbying on Third World issues and gay rights there were disappointments. No agreements were reached on increased overseas aid and cancellations of Third World debt and no agreement was reached on the recognition of gay relationships. While commitments made by Member States at the Conference are not legally binding, they do provide governments with a framework and the final document can be used as a tool to put pressure on governments. [....]

The ultimate test will be in the specific action undertaken and the resources allocated by the Irish government to ensure that commitments are followed through. Women's groups need to equip themselves with a copy of the final document produced by the Irish government so they are aware of the promises made. What is also crucial is that more women become politically active and learn the vital skills of negotiating and lobbying. Since Beijing, many talks, slide-shows and seminars have taken place to inform women about the Forum. Women development activists, academics and NGOs in Ireland have formed an alliance in the aftermath of Beijing to ensure that the Platform for Action in relation to Third World development co-operation is implemented. [....]

Beijing was more than an event; it was a powerful demonstration of women's strength, solidarity and capacity to work together to make a better world. What happens beyond Beijing is what really matters. It is a beginning, not an end. [....]

Kerry Hardie

from RESIDENTS AT THE CHATEAU LAVIGNY

1 She is the Editor of the Premier Journal of Moldova. [Valentina Se Presente]
    It is evening.
    She has changed and put on make-up.
    The flowers on the table
    wait, carefully quiet as her face.

    He takes down the atlas,
    flicks through the index
    to see where Moldova might be.
    She isn't offended. We stand,
    heads bowed to the page
    like the sunflowers we saw on the way
    that had left off their praising
    and dipped to beg grace.
    Moldova lies open before us.
    Her finger follows its border.
    The Russians have gone, the Ukraine
    has stolen the coastline, their people
    drink like Slavs, degraded.

    The man who shoots art films
    – long slow shots
    in blue light in Parisian cafes –
    turns like a lizard following a fly
    to stare at this woman
    who sits by an atlas and waits.
    She straightens, feeling his gaze.
    Her stubborn body
    won't shrink or back off.
    He understands. Both of them
    allow a dignity between them.

2 *Our Own*

    Darius, the Polish poet,
    fairly glows with pleasure when we say
    that Conrad wrote true and beautiful English.

3 *Le Cheval*

    The thing I like most about Switzerland –
    great unfenced fields of sunflowers,
    dying in the light.
    When we run out of broken-language conversation
    We play 'What animal would you be?'
    'Un cheval,' she says, quick and soft.

    The things I like most about horses –
    their strong necks, the planes of their faces,
    the way the life sits inside them.

    The things I like most about Valentina –
    her feminine hands, weight-bearing shoulders,
    the way her face lights.
    Those sunflowers. It's not because they are dying
    – dying things fill me with grief –
    but I like their bowed heads and that moulded place

    where the neck flows into the nape.
    Standing so straight, whole armies at prayer
    before the last battle is lost.

4 *Visiting the Sunflower Field*

    Now the rain is falling on the trees and on the vines,
    falling on draggled sunflower fields.
    It beats on the long windows
    that hold such blank and tender rectangles
    when they stand open in late August dusk.

Ailbhe Smyth

from 'Borderline Crosstalk: Europe 1992',
Volume 2, pp. 125-130

III Borderlines
are dangerous
complex constructs   fervent fabrications
policed realities
'the borders were fixed at Stalin's whim and
by military force'
the markers of our borders can all be shifted
made   re-made moved   re-moved
but what of gender   race   ethnicity
which remain intact   markers of another kind
for whom do borders shift?
for all the border crossings some differences
remain the same
no shift in power relations

'the peoples of Europe are from a wide variety of cultural
backgrounds'   and   foregrounds
some more fore than most
and some have no grounds
some are open territory   up for grabs
some are caught   borderline cases
'5,000 muslim refugees mostly women and children
fleeing Bosnia's hungry and war-devastated capital'
'the past year of conflict in what was Yugoslavia
has displaced 2.2 million people'
'40,000 women raped at least'
(what more can there be?)
in the name of nations   states   and freedom
where is the borderline between
nationalism   xenophobia   racism   fascism?
parallels if not synonyms
my nationalism
you feel as hatred death
not pride and glory
gynocide as genocide
your national identity
wipes me out

and off the face of the map
'the forced deportation of people is now being carried out
with military precision'
shifted across   back and forth   regardless of humanity

States of greed
Fortresses buttressed against invaders
and pollutants
nations need territories and territories need borders
and non-people need nothing

IV Crosstalk
is difficult
I can   not always   imagine
an unbordered world
shapeless   shiftless   infinite in its freedoms

I cannot redraw all the borders of my self
however they divide and separate
I cannot unlearn all the markers of MY WORLD
Whatever their origins   (or destinations)
there's always residue
what I can't excise   race   class   gender   sexuality
I carry   borders and markers   wherever I am
local or global   here or there
I cannot talk across them all   always.

Sometimes
I make do with remembering
good times
the sheets we hemmed and bordered
the cross-stitching learned from
my grandmother whose origin was in that foreign place
over the border
' a stitch formed of two stitches crossing each other
thus X'
and imagine infinite intricate cross-stitched
bordertalk

border (n) strip of ground planted with flowers shrubs
                herbaceous   *border*

Health and The Body

Cecily Kelleher

from 'Guest Introduction', *Volume 5*, pp. vii–viii

Almost invariably, when I raise the subject of women's health among health professionals the men groan and ask if surely there has not been enough attention to the subject. After all, I am told, men die younger and suffer more from the major killer diseases like cancers, cardiovascular disease and accidents. Hidden within the quantitative data, of course, is the heart of the feminist matter. For while women do live longer they also have a poorer quality of life as they age than men, carry the hidden, un-prestigious and extensive responsibility for the iceberg of health need in every country, and strive throughout to bear and rear new generations of people in a complex and unjust world. As they age they begin to catch up with men in rates of heart disease and cancers, and indeed in the case of osteoporosis suffer relatively more than men from its often fatal consequences. These are observable facts, not polemic or assertion. It is not so much a matter of whose fault it is as how it came to be so, and what might be done about it.

At the core of the women's movement, but also the health promotion movement, it is the concept of empowerment; the means of finding and articulating a voice to influence the determinants of social and physical well-being. [….] In Jakarta, 1997, at the World Health Organisation-sponsored conference on health promotion, we explored some of the political issues for which the twentieth century is likely to be remembered, including the end of colonialism, the rise and fall and re-rise of totalitarianism, and the emergence of the women's movement. When the present United Nations Commissioner for Human Rights, Dr Mary Robinson opened our Women's Studies Centre she spoke of the voice of the ordinary person and the particular position of women in the relative hierarchy of societies. The values she espoused, of participation, social support, personal development, improved primary health care and conducive public policy serve as the framework for the health promotion movement, better known as the Ottawa Charter (1986). The world over, the struggle to improve the quality of life has been a challenge for women in a way that differs from the history of the world as a story of territorialism and statesmanship written by men. [….]

Women undergo a mid-life change in physiological hormone patterns that link directly with their risk of heart disease and osteoporosis and also influence breast and uterine cancer rates. The quality of life for the older women is dependent not just on her lifestyle but also on a series of health care decisions, as for instance whether to undergo regular screening for breast or cervical disease, or whether to take hormone replacement therapy. Even the risk of sexually transmitted disease like AIDS is different for men and women, and in some parts of the world a problem of incomprehensible proportions. To what degree are decisions on these issues within the power of individual women or a matter of larger political considerations? In the next decade persuasive epidemiological evidence from clinical trials will help to resolve the basic biomedical dilemmas, but we are only beginning to ask about the emotional and psychological impact of these decisions or the means by which they are made or influenced. [….]

Understanding women's health also means understanding the position of women in society and the reasons which determine their health choices. [….]

Pádraig Ó Héalaí

Blasket Island Traditions

Abstract: In this paper some customs and beliefs associated with pregnancy and childbirth in a traditional Irish community are examined. The source material analysed is almost exclusively the folklore of the Great Blasket Island, Co. Kerry, but as much of this reflects general Irish tradition, the findings may be taken as indicative of traditional attitudes and practices concerning childbearing in many other communities, both in Ireland and in the wider European area.

from 'Pregnancy and Childbirth in Blasket Island Tradition', *Volume 5*, pp. 1-15

This paper treats some customs and beliefs associated with pregnancy and childbirth on the Great Blasket, an island lying some three miles off the coast of the Dingle peninsula in West Kerry. Life on the island is singularly well-documented as extensive collections of its folklore have been made by individual scholars, such as Robin Flower, Kenneth Jackson, Bo Almqvist and James Stewart, and still further collections have been made under the auspices of the Irish Folklore Commission, notably by Seosamh Ó Dálaigh, Mícheál Ó Gaoithín and Seán Sheáin Í Chearnaigh.[1] In addition, many accounts of island life have been provided by islanders themselves, the most widely known being the autobiographies of Tomas Ó Criomhthain, Muiris Ó Súilleabháin and Peig Sayers.[2] The population of the island was totally Irish-speaking, and ranged from 98 in 1861, to 145 in 1901, to 50 in 1947. The island was abandoned in 1953 by the few remaining families. This paper is based almost entirely on source material of Blasket provenance, but it should be noted that Blasket tradition in respect of childbearing is not *sui generis*, but rather may be taken as indicative of customs, beliefs and attitudes prevalent in many communities in Ireland, and even in the wider European area.

Attitude Towards Children

The numerous stratagems which were traditionally employed to ensure conception and increase fertility bear witness to the strong desire for offspring which prevailed in Irish marriages.[3] Consequently, it is not surprising to find evidence in folk tradition that the arrival of a new child was warmly welcomed, irrespective of the existing number of children or the economic circumstances of the family – the infant being commonly regarded as a gift from God. This receptive attitude to children is reflected in Irish proverbs, some of which also express the delight children afford parents: "A poor man never had enough children"; "A hearth without children – a sky without stars"; "The three sweetest sounds – the grinding of quernstones, the lowing of a cow and the cry of a child"; "The centre of affection in a house – the fire or a good child; "God never created a mouth for which he did not provide".[4] The sentiment expressed in this last proverb was powerfully reinforced by traditional stories which presented its message in a dramatic manner, as may be seen from the following summary of one such tale:

> There were two sisters, one married to a rich man and having no family, the other married to a poor man and having a large family. The poor sister was again pregnant so she decided to visit her rich sister in order to seek financial support and arrived at the door of the big house accompanied by all her family. The rich sister refused the request for assistance saying it was not right to bring another mouth into the world without having the wherewithal to feed it. Nine months from that day the rich sister gave birth to a child without a mouth.[5]

Bearing children was seen as having a spiritual dimension. An item collected from a Blasket midwife declares that a woman bearing a child was said to be in a sacred state, and that many sins are forgiven a mother who gives birth to twins.[6] According to a tradition attested in other parts of the country a woman who gives birth to a child in wedlock will never see hell.[7]

The openness to large families which was a characteristic of traditional communities did not mean, however, that the consequent strain on the mother was disregarded. Concern for the mother is evidenced in a number of proverbs which sound a cautionary note in regard to numerous births. For example, the proverbial expression frequently quoted by an elderly Blasket woman when referring to large families translates "If the fruit is abundant the tree is weak",[8] and another proverb, which probably refers to bearing twins, says: "A woman is the better for bearing a child but bearing two is harmful".[9]

Among the last generation of childbearing women who lived on the island, however, a new attitude to the size of families is apparent. The appropriateness of having a large family was challenged by some of this generation who held the view that parents were responsible for bringing children into the world and that they had an obligation to consider the quality of life they could offer their children. [....]

Previous generations had sought to exercise control over the size of families in restricted instances, as is evidenced by usages resorted to when childbearing was felt to be particularly difficult or dangerous for the mother. A contraceptive practice favoured by island women who were considered to be exceptionally at risk in giving birth consisted of drinking a specially prepared potion. Méiní, an island midwife, provided the following account:

> Mothers would sometimes give a drink to their daughters if childbearing was dangerous for them. They used to give them a drink to ensure they had no further children. They used to give them woad and cypress to drink.[10]

The effectiveness of this brew as a contraceptive measure is vouched for by the informant as she tells of three young girls who accidentally drank it, having mistaken it for tea, and when they subsequently married, none of them had a family.[11] Other means of contraception also feature in Blasket lore. For instance, in the case of a mother who had given birth to a stillborn child, and for whom another pregnancy was judged to be too risky, it was said that if the dead child were buried face downward, then the mother would not conceive again. This measure was also resorted to by unmarried women who had given birth and did not wish to repeat their experience. [....]

It may be of interest to mention here that the practices designed to prevent conception which most frequently feature in folk tradition are related to the malicious or vindictive use of charms intended to deprive others of children. Perhaps the most common of these was the tying of a knot (frequently at the time of the marriage ceremony) on a rowan withy or a piece of string. [….]

Stale Urine as Protection

Stale urine was widely used for practical purposes. A supply of it was a necessary requirement for the fulfilment of certain household chores – woollen thread used to be soaked in it to be cleansed of natural oil and it was also used to bleach coarse linen.[12] Stale urine was used as a detergent, a generous measure being added to the water when washing clothes, and as a medication. [….]

The powerful natural properties attributed to stale urine facilitated its employment as a protective agency against both the fairies and the evil eye. [….]

The urine was carefully collected: "There used to be a pot of it under the bed and when that was almost full it would be emptied into a small tub to mature".[13] As is usual with magical practices, it was believed that the observation of certain prescriptions would ensure the charm operated at full potency. It was said, for instance, that night urine was more powerful than day urine, that neighbours' urine had greater efficacy than one's own, and that the urine should be at least three days old before it had any power.[14] In view of the magical protection stale urine was believed to afford people in everyday life, it is not surprising that it was employed in the context of childbirth. Specifically, it was used to protect the confinement bed:

> A little bottle of holy water would then be procured and placed under the woman's head and a little bottle of stale urine would be stuck into the bed at her feet. The stale urine would also be sprinkled around the bed before cock crow for the nine nights she lay in confinement.[15]

It was used to protect both mother and child immediately after the birth:

> It had to be sprinkled every night when the child was born. Stale urine was the first thing that would be produced. It was not the holy water at all but the stale urine. It was thrown out on the dung heap and around the outside of the house. It was sprinkled on everyone inside the house and on all who came in. On leaving, people would get another splash of it to protect them from he fairies, lest the child or its mother be blighted. Yes, as defence against the enemy – the good people, or the fairies, as they were called here.[16]

> There used to be a skillet of stale urine at the lower corner of the bed and the nurse would take a drop of that in her hand and sprinkle it in

the direction of the doorway and on the confined woman and around the bed to protect her.[17] [....]

Protected Space

The custom of sprinkling stale urine demonstrates the operation of the concept of safe or protected space in folk tradition. The walls of the house afforded protection against supernatural interference, but the area outside was regarded as harbouring menaces and, consequently, all apertures – doors, windows and chimney – were sprinkled with urine. The understanding that the area within the house constituted safe space is highlighted by the reluctance of people to bring an infant into contact with the outside world so that even the journey necessitated by baptism was seen as particularly parlous requiring protective measures. According to the received wisdom no child should be brought outside the house until it was able to walk out itself, and even then, a child should never be allowed to sleep outside.[18]

Tensions and anxieties associated with pregnancy and childbirth in traditional communities were fuelled by factors such as a high infant mortality rate, the frequency with which a mother's life was endangered at birth, and an awareness of congenital malfunction and experience of serious illness in infancy. The measures employed to safeguard mother and child reflect concerns relating to these issues. In portraying the threats to mother and child as emanating from fairy interference and the evil eye, folk tradition enabled the community to exercise a measure of control over them as it also prescribed how these malign forces coule be overcome. Practices such as those outlined above can thus be seen to have been of great psychological assistance both to the individual and the community in dealing with tensions of childbearing.

Notes
1   There are c.50,000 pages of material recorded from inhabitants of the Great Blasket in the archives of the Department of Irish Folklore, NUI, Dublin.
2   T. Ó Criomhthain 1929 *An tOileánach*; 1934 *The Islandman*; 1973 *An tOileánach*; M. Ó Súilleabháin 1933 *Fiche Bliain ag Fás*; 1933 *Twenty Years a Growing*; 1976 *Fiche Bliain ag Fás*; Peig Sayers 1936 *Peig*; 1973 *Peig. The Autobiography of Peig Sayers of the Great Blasket Island*.
3   See S. Ó Súilleabháin 1942. *A Handbook of Irish Folklore*. Dublin, Folklore of Ireland Society, pp. 207, 209.
4   P. Ó Siochfhradha ('An Seabhac') 1926. *Seanfhocail na Muimhneach*. Baile Átha Cliath, An Gúm, nos. 65, 91, 1826, 90:
5   A variant of the tale summarised above was collected by Kenneth Jackson from Peig Sayers and edited by him in *Béaloideas* 8 (1938), 60 [= K. Jackson. 1968. *Scéalta ón mBlascaod*. Baile Átha Cliath, An Cumman le Béaloideas Éireann, 60]. [....]

6 IFC 1202:247. *Deir said bean a bheidh ag iompar linbh go mbeidh sí naofa agus logha mór atá ag máthair cúpla.* The reference is to ms. 1202, page 247, in the archives of the Department of Irish Folklore, NUI, Dublin.
7 IFC 1202:247; see Ó Súilleabháin, *op. cit.*, p. 209.
8 IFC 1495:35. *Más trom é an toradh is lag é an crann.*
9 *Irisleabhar na Gaeidhilge,* vol. 6 (1895), p. 40 [....]
10 IFC 1202:241.
11 IFC 1202:241.
12 Cf. Ó Súilleabháin, op. cit., pp. 406–7.
13 IFC 469:119–20. [....]
14 IFC 1494:265s
15 IFC 1202:235–6.
16 Seán Ó Criomhthain in Pádraig Tyers, *op. cit.*, p.113.
17 IFC 469:123–5. [....]
18 IFC 910:199, 229.

Anne MacFarlane

WOMEN HEALTH WORKERS

Abstract: The important health and hygiene work undertaken by women has been recognised by feminist writers.[1] Jones[2] considered the discrepancy between the fact that the role of women as promoters of good health and providers of good health care is largely unrecognised, while attributions of responsibility and blame when such roles are not performed are common. The purpose of the analysis is to examine historical and contemporary perceptions of women as health workers in Ireland. A qualitative interview survey was conducted among a nationally representative sample of 51 older people in Ireland from a possible sample of 79. Thus, a response rate of 65% was obtained. Participants provided information about responses to illness since their childhood. Material about traditional folk medicine, conventional medicine and also alternative treatments was explored. The changing role and pluralistic nature of women's health work across medical systems is discussed. [....]

from 'The Changing Role of Women as Health Workers in Ireland', *Volume 5*, pp. 17–36

[....] Impact of Health Work on Women

The impact of health and care work on the lives and health of women has been explored extensively and gender differences in health have been well documented. Essentially, while women live longer than men, they experience greater ill-health. Nettleton describes three explanations for gender differences in health – artefact, genetic and social causation. [3] The artefact explanation suggests that gender differences are merely a function of study design. Self-report studies are often used to record levels of morbidity and women may be more likely to 'admit' to symptoms than men due to the socialisation processes. [....] Particular attention has been paid to the detrimental effect of the double burden and multiple roles, involving paid and unpaid work, on women's health. [....]

Project Description

As part of an on-going analysis of health practices in Ireland, a study examining trends in health service utilisation in Ireland since the late 1930s was conducted by the Department of Health Promotion, NUI, Galway. The main purpose of this study was to explore medical pluralism in Ireland. Therefore, utilisation of both conventional and non-conventional forms of medicine, with reference to traditional folk practices indigenous to Ireland, as well as 'newer' alternative treatments was examined. Interviews were conducted among a sample of older people between the ages of 69 and 72 years of age. This cohort are considered to be ideally placed to discuss pluralistic medical systems due to the tradition of folk medicine during their childhood years, the rise of biomedicine during their adulthood and the current popularity of alternative therapies. Details of the study sample, research methodology and data analysis [are] discussed.

Discussion and Conclusion

In this paper it is argued that the majority of health care takes place outside of formal health care systems. [....] The influence of social factors and cultural assumptions have been discussed in relation to the lack of recognition given to women for the work completed by them. While attributions of blame are associated with instances of poor health, attributions of credit are largely lacking. The present analysis explored perceptions among older people of previous and contemporary responses to illness. Exploring both formal or conventional responses to illness, as well as more informal responses, has been particularly illuminating.

Generational differences have been identified and emerge as a strong theme within these data. Material presented from the present analysis shows that participants identified their mothers and wives as the main source of knowledge for self-care treatments in the past and also as the carers or practitioners responsible for the delivery of treatment within the home. While this health work may have been taken for granted by respondents during their childhood, some respondents seem to provide retrospective credit to their mothers for this work. Overall, however, material about the role of mothers as health workers was discussed in a matter of fact manner. [....]

Notes
1. Hillary Graham 1984. *Women, Health and the Family,* London: Wheatsheaf.
2. Helen Jones 1994. *Health and Society in Twentieth-Century Britain,* London: Longman.
3. Sarah Nettleton 1995. *The Sociology of Health and Illness.* Cambridge: Blackwell.

Margaret Hodgins and Cecily Kelleher

SOCIAL CARE WORKERS

Abstract: In recent years research attention has focused on social care services, in particular the range and extent of informal care. This research interest can be seen to occur in the context of the movement within health policy toward community based care. The vast majority of carers, both informal and formal (i.e. paid) are women. Research findings, particularly on informal carers indicate vulnerabilities in their physical and mental health and that care, for the most part, is unshared by other family members and inadequately supported by statutory health services. This paper discusses the marginal status of care-work, with particular reference to the gendered nature of social care. How this contributes to the compromised health status of carers and inadequate support services is discussed, drawing from both international studies and those conducted in the Irish context. Recommendations are made in relation to improving the quality of life, health status and working conditions of carers.

from 'Health and Well-Being in Social Care Workers', *Volume* 5, pp. 37–48

Introduction

[....] Those in receipt of social care are a heterogeneous group, but older people, persons with a learning disability and persons with mental health difficulties would be the most common client groups. Carers who are in paid employment are often termed 'formal social care workers', while those who provide care to family members or relatives, are termed informal or family carers. Family members who provide informal care have been the subject of research attention in recent years and a limited number of studies have been carried out on formal social care workers. Through the research literature on social care, there are three phenomena that appear with remarkable consistency. Carers, be they family carers or paid workers, or both, are usually women. Their mental and physical health is typically compromised when compared to matched samples of persons without onerous care responsibilities. Care is unshared by relatives, i.e. the carer has sole responsibility to a significant extent, and carers consistently report inadequate back-up or support from the formal health services. [....]

Informal Carers

Carers, where once invisible, have become a legitimate topic of discussion in public policy debate, especially in relation to support services.[1] [....] A limited number of studies have been carried out in Ireland. The first nationally representative study to be conducted on informal care was commissioned by the National Council for the Aged, and addressed a number of questions about the range and extent of informal care given to older people in Ireland,[2] and about the caring process.[3] [....]

Formal Social Care Workers

Less research has been conducted on formal social care workers than on informal carers. Virtually no studies have been conducted on nurses' aides, and very few studies have been carried out on the personal experiences of formal social care workers, or have compared the health status of formal care workers with other health care workers, non-care workers or informal carers. [....] The only comprehensive research study on the Home Help Service in Ireland was carried out by Lundstrom and McKeown.[4]

However, any real dichotomy between formal and informal care is questionable, and the distinction has been challenged, both in the context of the movement towards the use of carer allowances to pay family carers,[5] and the proliferation in the UK of 'paid volunteering' schemes mentioned by Baldock and Ungerson.[6] [....]

Gender and Care

Across a wide range of studies on informal care, it emerges that approximately three quarters of informal carers are women. Yoder, Yonker and Leaper, discussing paid care workers, comment that these are usually women.[7] In Ireland, Lundstrom and McKeown reported that almost all home helps are women. In addition to this, female informal carers are more likely to be providing informal care to highly dependent older people, are more likely to live with their care recipient and are therefore more likely to have to cope with increased dependency. [....]

Discussion

The research findings thus far present a fairly miserable picture of social care in Ireland. Demanding physical work, sometimes around-the-clock responsibilities, emotional drain and strain and increasingly limited opportunities to maintain a social life or to look after one's health. This is set against a background of possible family tension, juggling the emotional needs of family members and little or no recognition of the need for support in the form of back-up, respite or financial, by the State health services. [....] That heavy demands are placed on carers in the absence of cohesive and reliable support structure is clearly related to the fact that most carers are women. Care is predominantly undertaken by women because of powerful material and ideological forces that determine that they will do so. Ungerson argues that as long as women have an inferior position in the labour market – both in terms of access and equal pay – within the family, their paid work is seen to be more dispensable and less critical to the family's financial status. When, within a family there is a need to provide care, women seem to be the 'logical' option to either reduce their paid work or give it up altogether to provide this care. In such situations, Ungerson argues, the ideology of a woman's place being in the home, engaged in caring duties, is reinforced and thus the twin forces of the labour market and ideology interact.[8] [....]

Notes
1. J. Twigg and K. Atkin 1994. *Carers Perceived*. Buckingham: Open University Press.
2. J. O'Connor, E. Smyth and B. Whelan 1988. *Caring for the Elderly, Part I: A Study of Carers at Home and in the Community*. Dublin: National Council for the Aged.
3. J. O'Connor and H. Ruddle 1988. *Caring for the Elderly, Part II: The Caring Process: A Study of Carers in the Home*. Dublin: National Council for the Aged.
4. F. Lundstrom and K. McKeown 1994. *Home Help Services for Elderly People in Ireland*. Dublin: National Council for the Elderly.
5. C. Ungerson. 'Gender, Cash and Informal Care: European Perspectives and Dilemmas.' *Journal of Social Policy*. 24:1, pp. 31–52.

6. J. Baldock and C. Ungerson 1991. 'What D'ya Want if Ya Don' Want Money' in M. MacClean and D. Groves, eds., *Women's Issues in Social Policy*. London: Routledge.
7. J.A. Yoder, J.M.L. Jonker and R.A.B. Leaper, eds. 1985. *Support Networks in a Caring Community*. Dordrecht: Martinus Nijhoff.
8. C. Ungerson 1983. 'Why Do Women Care?' in J. Finch and D. Groves, eds., *A Labour of Love: Women, Work and Caring*. London: Routledge & Kegan Paul.

Catríona Marie Brennan

STAFF IN DOMESTIC VIOLENCE SHELTERS

Abstract: This article is based on research among women working in 19 domestic violence shelters in Ireland and Australia. The research aims to determine why women decide to work in this area and what keeps them there. A secondary research concern is to consider the impact of traumatic stress on workers' symptoms of burnout. The study found that the majority of women interviewed had personal experience of violence in their lives. Levels of idealism appeared high among women working in the area. Although training levels offered appeared good, some discrepancies were found with regards to the levels of management supervision reported. Initial indications were that although turnover and absenteeism were reportedly low, perceptions of staff relations and staff well-being showed signs of strain. [....]

from 'Factors Impacting on the Motivations of Staff Working in Domestic Violence Shelters', *Volume 9*, pp. 15-37

The Experiences of Staff Working in Domestic Violence Shelters

In Ireland and Australia [....] the ethos traditionally governing service provision has been one of mutual self-help and empowerment of women. Most refuges offer crisis accommodation and support as well as helpline services. In the better-resourced cases, outreach, court accompaniment and education programmes may also exist and contribute to a social change agenda of these organisations. [....]

When staff witness women attempting to leave and being repeatedly let down by the system, they feel frustrated and disillusioned. Low wages and poor conditions of employment are also negative factors identified by recent Irish research, *A Space to Grow*, impacting on the well-being of staff. The existence of poor structural support is an additional factor that has been identified as impacting on the prevalence of stress among workers employed in refuges.

From the research on traumatology, the effects of post-traumatic stress on victims of trauma is well documented, however most research excludes the effect on support workers, of witnessing the trauma of others regularly. [....]

Although many helpers report that they are pleased to be supportive of victims, secondary exposure to traumatic stress can negatively impact on them. The effects can be similar to those experienced by the victim of the primary event and may include intrusive images, emotional numbing, dissociation, nightmares or exaggerated startle response.[1] Refuge staff are exposed to such secondary traumatic stress on an ongoing basis when they work with women who relate their stories of rape, sexual abuse and other forms of victimisation and violence. [....]

> In 1997, the Irish Government Task Force on Domestic Violence acknowledged a lack of clear national policy on the development of refuges and made a number of recommendations to remedy this situation. One of the recommendations was that the Health Boards should take primary responsibility for the planning and development of refuges and the financing thereof. Continuation of contracting arrangements with voluntary agencies for the provision of these services was recommended to continue, conditional on groups meeting the specified criteria in relation to access and the quality of services. [....]

The Task Force also identified the core role of refuges in offering safe accommodation and support to any woman who requires it, encouraging each woman to determine her own future, recognising and caring for the emotional needs of children, and providing a comprehensive, client-centred back up service. A further recommendation of this Task Force also included the professionalisation of staff through the development of counselling skills and accreditation. However, absent from this remit for refuges is the inclusion of social change work. Rather, the focus is solely on the provision of services to women as individual victims. The difficulty with this approach is that instead of locating the problem within the broader social system where it needs to be challenged and addressed at every level, the victim is dealt with as an individual and continues to be isolated and most often further abused by the system [....]

Note
1   B Hudnall Stamm, E.M. Varra, L.A. Pearlaman & E.Giller 2002. *The Helper's Power to Heal and To Be Hurt - or Helped - By Trying*, Washington, D.C., National Register of Health Service Providers in Psychology.

Jane Sixsmith, Emer McCarthy, Ethna Shryane

WOMEN'S ATTITUDES TO HEALTH

Abstract: Women's knowledge, beliefs and attitudes relating to health influence their health behaviours. The majority of research to date has focused on women in their reproductive years and there has been little exploration of older women's attitudes in relation to health. This paper reports on studies which examine the knowledge, beliefs and attitudes of women aged 50-65 years on specific aspects of their health. These are the menopause, hormone replacement therapy, breast cancer and mammography screening. The participants for this study were accessed through general practice patient lists, both private and General Medical Services. Data were collected through a postal questionnaire and focus groups. These combined data reveal a lack of knowledge of health issues specific to this group. Fear was the overriding emotional reaction expressed as a result of this lack of knowledge. Participants stated that, while previously the health of others, usually children, had been their main concern, they were beginning to focus attention on themselves. The general practitioner was cited as an appropriate and accessible source of health information. The active provision of information by general practitioners has the potential to promote health to women of this age group. [....]

from 'Women's Attitudes to the Menopause, HRT, Breast Cancer and Mammography Screening', *Volume 5*, pp. 49-63

Women's Knowledge and Attitudes to the Menopause and HRT

Sociological studies have confirmed the importance of cultural and social factors in determining women's attitudes to the menopause. The age at which menopause is experienced by women is consistent across countries, i.e. at about age 50. However, symptoms reported by women from various cultures vary greatly. In the Western world the menopause is associated with ageing and a wide range of symptoms are reported, while in some Asian countries menopause is perceived as the end of social restrictions and taboos, and is consequently regarded as symptom free.[1] [....]

Breast Cancer and Mammography Screening

Breast cancer is the leading cause of cancer deaths in Irish women. Ireland has one of the highest rates of breast cancer in Europe. [....] The nature of many of the risk factors identified prevent their use in primary prevention, as they are not open to modification. Therefore, screening, while not reducing incidence, is generally considered to be the approach of choice in reducing morbidity and mortality. [....]

Women's Health and Irish General Practice

Doctor recommendation appears to influence health issues for women in this age group. In Ireland it is likely that the first contact women have with the health services is the general practitioner (GP). It has been found that women use GP services more than men. It has also been found that those in lower socio-economic groups experience more chronic illness, with resultant increased utilisation of GP services, than those in higher socio-economic groups.[2]

Health Education and Health Promotion for Women in this Group

Traditional models of health education suggest that if knowledge about the health consequences of behaviours were changed, then attitudes and, subsequently, behaviour itself would also change. Thus, for example, if more information is provided to women about breast cancer and mammography screening, then they are more likely to attend. This has now come to be considered as simplistic, as it has been found that in a number of settings, including mammography screening, increased awareness and knowledge have not been translated into changes in behaviour. [....]

Women's Health and Feminism [....]

Hormone replacement therapy has been considered by some in the feminist movement as the medicalisation of women's lives by the male dominated medical establishment.[3] The menopause is defined by this establishment as a 'disease' to be managed by the so-called "Masters of Menopause", as opposed to a natural event in a woman's life.[4] However, an alternative feminist perspective has been presented that criticises the medical establishment, not for prescribing HRT but for denying women access to it.[5] The study described here explores the levels of knowledge of women aged 50–65 years in relation to the menopause, HRT, breast cancer and mammography screening. The participants were all accessed through general practice, and the feasibility and acceptability of this approach is also considered.

Conclusion

These studies demonstrate that women, especially blue collar women in mid-life, lack knowledge of issues of direct concern to their health, which limits their ability to make informed choices. Information on these issues needs to be acceptable and accessible to all women and specifically targeted to their needs. The GP is in an ideal position to provide this information to facilitate women's decision making and so enable women to take control of their own health. [....]

Notes
1. Ane McPherson. *Women's Problems in General Practice*, Chap. 7, pp. 198–226.
2. Brian Nolan 1991. *The Utilisation and Financing of Health Services in Ireland*. Dublin: The Economic and Social Research Institute, pp. 81–93.
3. R. Klein, L.J. Dumble 1994. 'Disempowering Mid-life Women. The Science and Politics of Hormone Replacement Therapy (HRT)', *Women's Studies International Forum*, 17, pp. 327–343.
4. Germaine Greer 1991. *The Change, Women, Ageing and the Menopause*. London: Penguin.
5. J. Lewis 1993. 'Feminism, the Menopause and Hormone Replacement Therapy,' *Feminist Review*. 43, pp. 39–56.

Helen Mortimer

Body Image

Abstract: This paper addresses the issue of gender and body image, an issue which continues to have far-reaching implications for women's health, both physical and psychological. It analyses the marketing of body image for women by mass media, and reviews feminist responses to the issue from the 1970s to the 1990s. What emerges from this review is that little has changed in the media and its promotion of 'thinness' for women, since the advent of the women's movement. Body image as a social construct continues to be a key influencing factor in the development of eating disorders. The paper also stresses the need for further research on both eating disorders and women's attitudes to their own bodies.

from 'For Women Only - Why Fat is a Gender Issue', *Volume 5*, pp. 111-122

How a Woman is Measured

A woman is often measured
By the things she cannot control
She is measured by the way her body curves
Or doesn't curve, by where she is flat or straight or round.

> She is measured by 36–24–36
> And inches and ages and numbers,
> By all the outside things that don't ever add up
> To who she is on the inside.
>
> And so, if a woman is to be measured
> Let her be measured
> By the things she can control, by who she is and who she is trying to become.
>
> Because as every woman knows
> Measurements are only statistics
> And STATISTICS LIE
>
> *Anonymous*

For six years I wrote a column in a local newspaper which dealt with issues relating to women. Article after furious article was churned out denouncing the insidious pressure on women to be ever dieting, ever shrinking, in an attempt to conform to some unhealthy and specious ideal. And yet … when I found myself able to zip up a pair of size 12 jeans, my reaction was one of pure ideologically unsound joy. When my friends commented that I had lost weight I was delighted. And I definitely felt better thinner than fatter. And so, as Susie Orbach suggested, it seemed to me almost like a travesty – a feminist concerned about how I looked. Did this mean I had sinned against sisterhood? Does being a good feminist mean being in bad shape? Was I somehow colluding in the whole business of warped body-image and anxious self-flagellating pseudo perfectionism? Why should it be better to be a size 12 than a 14? Put like that, it's a trite question: one of the central tenets of feminism is that judgements about who we are and what we think should not be made on the strength of our appearance or our vital statistics. If, as Orbach taught us, we're entitled to be fat, surely we're also allowed to be thin. [….]

For as long as records have been kept and history has been written, the female body has been seen as something to control and master. Whether it is in the form of Chinese foot-binding, female circumcision, the wearing of corsets or under wired push-up bras, women's bodies have been viewed with an eye to changing them. In the early days of the Women's Liberation Movement, women came together to unravel some of the ways in which their experiences as women had moulded a particular self-identity. At the heart of this identity lay feelings of unentitlement, neediness, confusion around dependency needs, a taboo on feelings of anger, conflict around sexuality and a preoccupation with body image as a vehicle of self-expression.[1] [....]

Daily conversations and the popular press clearly indicate the importance of weight in women's lives. Bulimia and anorexia nervosa are now so prevalent that they affect more than 1 in 100 women in Western Europe. Gillian Moore-Groarke reports that almost 20% of Irish people are affected by the agony of eating disorders.[2] In a recent survey conducted by Moore-Groarke, of 3,000 people aged between 15–30, one in five had an eating disorder, 60% suffered from obesity, 35% had anorexia and 5% suffered from bulimia. Naomi Wolf quotes a figure of 150,000 women dying of the effects of anorexia in the US every year.[3] No one is very concerned by statistics showing that 80% of women in countries like the US, Britain, New Zealand and Australia are dieting at any given moment. The anguish behind these figures is obscured by an attitude that accepts this as the norm and sees no need for further questions. Women like to diet. Women expect to diet. Women have a tendency to fat. Women are always so self-involved.[4]

Only a handful of specialist treatment centres exist and little funding is available for research to combat these problems. Is this because the majority of sufferers are women? If 1 in 100 men suffered from eating disorders would more money be available and more done to eradicate eating disorders? The fact is that hundreds of thousands of individual women with eating problems do not represent a constituency. Although they share many of the same problems, it is their lack of collective engagement that keeps their problems hidden, unrecognised and inadequately considered. [....]

Notes
1   S Orbach 1978. *Fat is a Feminist Issue*, London: Hamlyn.
2   G Moore-Groarke and S Thompson 1995. *When Food Becomes Your Enemy*, Cork: Mercier.
3   N . Wolf 1990. *The Beauty Myth*, New York: Morrow.
4   S Orbach 1993. *Hunger Strike*. London, Penguin.

Mike Power

Osteoporosis

Abstract: In recent years there has been a large increase in the awareness of diseases of the elderly, such as cancer, stroke and osteoporosis. This has coincided with the increase in the age profile of the population of countries throughout the European Union and worldwide. However, this increased awareness of medical conditions has also coincided with the increased affluence of the society which we live in today. This affluence has led people to feel that they should not be limited by their increased susceptibility to conditions such as osteoporosis. Osteoporosis is the basis of this paper and I will deal with both its onset and ways to alleviate its main resulting problem, which is the increased susceptibility of bone to fracture.

from 'Osteoporosis: An Inevitable Consequence of Ageing?', *Volume 5*, pp. 65-79

[....] 1. Introduction to Bone

Bone is the main organ that gives the body its form and shape. The bone frame supports body tissues, protects vital organs, facilitates locomotion and provides attachment sites for muscles and tendons. This is the basic anatomical function of bone tissue and is of fundamental importance to the gross structure and movement of the person. Equally important, however, is that bone also provides the basic storage site for body reserves of calcium, phosphate and many other mineral ions. These mineral reserves facilitate the physiological function of bone, and are of vital importance to normal body metabolism. [....]

In osteoporosis, the amount of effective bone structure is reduced to levels below the fracture threshold and this low mineral density ultimately leads to increased risk of fracture. The fracture threshold is the level of bone mineral density (BMD) below which fractures will occur, after minimal stress is exerted on the bone tissue. Osteoporosis can also occur, however, in certain medical conditions, where either the condition itself (diabetes, renal failure), or its treatment regimens (anti-epileptics, corticosteroids etc) lead to decreased BMD. This reduction in BMD occurs mostly due to either a decreased ability to absorb calcium effectively in the intestine, or a reduced ability to make properly mineralised bone matrix. Many clinical conditions and treatments lead to a more rapid onset of fracture, as they lead to large increases in cellular activities. This increased cellular activity, and therefore BT, tend to increase the rate at which bone tissue is lost, due to the more rapid rate of BT. [....]

When BT goes out of control, the increased, or decreased, cellular activity can lead to harmful effects on the bone matrix. In fact, when there is even a slight imbalance in either of the two cellular activities, osteoblastic or osteoclastic, this can have serious effects on bone structure and metabolism. This imbalance can occur due to increasing age, where it leads to a condition called osteoporosis. The age-related osteoporosis sub-types are sub-divided into two main categories. *Type* 1, which affects mostly women after the menopause and is therefore commonly called post-menopausal osteoporosis. *Type* 2, which affects both men and women in later life and is therefore commonly called age-related, or senile osteoporosis. *Type* 1 osteoporosis mostly affects bones of the hip, spine and sites rich in spongy bone, while *Type* 2 affects both bone types equally. *Type* 1 osteoporosis is mostly related to increased osteoclastic activity and is the cause of rapid bone loss after the menopause. This rapid onset is thought to be mainly due to the loss of steroid hormones which occurs at the menopause and has an increased effect on spongy bone. *Type* 2 affects spongy and compact bone alike. It is not accelerated, because the compact bone matrix is not very active. It is thought to be due mainly to decreased osteoblastic activity. [....] it is now accepted that BMD decreases with age in both men and women. [....]

In women, this age-related decrease in the amount of functional bone mass (BMD) begins either just prior to, during, or shortly after the menopause. Just as BMD decreases with age, so also the risk of developing a fracture increases. Therefore, it is recommended to maintain BMD at as high a value as possible for your age. This decrease in BMD observed with increasing age is true for every skeletal site measured to date. However, actual BMD values vary for these different sites due to the different ratios of compact and spongy bone occurring at these locations. Though there are many risk factors associated with the development of osteoporosis, such as balance, certain medical treatments, leanness etc, the increased susceptibility to fracture is thought to be most closely related to BMD itself. [....]

Some of the most important factors associated with osteoporosis over which we have control are lifestyle, nutritional and social factors. Over the past ten years there has been an increased awareness that physical activity is good for both lipid metabolism and the circulatory system. This has lead to a huge increase in the number of people walking, jogging, dancing and taking light weight-bearing physical exercise. Where this increased physical activity involves taking weight-bearing exercise, it is also good for the bone tissue because the increased stresses to which the bones are subjected during this exercise help to increase the ability of bone tissue to resist subsequent stress and fracture. The non-weight bearing activities such as swimming (though very good for your heart, muscle and lipid metabolism), do not have much direct effect on bone density. One must keep in mind, however, that in women, though this light exercise has beneficial effects on bone tissue, too much exercise can lead to a reduction in BMD. This is due to the effect of excessive exercise on the normal female monthly ovarian cycles. As a result it is essential that women take adequate exercise, but not take it to excess. [....] Exercise is probably one of the most under-estimated factors in the prevention of osteoporosis today. Lifestyle factors such as smoking, inactivity, nulliparity, excessive exercise, early menopause and late menarche are all recognised as factors which may accelerate the onset of bone loss and osteoporosis. [....] Specifically, lack of exercise leads to a reduced ability of bone tissue to resist stress imposed on it and therefore an increased likelihood to fracture. [....]

There are many proposed therapies for the treatment of osteoporosis. All of these treatment regimens either utilise medication to decrease the rate at which bone turnover occurs, or directly inhibit the activity of osteoclasts. The most prevalent method used in the recent past has been hormone replacement therapy (HRT), though this has come under severe scrutiny due to the inherent fear of developing cancer.

Together with the decreased activity profile of younger people in recent years. there is also an increased consumption of highly carbonated (fizzy) drinks. This is especially prevelant in the western world among younger females. However it has now realised that the increase in these carbonates can also lead to a decreased ability on the intestine to absorb the essential calcium mineral from the diet. This will leads over time to a decreased bone density (BMD) and consequently an increased susceptability to fracture. [....]

Though HRT has been shown to be beneficial for both the circulatory system and bone structure, there are some medical conditions [....] under which it cannot be recommended, and therefore new medications have been developed. [....]

Osteoporosis, particularly post-menopausal osteoporosis is a very common, morbid, and extremely painful disease. The therapeutic agents now used, or in the process of being developed, offer some expectation of reducing the incidence of fracture in recent years. It must, however, be remembered that individual patients' responses to these different medications will vary, and so the selection of an ideal answer to a complex problem will need careful and thoughtful selection of the various medications. We are, therefore, moving slowly closer to the answer to the osteoporosis problem. We can only live in the knowledge that work is ongoing in several areas and with many compounds which may reduce the incidence of this condition in the future. [....]

Cecily Kelleher

HRT

Abstract: There has been considerable recent interest in the use of hormone replacement therapy for healthy women who are without symptoms associated with menopause. The controversy has generated strong feminist arguments on either side. A core element of the modern women's movement is the extent to which women are being disempowered by interference in their own reproductive function. The Health Promotion movement concerns itself with the capacity of individuals to take control of their own health. There is much focus on lifestyle change as part of this. This paper explores the epidemiological evidence relating one key condition, coronary heart disease, to gender. It then examines why hormone replacement therapy, rather than natural menopause, might protect against this risk. This exposes the ultimate paradox; is there a sense in which it could be empowering to choose an artificial rather than a natural course of action to protect against one aspect of long-term ill health? Does protection of the physical heart undermine the spiritual heart of health promotion?

from 'Hormone Replacement Therapy: Is it Good for Women's Health?', *Volume 2*, pp. 153-158

At the turn of the century, Picasso produced a painting entitled 'Science and Charity,' now housed in his dedicated museum in Barcelona.[1] The painting is remarkable in several respects. Firstly, stylistically, it belongs to a more literal period in his development. Secondly, its subject is sombre and narrative in form. It depicts a moribund young woman being tended on the one hand by an elderly paternalistic male physician and on the other by a Carmelite nun, holding a distressed and yearning child. It encapsulates remarkably well the spirit of medical practice at the time and provides an apposite contrast for such practice today. The stereotypes have been radically undermined since then and the gender suppositions, in the case of the carers at least, are no longer automatic. Moreover, we have lost the fear of childbirth that so significantly shaped the evolution of obstetrical practice. What is true now and then, however, is that the spectre of young death is haunting and emotive, whether from tuberculosis then or AIDS-related disease now. The so-called medicalisation of health has been challenged by feminist theory on the basis of its dis-empowerment of women by a dominant male medical establishment, A central component of Germaine Greer's book on the menopause, *The Change*[2] is that a misogynistic, medical establishment continues to exploit women through what should be a natural life-stage, abetted by a largely ageist Western world culture.

In parallel with this, the health promotion movement has also grown up. This contains elements of the same criticism of the direction of health policy generally, but not solely from a gender-based perspective. It is underpinned particularly by the recognition that technological, hospital-based medicine has been overwhelmed by client demand due to the prevalence of extremely common, serious and relatively irremediable disease conditions like heart disease and cancers. Paradoxically, these have a largely preventable component.[3] This movement has grown beyond the basic preventative medicine perspective (which retains the biomedical model) to a more holistic perspective and finally to a positive definition of health as a resource for every day living.

It is not incompatible to stress that health might be positively promoted while at the same time retaining a treatment model for care. What is also recognised is that individuals themselves require personal skills to make health-promoting choices and also, crucially, the freedom of social opportunity in which to do so. There is more than one school of health promotion, but the notion of personal empowerment is key to the Ottawa Charter, which stresses the need for healthy public policy, supportive environments, community participation, personal skills and finally a health service reoriented toward primary care which is client-oriented and philosophically more holistic.[4]

What should concern us is our vision of health for women in the next century, including the attributes and values we wish to maintain. There are two key issues to be addressed: what constitutes real choice for ageing women in terms of their health, and secondly, how arbitrary is naturalness in this context? Only when we can answer these questions can we respond adequately to the very real dilemmas raised by the availability of hormone replacement therapy. [....]

Notes
1   Pablo Picasso 1897. 'Science and Charity', Museo Picasso, Barcelona.
2   Germaine Greer 1991. *The Change: Women, Ageing and the Menopause*, Penguin.
3   See Cecily Kelleher 1992, 'Promoting our Health in Ireland' in *The Future for Health Promotion*, ed C. Kelleher, Galway Centre for Health Promotion Studies, and 1986. *Ottawa Charter for Health Promotion*, (Nov.).
4   *Ottawa Charter for Health Promotion*, op cit.

Esther Mary D'Arcy

ABLE-BODIED WOMEN

Abstract: This article attempts to emphasise the importance of fitness for women and offers advice on the type of exercise and the need for a daily relaxation technique. It explains the consequences of incorrect exercises, posture, and lifting. It stresses the need for educational programmes for women on fitness and health, with the emphasis on prevention rather than cure.

from "Able-Bodied Women?", *Volume 2*, pp. 159-171

[....] The course of human evolution and the development of some cultural habits that encourage physical softness help to explain why today's women more than ever need to exercise. In evolutionary terms the brain and hand have undergone amazing refinement, but the more basic parts of the body have progressed little [....] Consequently, certain points of structural weakness emerge – (A) the spine, (B) the abdominal muscles, and (C) the pelvic floor. Such weaknesses can contribute to bad posture, fatigue, backache, and stress incontinence.

(A) The Spine

[....] To protect the back it is helpful to think over the things you do regularly during a day (toe touching or tying shoe laces, picking up things from the floor, lifting babies out of cots) and analyse the movements involved and adapt the movement or the job to suit your back and not the other way around. Ways of correcting this unnecessary pressure on the back include pelvic-tilting (backward tilting of the pelvis to reduce the curve of the lower spine) in standing, sitting and lying. Apart from actual pelvic tilting, it can be achieved by having the knees higher than the hips when sitting (five degrees is sufficient), bending up the knees when lying on your back, and putting one foot on a bar or step in front of you when standing. Pelvic tilting as an exercise strengthens both abdominal and back muscles.

The posture of forward tilting of the pelvis may often be further exacerbated, unnecessarily, in pregnancy. There is no contra-indication to pelvic tilting (i.e. pulling in the tummy!) and in fact it is beneficial to continue correcting the position throughout pregnancy to maintain or strengthen abdominal and back muscles. The increased pressure of the growing baby is then more evenly distributed between the mother's feet, rather than in front of them. Often, pelvic tilting alone is sufficient to prevent or relieve the backache that is so common in pregnancy [….]

(B) The abdominal muscles

These muscles are rarely used in an average day and are exercised only when they work against resistance such as lifting and walking uphill. It is difficult to strengthen abdominals properly because of an associated muscle group, the hip flexors (which bring the leg forward in walking). Double straight leg raising and sit-ups are often recommended in women's magazines for toning up the abdominals. They can be injury-provoking and ineffective; they exercise the hip flexors mostly and can cause back pain by pulling on the joints of the lumbar spine. Proper and effective abdominal exercises must protect the lower back from the adverse pull of the hip flexors and control leverage and resistance from gravity. Sit-ups can be modified by bending the knees, this flattens and mechanically protects the lower back [….]

(C) The pelvic floor

The pelvic floor, unlike the abdominals, has much more work to do since humans, especially females, became upright. It has to (1) provide sphincter control of the three perineal openings; (2) support the contents of the pelvic cavity; and (3) withstand the forces of gravity and increased pressure within the body during, e.g. lifting, laughing, coughing. All this work is done by a sling of muscles, suspended from the coccyx behind to the pubis in front [….] The potential problems in human design have existed since becoming upright, but 'progress,' in the form of labour-saving devices, though most welcome, have 'freed' women from the type of physical work in which muscular development compensated for these structural weaknesses. In Western women, the pelvic floor muscles are under-utilised compared with those who perform all domestic and social functions while squatting or without the support of a chair [….]

Stress incontinence is the involuntary leakage of urine during times of increased intra-abdominal pressure, e.g. coughing, sneezing, and laughing, when the power of the pelvic floor muscles is insufficient to counteract the pressure. It can occur in any age group and the effects are many. Apart from the obvious distress and inconvenience, discomfort and embarrassment, women have to contend with associated problems [....] Weakness in the vaginal and urethral walls can lead to prolapse of the womb or bladder, respectively. This feeling, described so often by women as 'something coming down,' (S.C.D.) is alleviated while lying down, but come the morning, and from the time of rising, gravity encourages the prolapse on its descent, unimpeded by the weakness of the structure, as far as, and beyond, the perineal openings [....] The onus is on those of us who know to spread the word, to educate to prevent. We must ensure such notions as, 'you have to put up with it' and 'it's part of being a woman' are incorrect and unacceptable [....] It is incumbent upon us to ensure that women are not, due to lack of information, condemned to a life of wet pants. We must dispel the idea that the 'gynae repair' is inevitable when the reason for it could have been preventable. We must work to provide the opportunity for all women to avail of preventative medicine, information about understanding and controlling their own bodies and consequently their own lives [....]

Sheila Street

WOMEN AND HIV

Abstract: Women are being infected with the Human Immunodeficiency Virus (HIV) at an increasing rate worldwide, and there is a need for information which is aimed specifically at women. This article provides information for women who are HIV+, and for those who do not know their HIV status, examining in particular the effects new treatment options and medical advances have had on managing the virus and preventing its spread during pregnancy and childbirth. While medically the prognosis for people who are HIV+ and are availing of combination drug therapy is very good, socially the stigma which is faced by people who are HIV+ remains the same. There is a definite need for services which can be accessed by women who are HIV+, and which take a holistic approach to the difficulties these women may be facing.

from "Women and HIV",
Volume 5, pp. 81-90

In most parts of the world the Human Immunodeficiency Virus (HIV) is infecting women at a faster rate than men. In some areas, for example sub-Saharan Africa, for every 10 men infected with HIV there are 12 women. This trend makes it extremely important for information about the virus to be aimed specifically at women. Physiologically, women are more likely to be infected with HIV by sex with a man than vice versa. While estimates of transmission rates vary, it is suggested that vaginal intercourse with an HIV infected person is between 2 and 20 times more risky for a woman than a man. Increasing this vulnerability to infection is the fact that many women begin having sexual intercourse at a young age, and are often younger than their partners. Trauma during sexual intercourse is more likely in an immature genital tract where the vaginal walls are thin, as is the case with young women and girls – this also makes their infection with HIV more likely.

Women who have been infibulated (subjected to 'female circumcision') have a heightened vulnerability to HIV infection, as intercourse will cause bleeding. Since the practice of infibulation is often covert and illegal, the operation is likely to be carried out under conditions which themselves pose a risk of blood transmission of HIV.[1]

While it is obvious that women have an increased risk of becoming infected with HIV through unprotected vaginal intercourse, it is often forgotten that women also practice anal sex with their partners as a form of contraception, during menstruation and for pleasure. It has been suggested that up to 25% of women practice anal sex. If this is so then there are far more women than men having receptive anal sex, yet there is very little information for women on how to make this practice safer. [....]

Women with AIDS are more susceptible to cancers and infections of the reproductive tract, such as pelvic inflammatory disease (PID) and other sexually transmitted diseases (STDs). There are treatments available but it is important that these infections are detected early. It is very important that women living with AIDS, or who are HIV+, have regular pap smears so any abnormalities can be dealt with at an early stage. It is also very important for women to visit their doctor regularly and build up a good relationship with her/him, and to remember that if you are not comfortable with your doctor you should change to another. [....]

In Ireland the health needs of women who work in prostitution had been virtually ignored until HIV became a public health issue. At present there are two organisations in Dublin which offer services to women in prostitution – the Women's Health Project (WHP) and the RUHAMA project. WHP offers a wide range of services which include counselling, women's health services, support and outreach work. RUHAMA offers support, counselling, health services and outreach. Outside of Dublin the services available are either from local HIV and AIDS organisations or STD clinics, and there are no services which are directly aimed at women working in prostitution.[2]

The report *The Health Needs of Women Working in Prostitution in the Republic of Ireland,* which was commissioned by EUROPAP and the Eastern Health Board, sets out the current level of service provision in this area, and proposals for the future. This report highlights the lack of services outside of Dublin which specifically target women working in prostitution. Research needs to be carried out to ascertain the numbers of women working in prostitution in urban centres, such as Galway, Limerick, Cork and Sligo, and this information could then be used to provide the services which the women feel would be helpful. Carrying out research of this nature is very difficult unless there is a trusting relationship between the women and the researchers. This is often very hard to establish unless there are links between the women and the services already being provided. Many service providers would probably have at least one contact in their area, which could be valuable in terms of peer research.

Women working in prostitution are in a very vulnerable position in relation to HIV and STD infection, and deserve services in their localities which can provide them with information and resources for protecting themselves, as well as a user friendly service which will serve their needs. [....]

There is a very low risk of HIV transmission through sexual activity between women. Research in the area of woman-to-woman transmission has not been on a large scale, and most findings suggest that transmission of the virus occurred through other activities, such as sharing injecting equipment, blood transfusions or sex with men.[3] There is a risk of becoming infected with HIV during oral sex, and this risk can be decreased by using a square of latex to cover the genital area. Shared sex toys should always be used with condoms, which are changed for each person using them. Latex gloves can help to reduce the risk of infection involved in fingering and fisting the vagina or anus. Women in same sex relationships who wish to have children may consider self-insemination with sperm from a donor. In this case it would be in their best interests to ask the possible donor to take a HIV antibody test.

HIV has the potential to infect us all, and has already infected far too many women. Women who do not know their HIV status need to be given information which will help them to make informed decisions that may prevent them from becoming infected by HIV. Women who are HIV+ need to be supported in the decisions they make around new treatments, pregnancy, sexual relationships and other areas in their lives. Ten years into the pandemic, the reality of people with HIV and AIDS having sexual relationships is still a taboo subject in many AIDS organisations. This definitely needs to be challenged, as people do not cease to be people when they receive a HIV+ test result.

Notes
1   Keith Alcorn (ed.) 1997. *AIDS Reference Manual.* UK, NAM Publications, pp 37-38
2   Ann Marie O'Connor 1994 *The Health Needs of Women Working in Prostitution in the Republic of Ireland*, EUROPAP and the EHB (Women's Health Project), pp 19-21.
3   Alcorn, *op cit*, p. 108.

Lorna Shaughnessy

FEMALE GENITAL MUTILATION

Abstract: The health risks and suffering caused to women by female genital mutilation (FGM) require an urgent response. This paper argues for the necessity to respond in a manner that is culturally sensitive. It is important to understand female genital mutilation as a deep-rooted traditional practice in many societies, and as such it should be studied and apprehended in sociological, anthropological and political terms. Many reasons have been offered over the centuries to justify the practice of FGM: sexual, health-related, religious and social, among them. To these four categories a fifth can be added, the political, which is largely inspired by a desire to preserve cultural difference in the face of political dominance by Western socio-economic forces. It is also symptomatic of the way in which women's bodies frequently become sites of battle for cultural and political dominance. The paper also outlines current debate on the appropriateness of legislation as a first step in the campaign against FGM. It explores the ways in which differing approaches to the problem of FGM will challenge or compromise some of the values and principles that inform activism in Western societies.

from 'Female Genital Mutilation: Beyond Mutilating Mothers and Foreign Feminists', *Volume 5*, pp. 123-134

Female genital mutilation (FGM) is the direct cause of death, illness and psycho-sexual trauma amongst hundreds of thousands of women in the world today.[1] As such, it requires an urgent global response from the international community, and world health and developmental organisations. However, despite the unanimity of concern for women's health articulated by both the international community and those communities where FGM is still practised, there has been little unity of strategy in approaching the problem to date. One of the reasons for this, in my opinion, is the high moral tone that has been adopted by individuals and agencies in Europe and North America when they address this subject – a tone that has served to alienate rather than persuade communities who continue to 'circumcise' women. [....]

Dorkenoo has outlined four categories of explanations given for FGM (sexual, health, religious and social). I would add a fifth, the political, which I believe is becoming an increasingly common justification in Africa, and is largely inspired by a desire to preserve cultural difference in the face of political dominance by Western socio-economic forces. This trend is also symptomatic of the way in which women's bodies so frequently become sites of battle for cultural and political dominance, particularly in a colonial or postcolonial context. For example, in the struggle for Kenya's independence, Kenyatta, the great liberator, encouraged the most militantly nationalist tribe (the Kikuyu) to excise all their girl children as a mark of their commitment to African tradition and their resistance to British dominance. Women's bodies and women's health can easily become pawns in such battles for cultural dominance. This is, of course, directly related to the fact that women are responsible for the primary care of children and for their socialisation the world over. As a result of this, the task of preserving culture and custom most frequently falls to them. For this reason it is vital that campaigns to eradicate FGM be culturally and politically sensitive. If a political backlash is inspired by over-zealous or inappropriate campaigning then generations of women will pay the price.

So what are the most appropriate ways in which to campaign against FGM? This is a subject hotly debated in countries where women are still 'circumcised', and there is some diversity of opinion. In Nigeria, for example, I discovered that much of the debate centred on whether or not FGM should be outlawed through legislation. The pro-legislation lobby argue that Governments and States must lead by example, and take a clear stand on the issue by criminalising FGM and distancing themselves from it. They point out that all the international resolutions in place are utterly ineffective unless they are backed up by internal legislation. In addition, they stress the need for Governments to enshrine children's and women's rights in law. Apart from introducing new legislation, Nigerian campaigners suggest that the already existing charges for grievous bodily harm and surgical malpractice could be enforced immediately. [….]

Another question of strategy raised by Dr Irene Thomas, (a Nigerian member of the UN Committee on 'Harmful Traditional Practices' in Africa), is whether or not to place the campaign against FGM under the same umbrella as another traditional practice in Africa – that of tribal scarification. A generalised approach would certainly assist a public appreciation of the health risks involved such as HIV and severe infection. The fact that the practice of scarification is dying out would also lend weight to arguments in favour of changing or abandoning traditional practices. But the price to be paid is, as ever one of principle; the gendered nature of the suffering caused by FGM is diluted or lost in this kind of umbrella campaign. One way of exploiting such a campaign, however, would be to group FGM with other traditional practices that discriminate exclusively against women, as for example child marriage and premature pregnancy (a significant factor in the high incidence of vesico vaginal fistula in some areas of Nigeria), or some of the tribal customs surrounding widowhood where a widow's children can be taken from her and sent to live with other members of her late husband's family.

Health education is, I believe, the key to encouraging change from within traditional communities, and change from within will probably be more durable than that imposed by central governments whose legitimacy or agency in the lives of many citizens is at best abstract and at worst hostile. It is only by involving women in grassroots movements for health education – a subject that is specific to women and women's interests – that a link between FGM and gender awareness can be made in a non-intrusive and non-blaming way, and the pointless stereotyping of both foreign feminists and mutilating mothers can finally taken out of the equation. In this way, women may begin to perceive FGM as an area of their lives that they can influence, and where they can begin to exercise a degree of informed choice for themselves and their daughters.

Note

1   Efua Dorkenoo 1994. Cutting the Rose: Female Genital Mutilation: The Practise and Its Prevention, London: Zed Books.

Margaret Brehony

WOMEN AND HEALTH IN NICARAGUA

Abstract: This paper examines the debt crisis and structural adjustment in developing countries and its impact on women. In a review of the recent history of health care in Nicaragua, it looks at the role of the Nicaraguan women's movement, grassroots organisations and their response to the health crisis. It describes community based health projects, some of which provide health services for women, and others which use natural and indigenous medicine as an alternative means of meeting some of the community's health needs. Finally the paper attempts to convey the huge daily risks to health faced by Nicaraguan women, and their relentless struggle to empower themselves as they ate abandoned by the state, international lending institutions, and richer nations.

from 'The Health Crisis and Women in Nicaragua', *Volume 5*, pp 135-148

In a country populated by four million people, women make up 52% of the population of Nicaragua. A complex interaction of economic, cultural and social forces have created a situation that is catastrophic for women's health. This article will focus on the current economic policies adopting structural adjustment programmes (SAPs), and the devastating effect they have on the health of the Nicaraguan people, particularly that of Nicaraguan women. Structural adjustment imposes certain conditions on countries in debt to the World Bank and the International Monetary Fund. This adjustment of a debtor state's economic policy generally involves the privatisation of state-run companies, a reduction in social services such as health care and education, and the reorientation of the economy towards greater production for export. Structural adjustment has been promoted as a set of neutral economic measures designed to make the national economy more efficient, more competitive and hence able to meet its debt repayments. In practice it is not neutral and has led to greater polarisation between rich and poor and to greater exploitation of women. [....]

In December 1989, while working on a coffee co-operative farm in La Dalia, Nicaragua, I witnessed the tragic death of a twenty-eight year old woman, Luz Marina, who worked picking coffee for less than US$1 a day until her labour pains started. There was no transport to take her to the health centre four miles away. By the time she got there she had been haemorrhaging for a few hours. Her sixth child was safely delivered, but she, Luz Marina, died a few hours later. The doctor said that the haemorrhage would not have been fatal had the woman not been anaemic and malnourished due to a parasitic infection. She had haemorrhaged twice already during the pregnancy but could not afford to go for medical attention. She was illiterate, had never used contraceptives and was extremely poor. Her mother was in her forties and having reared six children of her own, took over the care of her five grandchildren and the new-born baby. She, and the oldest of her grandchildren, earned their living picking coffee. The baby died nine months later from chronic diarrhoea and dehydration due to parasitic infection. The inhuman conditions under which Luz Marina and her baby died are directly related to Nicaragua's spiralling debt to the World Bank and the International Monetary Fund. [....]

Women's Response

AMNLAE, the women's organisation of the Frente Sandinista (FSLN), was the first hope of action for the liberation of Nicaraguan women. Its main activity in the 1980s, however, was limited to traditional women's work for the party. It became a focus for mothers of those killed in action and women involved in neighbourhood committees. Closely allied to the FSLN, it reflected the patriarchal structures of the party and the traditional image of women was maintained. However, parallel to this, a dynamic and diverse women's movement began to develop, challenging the party's failure to adopt a gender-specific perspective.[1] After the 1990 elections the political changes in the country and the repercussions of SAPs had a very negative effect on women, reversing many of the achievements of the revolution by closing down children's day-centres, women's health and education programmes. There was a marked return to the exploitation of women's bodies in the mass media, and unemployment amongst women rose to over 70%. This shocking regression reverberated among women nationally, and while provoking a terrible sadness it also created an urgent need to re-think and strategize. This process of reflection culminated in a national autonomous women's conference in Managua in January 1992, the slogan of which was 'Unity in Diversity'. This call for unity came from former AMNLAE leadership, women trade union activists, women's groups, women's centres and independent women, and all those not wishing to encourage division amongst women along party political lines and with a strong feminist agenda.

The main issues discussed were:

(i) The effects of current economic policies on women's daily lives and work.
(ii) Methods and aims of organising women, how to protect the political spaces already won, and how to open up new ones.
(iii) Health and reproductive policies.
(iv) Violence against women.
(v) Relationships and sexuality.
(vi) Popular culture and its role models of discrimination against women [....]

Within Nicaragua, hope lies with the grassroots, the Women's Movement, and Community organisations. Their clear vision of their needs and of the challenges they face, together with their hard-won experience of grassroots organisation, and a truly courageous spirit, puts them in a strong position to defend the interests of women and of the popular organisations. Their voice strengthens the call for the cancellation of foreign debt, for economic restructuring and a transformation of the inhuman face of structural adjustment.

Note
1   Sofia Montenegro. 1994. "the future from a female point of view", *Companeras*, Latin American Bureau.

Timothy Collins

BRIDGET LYONS-THORNTON

Abstract: Commencing with Maria Sibylle Merian, who published accurately illustrated books on butterflies and other insects at the beginning of the eighteenth century, the life and times of various Irish women who made major contributions to natural history are included in this essay. The positive influence of the amateur naturalists' field clubs in establishing the equality of both sexes in matters of science is noted, and the development of medicine in Ireland by women in the twentieth century, notably the early BCG vaccination schemes, is detailed.

from 'Irish Women Scientists', *Volume 1*, pp. 39-53

That women have made as great a contribution to the science of natural history as men has never been seriously questioned. What is not realised fully are the extra problems which women naturalists have had to overcome down through the years. To compete on an equal footing with their male colleagues, women naturalists have had to possess exceptional qualities.

The earliest woman naturalist that I have come across has no connection with Ireland whatsoever, but is worthy of mention because she was an exceptional scientist, yet is relatively unknown today. Her name is Maria Sibylle Merian and it was only after seeing the quality of her work that I began to take note of similar work completed by Irish women naturalists. [....]

One must move forward some one hundred and fifty years to find Merian's work echoed in that of Irish women naturalists. This is partly due to the fact that it was only in the mid-nineteenth century that women could avail of the equipment and facilities previously reserved exclusively to men (as members of learned societies) and now available to the amateur naturalists' field clubs. [....]

Bridget Lyons-Thornton led a truly remarkable life. While still a medical student in UCG, she took part in the Easter Rising and later the War of Independence, ultimately rising to the rank of Commandant in the old IRA. [....] After completing her studies, Lt. Bridget Lyons-Thornton was attached to the Army Medical Service. Later in life she specialised in paediatrics, doing much pioneering work with the early BCG vaccination schemes in the 1930s and 1940s.

In 1916 Bridget Lyons was studying medicine at UCG, when, on the evening of Easter Monday, reports reached her of the fighting which had broken out in Dublin. Coming from an intensely republican Longford family, she knew that her maternal uncle Joe McGuiness (who later became a TD) was in a republican garrison that was to occupy the Four Courts. With another uncle and some friends, Bridget Lyons set off for Dublin in a hired car to join the Rising. Abandoning the car at Phoenix Park they made their way over barricades of beer barrels and carriages stripped of their wheels to join the Four Courts garrison. Bridget later said that she was dismayed to see such flimsy defenses used to oppose the might of the British Empire.

As she was only a medical student, the casualties she cared for taxed her small experience to the limit. After the collapse of the Easter Rising, the Four Courts garrison surrendered and Bridget Lyons was marched off to Kilmainham Jail where she remained for some weeks.

Lt. Bridget Lyons-Thornton

Bridget Lyons was very active during the War of Independence, smuggling ammunition and grenades to the Longford Brigade of the IRA under the command of Seán Mac Eoin. She also acted as emissary, with considerable delegated power, in Sligo at the Partition election of 1921. During this time, she also acted as a secret agent, personally responsible to Michael Collins on many missions. One of these was the collecting of intelligence relating to Seán Mac Eoin, who had been wounded and captured. Bridget Lyons found ways of visiting him in the King George V Hospital (now St Bricin's). Her information was used by Emmet Dalton in his attempt to free Mac Eoin.

In the midst of all this activity she managed to complete her studies and graduated in 1922. Michael Collins thought so highly of her that he offered her a commission in his newly founded Army. Bridget Lyons was commissioned as a First Lieutenant some weeks after Michael Collins' death and has the unique distinction of being the first, and for nearly 60 years, the only woman to hold a commission in the Irish Army. It seems almost appropriate that the next woman to hold a commission (Margaret Flanagan, in 1981) was also a doctor.

As an officer, Lieut. Bridget Lyons worked with the first Director of the Army Medical Service, Major General Maurice Hayes. [....] One of her areas of responsibility was Kilmainham Jail where many women prisoners of the Anti-Treaty forces were incarcerated. These women were extremely resentful of the fact that their former friend and comrade was now in the Free State Army.

It was at this time that she met her future husband, Capt. Eddie Thornton. Both of them had contracted tuberculosis and both availed of a special arrangement for sending tuberculosis patients to Switzerland. At the time it was believed, erroneously, that the higher levels of ultra violet rays available in sunlight at high altitude had a beneficial effect on the control of tuberculosis. Bridget Lyons-Thornton responded to treatment that she knew was very primitive and of low efficiency. Her husband never fully recovered and he died in 1924. Subsequently, Bridget Lyons-Thornton resigned her commission and pursued a long and active career specialising in paediatrics and public health. She took part in the early BCG vaccination schemes organised by Dorothy Price. She always felt strongly that women had a very important part to play in many occupations which had traditionally been the exclusive preserve of men. Bridget Lyons-Thornton died in 1987 and was buried on Easter Monday, almost exactly 71 years after the fateful day she left UCG to take part in the Easter Rising. [....]

NURSES IN THE WEST OF IRELAND

from 'Lady Dudley's Scheme for the Establishment of District Nurses in the Poorest parts of Ireland', *Volume 5*, pp. 149-153

[....] In 1903, Rachel Dudley, wife of the Lord Lieutenant, concerned at the extreme poverty in the West of Ireland, wrote letters to the Irish newspapers to collect money to provide a district nursing service along the Western seaboard:

Vice-Regal Lodge, April 23rd, 1903

Sir,

During the months I have spent in Ireland constant appeals have been made to me, from the poorest and most congested parts of the country, for help towards providing District Nurses, and the great need for assisting the people in this direction has been brought home to me very forcibly in many different ways.

Queen Victoria's Jubilee Institute for Nurses provides for the thorough training of suitable District Nurses, and much excellent work is being done under its supervision in many places in Ireland; but it is obliged, except in a few special cases, to leave the maintenance of Nurses, once started, to local effort.

The average annual cost of maintenance of each nurse is about £100, and it is just in those places where the need for such nurses is greatest, on account of the extreme poverty of the people, that it is impossible to obtain the necessary funds locally. In many of the very poor districts there are no resident gentry and no well-to-do inhabitants of the middle classes, and because of their poverty the people themselves are not able to make any contribution.

I recently approached the Central Authority of Queen Victoria's Jubilee Institute for Nurses with a view to securing their co-operation in providing and maintaining Nurses in these districts, where the need for them is so acute; and I am happy to be able to announce that the Committee have generously voted a sum of £180 per annum to form the nucleus of a special fund to be raised for that purpose, and they have also undertaken to supervise the Nurses through their Dublin Branch.

Four Nurses, maintained by funds raised outside the neighbourhoods in which they work, are already established in congested districts. Two are supported by a Manchester fund, the West of Ireland Association, one by the Irish Homestead newspaper, and one in Achill mainly by Queen Victoria's Jubilee Institute. The work done by these Nurses is admirable and my knowledge of the usefulness of their ministrations encourages me to appeal to the public for funds to provide similar assistance throughout the many other congested areas of Ireland

I feel sure that all who know anything of the misery which prevails among the people in some of the poverty-stricken country districts, will recognise how much may be done for the relief of their immediate necessities, and the improvement of the conditions under which they live, by the establishment among them of thoroughly trained and capable District Nurses.

It is with confidence, therefore, that I appeal for subscriptions to a fund to be expended in establishing and assisting to maintain Nurses in the poorest of the country districts of Ireland.

I shall be happy to receive contributions, in the form of Donations or of Annual Subscriptions, or they may be sent to the Secretary of the Bank of Ireland, marked 'Lady Dudley's Fund for Jubilee Nurses'.

Yours faithfully, RACHEL DUDLEY

The response to Lady Dudley's scheme was both 'generous and encouraging' according to the first annual report, and the committee set to work immediately to putting the scheme in place and appointing the first Nurses as quickly as possible. James Murray details the establishment of the first nurses in Connemara, who were appointed over the first few years of the Scheme:

> The first Lady Dudley nurses in Connemara were Elizabeth Cusack, appointed to Bealadangan in August 1903, and Catherine Wills to Carna in October 1903. The 'Lady Dudley Nursing Scheme' expanded rapidly along the Western Seaboard: in County Galway nurses were appointed to Roundstone in 1904, to Spiddal in 1904, to Recess in 1909, to Lawrencetown in 1908, to Clifden in 1911 and to Moycullen and Killanin in 1919. Annie M. P. Smithson, later a well-known novelist, was the first nurse in Lawrencetown.

The First Annual Report of the Scheme details the appointment of the first two Nurses, including Nurse Elizabeth Cusack, pictured below:

NURSE CUSACK AT WORK

The 17th of August, 1903, was a red letter day to the supporters of the Scheme, for it saw the establishment of their first two Nurses, Nurse McCoy at Geesala, Co. Mayo and Nurse Cusack at Bealadangan, Co. Galway. Geesala, in the parish of Bangor, is on a peninsular [sic] filled by a wide and desolate bog, along the edge of which are scattered its 2,000 inhabitants, and which forms the Nurse's district. Bealadangan is situated on an isthmus connecting the islands of Lettermore, Lettermullen and Gorumna with the mainland. This densely populated neighbourhood is one of the most poverty-stricken in Ireland, and there is certainly no district in the country in which the services of a Nurse are more urgently required.

Within a short time, the first appointees had become fully involved in their task, with Lady Dudley continuing to encourage all forms of philanthropic support given to them. In 1905 her personal secretary, Dorothea Keyes, wrote a letter to Mr P. D. Conroy of Rosmuc to thank him for help given to Nurse Cusack during the course of her duties in the locality. [....]

As Ireland's 'social and economic salvation' was pursued in various ways over the following decades, the scheme born of Lady Dudley's personal initiative in 1903 was further developed, becoming an integral part of healthcare provision in the West. James Murray summarises its history over the course of this century:

> The tragic death by drowning of Lady Dudley at Screeb in 1920 did not affect the scheme and for half a century after the establishment of the Irish Free State, the Lady Dudley Nurses continued to play an expanding role in the care of the sick in their own homes along the Western Seaboard. Between 1925 and 1943, thirteen new districts were opened in Connemara, Aran and East Galway. Some districts were closed due either to amalgamation with adjoining districts because of diminishing need, or to lack of adequate local support, e.g. Woodlawn, Ballinasloe, Ballygar, Cleggan, Finey and Cornamona between 1951 and 1959. The Lady Dudley nurses continued in Connemara until their absorption into the Public Health Nursing Service of the Western Health Board in 1974.

The Jubilee and Lady Dudley Nurses were familiar figures in the West of Ireland, and played a vital role in the lives of people living there. Their story also provides a striking illustration of the gradual transition from private philanthropy to state-administered healthcare in the course of the twentieth century.

References
James Murray, *Galway: A Medico-Social History*, Galway, Kennys, 1994
Lady Dudley's Scheme ... First Annual Report, April 23rd 1903-April 23rd 1904 (courtesy of the Irish Folklore Department, UCD).

Scene Three
EXT.   SUBURBAN ROUNDABOUT   NIGHT

Headlights enter frame continually, circular motion of traffic, relentless.

          INTERROGATOR
I need more proof that you belonged.
We get plenty of pretenders here,
we take no chances. Have you any
photographs or coins from that time?

          TEENAGER
This is a note from my mother. It's a
Shopping list. I used to shop every
Wednesday.

          INTERROGATOR
This means nothing. There's

          INTERROGATOR (continued)
No signature and no stamp.

Sound effects. Camera from point of view of moving car. Warehouses, buildings for interior car parking, bars on window. The odd person walking on pavement.

          TEENAGER
I can't help it. I had just my coat on
When I left, no bag. I didn't even have
a pair of gloves. It wasn't a cold day.
The trees were the same. The same
Wire fence. I was wearing patent shoes,
But the shine is gone now.

Scene Four
EXT.   BOG   SUMMER MORNING

Bird song and nature effects. We see the back of two young children as they set off pushing a buggy along an endless looking path. It could be a fairy tale journey. We see gorse and striking colours of bog. The children move slowly out of frame as they chat to each other.

>   INTERROGATOR
> Your presentation is not going very well.
> Don't you have any witnesses at all?
>
>   TEENAGER
> One minute they were there, the next
> minute they had disappeared, my uncle,
>
>   TEENAGER
> my aunts, my sisters. Then suddenly nobody.
>
>   INTERROGATOR
> I see. Did you not think of adopting
> a family and relatives?

Scene Five
EXT.   ROWS OF TREES   EVENING

Camera movers through lines of stark trees, silhouetted against a deep red sky.

>   TEENAGER
> I was stuck in the mud. One shoe.
>   (she hesitates)
> I remember a doll with blue, stripy
> legs and a clown's face. I remember
> a black cat with long whiskers and
> a white chest. I remember. I remember
> I remember ring-a-ring-a-rosy we all
> Fall down. They wouldn't play with me.
>   (in tears)
> They wouldn't play with me, so
> I ran away.

Irish Women's Movements

Myrtle Hill

Feminist Activism in Northern Ireland

Abstract: Much has been written on life in the North of Ireland during the 'troubled' 1970s, and on the difficulties faced by those struggling to achieve a more equitable society. While a Women's Movement emerged here, as in other parts of Western Europe, the prevalence of religious discrimination tended to marginalise and undermine calls for gender equality. Moreover – and this has been the focus of much recent feminist analysis – feminist activists in the North were themselves divided. Quite apart from the usual debates between radical, liberal, socialist and Marxist brands of feminism, other aspects of identity – loyalist, republican, nationalist and unionist – complicated almost every issue and placed women in opposing political camps. [....] But historiographical emphasis on the fragmentation of the Women's Movement has tended to undermine the extent of both the short and the longer-term achievements of the period. The purpose of this paper, therefore, is to try to identify and assess the legacy of these years of feminist activism and its impact on contemporary experience. Of course, other influences contributed to the progress made by women in employment, politics and academia, but in this so-called 'post-feminist' era, the importance of women's own agency in challenging discrimination in the public arena, and, perhaps more particularly, in opposing oppression and promoting choice in the area of sexuality, needs to be acknowledged and recorded.

from 'Lessons and Legacies: Feminist Activism in the North c1970-2000', *Volume 9*, pp. 135-150

The Women's Movement(s)

[....] The 1970s witnessed the development of a new tradition in the North – part of the broader feminist movement – which would provide women with the analytical tools to begin to tackle the gender deficit.[1] The first stirrings of such concern could be traced to 1971 when the Lower Ormeau Women's Group protested against the decision of Margaret Thatcher, then Minister of Education, to stop free school milk for children over the age of seven. Despite the use of imaginative tactics and the support of Belfast City Council, the 'Mothers of Belfast', were ultimately unsuccessful, while the introduction of internment in August of that year distracted attention from such purely social issues.[2] In 1974, however, female staff and students at Coleraine University joined local women to focus attention on the issue of domestic violence, and the Coleraine Women's Group went on to set up a Women's Aid group and a Women's Housing Association. A year later, following a weekend of films on women's issues organised by women meeting at Queen's University in Belfast, the decision was made to form the Northern Ireland Women's Rights Movement (NIWRM). Their aims were "to spread a consciousness of women's oppression and mobilise the greatest possible numbers of women on feminist issues".[3] With the intention of acting as an umbrella organisation that would bring together and provide a stronger focus for individuals and groups already working to draw attention to gender discrimination, they attracted activists from a wide range of backgrounds – students, academics, trade unionists, communists and supporters of the Civil Rights movement. An immediate focus for their campaigning activities was to call for the extension of the Sexual Discrimination Act to Northern Ireland, a goal achieved in 1976. The establishment of the Equal Opportunities Commission in the same year was seen as particularly helpful by those feminists and trade unionists for whom the right of women to be given opportunities and rewards equal to those of their male colleagues, was considered a fundamental entitlement. However, this type of reformism proved unacceptable to feminists for whom the women's struggle was inseparable from the overall context of colonial oppression, and to those whose commitment to the struggle for international socialism demanded a more revolutionary approach. The most publicised example of feminist division was over the issue of female republican prisoners, in particular, their situation when on 'the dirty protest' simultaneously arousing massive support and intense revulsion. This emotive issue served to bring differences to the surface, but disagreements over the internal structure of the organisation also proved contentious and irresolvable. Within a few months, those who aimed to combine their prior commitment to socialism with feminist and nationalist concerns formed the Socialist Women's Group (SWG). They retained their membership of the NIWRM for about a year, finally leaving following disagreements over the Peace Movement. [....]

It could of course be argued that division, by offering a range of outlets for feminist energies, facilitated activism on a wide range of fronts, and that the loss of its more radical voices enabled the NIWRM to broaden its base. Some of the organisations of the period were short-lived; both the BWC and WAI dissolved in the 1980s, but there were occasions during the following decades when a small number of feminists, from diverse backgrounds, engaged in campaigns of common interest.

While drawing attention to the 'multiplicity of struggles' that existed, it is impossible, in this brief paper, to address in full the legacies left. However, one of its major aims is to highlight the key issues which feminist activists brought into the public arena during this critical period of conflict and transition, and to reflect on their broader influence and long-term impact. In this so-called 'post-feminist' era, it is surely important that the history of feminism to date – in all its forms – is not forgotten, and that we continue to question, challenge, explore and analyse the 'lived experience of women's lives'. [....]

Notes

1. Eileen Evason 1991. *Against the Grain: The Contemporary Women's Movement in Northern Ireland*, Dublin; Monica McWilliams 1995. 'Struggling for Peace and Justice: Reflections on Women's Activism in Northern Ireland' in Joan Hoff and Maureen Coulter (eds.), 'Irish Women's Voices: Past and Present', *Journal of Women's History*, 6:4 / 7:1, Indianna, pp. 13–39; Carmel Roulston 1997. 'Women on the Margin: The Women's Movements in Northern Ireland, 1973–1995' in Lois A. West (ed.), *Feminist Nationalism*, London, pp. 41–58.
2. Lynda Edgerton-Walker 1986. 'Public Protest, Domestic Acquiescence: Women in Northern Ireland' in Rosemary Ridd and Helen Callaway (eds.), *Caught up in Conflict: Women's Responses to Political Strife*, London, pp. 61–79, p. 72.
3. Statement by NIWRM, Political Collection, Linenhall Library, Belfast

Eilish Rooney

WOMEN'S EQUALITY IN WEST BELFAST

Abstract: The peace process, the cease-fires, the Good Friday Agreement (GFA), and the multitude of political, civic and individual efforts to resolve the violent conflict in the North of Ireland are changing the political landscape on the island. This is most keenly felt in the North. Important progress has been made slowly. In the last year there were no sectarian killings. *[Note: sectarian killings have resumed since this article was first published]* The conflict may reach a workable form of resolution. Local governance may eventually be seen to 'work'. The sectarian power relations that were embedded in the state building project of 'Northern Ireland' are re-framed by the GFA within equality and human rights legislation, the reconstitution of policing, reform of the criminal justice system, cross-border bodies, the council of the isles, commitments on victims and prisoners and demilitarisation. Arguably, the GFA is a radical reformulation of nation-state relations whereby two governments have signed up to a process in which each state cedes territorial identity to the popular electoral mandate of people voting in the six counties.

from 'Counting Women's Equality in West Belfast and Finding Failings in the Northern Ireland Equality Commission', *Volume 9*, pp. 151-159

[....] West Belfast has a population of some 90,000. It contains some of the most deprived neighbourhoods in Ireland and Britain. The constituency is predominantly nationalist and republican with some unionist and loyalist neighbourhoods – all of them experiencing high levels of deprivation in relation to employment, education, health, income and the legacies of the long war. The equality legislation following from the GFA needs to be realised in these neighbourhoods. Catholics and Protestants in areas of deprivation face difficult and different problems in confronting the legacy of sectarianism. At the very moment when sectarian 'identities' are arguably, of necessity, being institutionalised (in the NI Assembly), the material and cultural weight of institutionalised sectarianism has to be undermined. Equality legislation is one vital mechanism for doing this and for building a society out of sectarianism. This paper contributes to the work of putting women into that frame.

Challenges and Opportunities

One of the difficulties in raising the debate about women's equality is similar to opening the debate about social class equality. The current terms of the equality debate in the North have developed out of the history of debate on the unemployment differentials between Catholic and Protestant males. This differential has persisted despite 30 years of legislation making it unlawful to discriminate against people on the grounds of religion or political opinion. According to the latest Labour Force Survey religion report, the unemployment differential between Catholic and Protestant males is currently two to one. The female unemployment rate is 6.1% of Catholics compared with 3.9% of Protestant females. Among males 9.9% of Catholics compared with 4.7% of Protestants are unemployed. These differentials have serious consequences for women's equality. [....]

Trouble with Women

In the places in the North of Ireland where women might influence how decisions are taken with regard to these matters, there are very few women. Just 14% of the NI Assembly was female and 18% of local councillors are female, and with over 31% female membership of public bodies it appears that women fare better on the appointments system. Over 49% of the civil service is female, but this drops to just 16% at senior level. There are even fewer women in senior positions in business and industry. [....]

Women comprise 51% of the population in the North. However, the presence of individual women, or small percentages of women, in decision-making is no guarantee that women's inequality is recognised and addressed. [....] Some women are more in need of equality than others. Obviously working class Catholic and Protestant women, who experience the highest levels of deprivation in West Belfast, are more deeply disadvantaged by women's inequality than women in relatively advantaged middle class areas. The latter may purchase the domestic labour of poorer women to look after children and do the housework. [....]

Women and West Belfast

[....] Two measures of deprivation are of particular relevance to women's equality: child poverty and women's and men's employment. Over 26,000 children (0–15 year olds) live in the 17 electoral wards in the West Belfast constituency. In eight of these wards 80% or more of the children live in poverty. Altogether, the 17 wards in West Belfast have more than half of the under 16 year old population living in poverty. This means that more than 13,000 children live in poverty in this area. The impacts on women with primary responsibility for the care of children are obvious.

Other things follow – high levels of health deprivation and of drugs prescribed to women for anxiety or depression. The problem of children in poverty is compounded by the government's system of repayments to the Social Fund. [....] In 2000/01 over £34m was deducted from benefits to repay Social Fund loans. In other words, the poorest families in the six counties repaid £34m out of benefits back to the government. The percentage of this money flowing from the poorest homes in West Belfast is not recorded in the report, but given the levels of deprivation in the area it is likely to be substantial. This system adversely impacts on the poorest women and children and on those with dependants. [....]

Women's Equality Matters

[....] Women's equality has a direct impact on the lives of women, men, children, dependants and neighbourhoods. Strategies aimed at improving women's equality should prioritise improvements in the lives of women who experience the deepest levels of multiple deprivations. Many women in West Belfast experience deeper levels of deprivation than women elsewhere in the North. [....]

Indeed, the implication that working class Catholic and Protestant neighbourhoods have to compete with each other for their share of scarce resources generated from the peace process is counterproductive to building good relations and finding a future out of sectarianism. Change takes time. Ignoring the realities of women's lives is no way to waste the opportunities of the present.

Caitríona Ruane

Obstacles to Peace in Ireland

This is a revised version of a paper that was presented to a plenary session of the NGO Forum at the 4th UN World Conference on Women on September 4th 1995.

from 'Obstacles to Peace and Human Security in Ireland',
Volume 4, pp. 117-124

[....] Ireland and Britain have had a troubled history since the Anglo-Norman invasion in 1169. During those 826 years there has never been a time when there have not been 'British' troops in Ireland. British colonialism has not been a happy experience for the native Irish or, indeed, British soldiers. It has resulted in famine, mass emigration, hangings, slaughter, land wars, plantation, hunger strikes, floggings, rebellion, partition of Ireland and untold suffering for Irish and indeed British people. It is one of the oldest and most complex of all colonial conflicts and it predates the development of capitalism. Every subsequent development in Irish society was structured by the colonial process – urbanisation, industrialisation, the transition from feudalism to capitalism – each of these huge processes was given the colonial imprimatur. In consequence, decolonising Ireland or healing the wounds attendant to the colonial process in Ireland is not an easy task. Every party to the conflict – Irish and British, settler and native, coloniser and colonised – has had its identity forged at the colonial nexus. The colonial legacy continues to structure British and Irish lives in a way that is just as profound as gender, race or class. [....]

I began working in the North of Ireland in March 1988. I had returned home after working for three years in El Salvador, Nicaragua and Guatemala. I wanted to work on issues of conflict in Ireland and link those with the issues and people I was working with in Central America.

I co-founded the Centre for Research and Documentation (CRD), based in Belfast, which was founded by Irish people who had worked in Africa, Asia and Latin America, and human rights workers in Ireland. We felt that there were similarities between our situation and those in countries in the Southern hemisphere and that there were valuable lessons we could learn.

Censorship, harassment, labelling and marginalising had done their job and effectively silenced a huge section of the Irish population. The only 'acceptable' analysis permitted on the media was that the IRA are the problem and if they would stop we would have peace. There was little or no analysis of the root causes of the conflict except by a few courageous journalists, politicians and human rights workers. In 1988 CRD spoke of the need for negotiations proposing that everyone should sit down and talk rather than fight. That statement may not seem very radical now, but at the time it made us many enemies. The longer I worked in the North of Ireland, the more I experienced directly and indirectly the almighty power of the British state. I had spent years condemning US government policy in Central America, the Philippines, in Iraq, yet I was rarely accused of being anti-American. The minute we became critical of British Government policy in Ireland it was a different story. I patiently but firmly explained the difference between being anti-British and anti-British Government policy. [....]

How the women have suffered in this conflict, and how they have worked – worked to survive, to educate their children, to keep their children form joining military organisations, even when they themselves supported those organisations. Women gave birth, protected their children, visited them in jail, brought food, clothes and book parcels for prisoners. A prisoner in jail cannot do without, no matter how bad the family finances are. They protested, confronted armies, demanded to know where their children were. They were strip searched, their children were killed by IRA bombs and British Army bombs. On top of all that many women suffered violence in the home. Now because of the courageous work of organisations like Women's Aid, the Rape Crisis Centre, the silence is being broken, slowly but surely, and women are finding their voices and supporting other women. [....]

Note
I would like to thank Professor Liam O'Dowd and Dr Robbie McVeigh who worked with me at CRD, for their assistance, guidance and support.

Orla Egan

THE CORK LESBIAN COMMUNITY 1975-2000

Abstract: This paper traces the evolution of the lesbian community in Cork, the second largest city in the Republic of Ireland, from the mid-1970s to the end of the twentieth century. It focuses on the community's attempts to eke out a space for itself, attempting, at various stages and with varying degrees of success, to negotiate and share space with gay men, women's groups and other 'alternative' groupings. It highlights the range and diversity of activities organised by the community over the years, combining a commitment to political activism with a sense of fun and a consciousness of the need to create spaces for the celebration and enjoyment of lesbian culture and community. I have been involved with the Cork lesbian community since the early-mid 1980s. My experiences with the community, and its place in my life, have inspired and encouraged me to undertake research on the history of the Cork lesbian community and to explore how it has changed over time. This paper is based on that on-going research.

from 'Searching for Space: Cork Lesbian Community 1975-2000', *Volume 9*, pp 79-104

Early Lesbian and Gay Community Building in Cork

In 1975 in Cork city there were no formal lesbian and gay organisations or social centres. Informal social networks did exist, mostly centering around parties and gatherings, particularly in the homes of some of the wealthier gay men. These parties were open only to those 'in-the-know' and in the 'in-crowd.' If the house owner didn't like you, you were excluded. Public toilets and parks also provided loci for casual clandestine sexual encounters between men. In the 1970s gay men would meet regularly in the Imperial Hotel, where they were sometimes joined by a small number of lesbians. Cork lesbians would sometimes travel to Dublin to socialise in the lesbian and gay scene there. Many Cork lesbians emigrated to cities such as London, where they could find a larger and more open lesbian community.

The first Cork gay rights organisation was established in 1976. The Irish Gay Rights Movement (IGRM) had been set up in Dublin in 1974, and a Cork branch was formed in 1976. A combination of circumstances created the context and conditions for the emergence of these lesbian and gay organisations in Ireland: the changing nature and gradual liberalisation of Irish society, the emergence of Irish social change movements, in particular the Women's Movement, and the new gay ideology of pride and assertiveness following the Stonewall Riots, and the emergence of the Gay Liberation Front in the USA and Britain.

The Cork IGRM succeeded in leasing premises at 4 McCurtain Street, thus establishing Cork's first gay centre. Weekend discos and social events were held there up until the mid 1980s, providing an essential space for gay men to socialise. Although the Cork discos were predominantly male, a number of lesbians did socialise there. The IGRM also set up a telephone counselling service and a number of newsletters and publications were produced. Members of the Cork IGRM were also involved in a radio programme on 'Homosexuals in Cork' which was broadcast on the Cork RTE local radio programme *Cork-About* on 20 January 1978.

There were some attempts to set up a specifically lesbian social scene in Cork in the late 1970s. For example, a short article in the 1978 first edition of *Sapphire,* the Cork IGRM newsletter, notes that 'since the formation of the Cork Branch of IGRM the gay women in this city have been considering setting up a social scene for themselves.' There were negotiations with the Cork IGRM to try to make the centre available exclusively for women one night a week. A women's meeting was held in the IGRM premises on 30 January 1978 to discuss setting up a lesbian social scene in Cork, which is the first lesbian meeting in Cork of which I am aware. There were also plans to hold meetings on a weekly basis, but it is unclear if this happened.

It is apparent that lesbians continued to encounter difficulties in trying to negotiate space and support within the McCurtain Street centre. One of the motions passed at a 1981 National Gay Conference in Cork proposed 'that the men in McCurtain Street allocate one evening of each week for a social run by women for women. We demand that further resources be made more freely available to women.' This would seem to indicate a lack of support for independent women's activities in the McCurtain Street club and that the club continued to be geared primarily towards the needs of gay men in the city. [….]

Issues Emerging

The search for a space of our own has been a continuous theme for the Cork lesbian community from the 1970s onwards. The community has continually tried to negotiate space for lesbians to meet, socialise and organise, often in very hostile or difficult environments. Cork lesbians have tried to negotiate and share space and resources with other groups with whom it would seem to share common interests and concerns, in particular other women's groups and gay men. While it would usually be assumed that there would be a large degree of commonality in the politics, concerns and interests of these groups, in practice, conflicts of interests continually arose and the ability of the lesbian community to organise activities and resources was compromised. The difficulties experiences by the Cork lesbian community should lead us to question facile assumptions about the shared experiences and politics of lesbians and heterosexual women, and of lesbians and gay men.

The lesbian space created by Cairde Corcai/LINC has led to a blossoming of lesbian activism and the development of a wide range of groups and activities catering for the diverse interests and needs of the community. The importance of this work was recently acknowledged by President Mary McAleese who formally opened the new LINC premises in White Street in July 2003.

However, the creation of a 'space of our own' has not led to a severing of all ties with other groups. If anything, the creation of a separate lesbian space has removed many of the tensions arising from sharing space with other groups, and has enabled the lesbian community to rebuild alliances and relationships with other groups. For example, a strong working relationship has been developed between LINC and the Gay Men's Project in The Other Place, and both projects participate in a newly established City-Wide Lesbian and Gay Steering Group.

The evolution of any community is complex. In this paper it has only been possible to provide an overview of the main developments in the evolution of the Cork lesbian community. There are many other issues which need to be further explored. These include issues of diversity within the community and of differing experiences of community.

Through my on-going research I hope to reflect the experiences of those who have been centrally and actively involved in the community, as well as those who have remained more on the margins; those who have had mostly positive experiences within the community, as well as those who have felt excluded and marginalized; those who stayed and those who left. I think it is also important to not just concentrate on the more visible manifestations of the community, such as groups, bar, community centres, but to also explore other sites of community activity and formation, for example, in sporting groups, in homes or in workplaces.

The Cork lesbian community has a strong history of activism from the late 1970s through to the present day. This history has largely been unacknowledged, unrecorded, invisible and ignored. Despite the difficulties encountered in the 'search for space', a vibrant and active community was created; a community that combined committed political activism, with a sense of play, fun and exploration; a community determined to create spaces which fostered the development of lesbian culture and community in Cork.

Mary Owens and Anne Byrne

Rural Women's Lives

Abstract This article is based on extracts from a recent study of rural women in Ireland.[1] The study involved an in-depth exploration of women's lives in one rural location in the West of Ireland in the period 1991-1995. It grew out of our concern as development practitioners that women have not been adequately included in the rural development process which has taken place in Ireland in the last ten years. Women's lives within and outside the home, encompassing caring responsibilities, paid and unpaid work, access to services and facilities, status within the community and participation in local activities needs to be taken into account by policy makers in a process which we have described as the 'feminisation' or rural development. This summary account describes some of the key areas which impinge on rural women's lives – family, work and community. We argue that what is required is a distinct set of policy responses to enable rural women to benefit more fully from rural development initiatives and to increase their influence over the design of Irish development policies. [....]

from 'Family, Work and Community – Rural Women's Lives: Rural Women's Research Project – Summary Account',
Volume 4, pp. 77-94

Women's Perspectives on Rural Development

In 1993, the Second Commission on the Status of Women published a comprehensive report on women's participation in Irish society with a section devoted to the special concerns of rural women. This was quickly followed by a report of the Joint Oireachtas Committee on Women's Rights, Women and Rural Development. Both these reports describe the large number of barriers to women's participation in the rural development process. They emphasise the limited mobility and physical isolation experienced by many women in remote rural areas, especially those reliant on a poor public transport system. In addition, they point to the barriers confronting rural women with substantial caring responsibilities in the home and to the inadequate provision of child and elder care facilities in rural areas. Both reports highlight the disadvantages experienced by rural women on a daily basis due to the insufficient provision of basic public services in rural areas such as health, training and education, housing and other social services. The Report of the Second Commission on the Status of Women proposes a wide range of concrete measures to address these issues. It calls for the creation of centres in rural areas to support community care services, an examination of the training needs of rural women and measures to ensure the 'equitable' representation of women and men on County Enterprise Boards and local development initiatives. The Joint Oireachtas Committee makes a number of recommendations aimed at integrating a gender dimension into rural development policies in general. These include wider consultation with rural women's organisations in the design and implementation of rural measures, specific support measures for rural women which address their lack of mobility and social care responsibilities, increased funding for women's development initiatives, quotas and targets for women's representation on public boards and agencies and more research on rural women which would allow their participation in development programmes to be accurately monitored and evaluated. [....]

The Study

The study on which this article is based was conducted between 1991–1995. The main aim of the study was to carry out an in-depth analysis of women's lives in one rural community in order to explore women's participation in the family, the labour force and the community and to identify the factors which promote or inhibit their involvement in local development activities. While published research has highlighted important aspects of Irish rural women's lives, it has tended to focus on farm women, their work and farm family relationships. For this reason, we chose to base our study on a broader constituency thereby including women living in the country, both on and off farms, who are involved in a variety of family situations and occupations. The heterogeneity of the composition of rural women is a matter which requires consideration both in research and in development issues. [....]

Concluding Comment – The Feminisation of Rural Development

We would like to conclude by making a number of general recommendations on how to proceed towards removing these constraints. Firstly, rural policy must respond by removing barriers to women's participation at the practical level, chiefly through investing in child and elder care; secondly, public services in rural areas must be improved; and thirdly, an expansion in the provision of programmes in information and community development work for women is necessary. This third measure is required in order to create the space for women to identify their needs and aspirations and then to build mechanisms for representing these issues in the policy domain. There is a great need for structures at the local and the regional level which bring women together, provide a forum for regular discussion and consultation and act as a support for women who are in a position to negotiate for resources in development partnerships, County Enterprise Boards, advisory committees to statutory bodies, etc. This recent introduction of gender guidelines and quotas for development partnerships have facilitated the entry to management level of a relatively small number of women of whom a lot is expected in a short period of time. This progressive move now needs to be accompanied by more broadly based measures to engage rural women with the 'bottom up' development process and a commitment to providing resources for initiatives of practical benefit to women on the ground.

Note
1   The Rural Women's Research Project was conducted by members of the Women's Studies Centre from 1991–1995.

Eilís Ward and Orla O'Donovan

NETWORKS OF WOMEN'S GROUPS AND THE WOMEN'S MOVEMENT

Abstract: Over the last decade there has been a flourishing of locally based women's groups in Ireland in both urban and rural areas. Symptomatic of this trend has been the establishment of networks of women's groups – coalitions of diverse groups in specific geographical areas. The research presented in this paper sets out to examine what some women who are involved in 2 such networks in the West of Ireland think about politics and about the political function of the networks. While it is clear that the women surveyed felt an exclusion from certain political activities based on their gender, it is not clear that these groups are necessarily engaged in political activities informed by a feminist consciousness. This latter point raises questions about the relationship of these groups to the women's movement.

From "Networks of Women's Groups and Politics: What (Some) Women Think", *Volume 4*, pp 1-20

Introduction

This paper presents and analyses some of the findings from a bigger research project which we conducted with 4 networks of women's groups in Ireland during 1995/6.[1] [....]

The study was motivated by 3 different, but related, factors. Firstly, there is a lack of research in Ireland on locally-based women's groups. While much has been written about women's participation in the parliamentary politics in Ireland[2] and on women's participation in rural and community development,[3] little attention has been paid to the politics of women's groups. [....] Secondly, feminist analysis in both Ireland and elsewhere argues for women to develop alternative bailiwicks to the party/trade union/sporting organisation structures which act as the customary traditional routes to parliamentary politics.[4] [....] Thirdly, as members of UCG Women's Studies Centre which has co-organised a series of seminars on *Women and the Irish Constitution* with the local network of women's groups, it became apparent that there was a range of issues which some of the network's members deemed to be inappropriate for consideration by women's groups. [....] This experience raised questions for us, about what locally based women's groups considered to be 'political' in the first place and what they deemed appropriate political activity for networks of women's groups. [....]

Conclusion

Having explored some of the quantitative findings from our study, we need to come to some general conclusions. [....]. Do these findings allow us say anything more than that great differences exist between women and that, for example, some women identify with feminism and other do not? This is not new! The possibility that the differences in perceptions and attitudes may be explained with reference to the varying profiles of the 2 groups of women needs further exploration.

In a wider context, our findings can be usefully viewed in the context of the Euro-Barometer findings on support for gender equality throughout Europe as analysed by Wilcox.[5] He concluded that Ireland has at once the highest percentage of strong feminists in Europe and among the highest percentage of non-feminists. [....]

How does all of this link into the issue of whether these groups are part of a women's movement? Much of the literature on the women's movement in Ireland assumes an unproblematic relationship between the two, or at least an automatic progression from the establishment of a women's group to the espousing of a feminist consciousness and the presentation of a gendered critique of Irish society.[6] [....]

But what exactly is a women's movement? This is a debate which cannot be entered into here in any detail except to note that the literature on (new) social movements,[7] is not in easy agreement about what formally constitutes a movement, as opposed to an unconnected, vaguely linked collection of groups which may cluster around, in this case, women's activities and organisations. [....] However, the issue here is not so much whether locally-based women's groups and the networks, *per se*, constitute a social movement but more basically whether they indicate the presence of a gender consciousness which would render them as part of a women's movement to begin with. The difference may appear subtle but it is important because of the assumptions which we feel have been made about the two, as outlined above.

If we take the notion of a women's movement in its broadest sense of collective action based on a gendered critique of the existing order, it is clear that these women's groups do not necessarily a women's movement make. While the women's movement may emanate from many diverse types of feminist action, it does assume a coherent central tenet of actions to remove discrimination and break down the 'male domination of society'.[8] It must rest on a common gender consciousness and a desire for collective action flowing from that. [....]

We suggest that analysis which argues that there is an organic link between feminism and women's movement is correct. The former is required for the latter to exist. What makes the women's movement distinct from other new social movements is that it is defined by a gendered critique of the existing order and a commitment to changing that order. Thus, as we have claimed throughout this discussion, a feminist consciousness is elemental. But to say that a similarly organic link exists between women's groups and the women's movement is more problematic. To argue that women's groups *per se*, are inherently part of the women's movement is akin to arguing that woman, by definition, is feminist. We cannot leap from biology to ideology and certainly not from the fact of groups of women coming together, albeit in a women-only activity, to the existence of a movement which may or may not build itself around such groups. The latter requires a conscious commitment to a set of practices, ideologies and goals. This is not to say that the kind of work carried out by all women's groups is not important and inherently good for their members.

Perhaps the most radical impact of membership of women's groups and networks has been felt in women's personal and private lives. While the personal is political and while many women have made important changes in their lives as a result, these changes may not necessarily lead to a desire for change in gender relations in society. [....]

In order to explain the phenomenon of the mushrooming of women's groups we may look to the effect of the second wave of the women's movement in Irish society in general. Clearly the institutional change which led the Combat Poverty Agency to positively target women in rural areas can be seen to have resulted from the integration of the demands of the second wave into how the Agency views women's role in Irish society. But the phenomenon might also be explained by the changing nature of Irish society in which extended families are being replaced by nuclear families and in which many women live lives of isolation, removed from their own families and communities, perhaps in residential areas which have not grown according to organic demographic changes but according to centralised civic planning and property prices. It could be argued that the women's groups which have mushroomed serve the function of the extended family and the 'community' in which there are regular patterns of sociable interaction, information networks and points of support, encouragement and validation of the self and ones function in society.

Notes

1 For details of the complete findings and analysis see 'Networks of Women's Groups, Politics and Feminism', in Galligan, Y., Ward, E. and Wilford, R. (eds) *Contesting Politics: Women in Ireland, North and South* (Westview Press, 1999).
2 See, for instance, Brown, A. and Galligan, Y. 1993. 'Changing the political agenda for women in the Republic of Ireland and Scotland', *West European Politics.* 16, 2, pp. 165-189 [....].
3 See, for instance, Braithwaite, M. 1993. 'Women in the Rural Economy: a study of the economic role and situation of women in rural areas of the European Community', Brussels, Equal Opportunities Unit, Directorate General for Social Affairs [....].
4 See Galligan, Y. 1993. 'Women in Irish Politics', in Coakley, J. and Gallagher, M. (eds). *Politics in the Republic of Ireland.* Dublin, PSAI Press/Folens p. 216.
5 Wilcox, C. 1991. 'The Causes and Consequences of Feminist Consciousness Among Western European Women', *Comparative Political Studies.* Vol. 23, No. 4, pp. 519-545.
6 See, for instance, The Second Commission on the Status of Women. 1993. *Report to Government.* Dublin, Stationary Office [....].
7 An explanatory note is required here to point out that, in general, a distinction is made between the social movements of the last century and into the early 20th century (e.g. workers' movements, movements for women's suffrage) and the new social movements of the recent decades based on, for instance, environmentalism locally based community developments and the second wave of the women's movement.
8 Lovenduski, J. and Randall, V. 1993. *Contemporary Feminist Politics: Women and Power in Britain*, Oxford, Oxford University Press, p. 2.

Maria Gibbons

Lesbian and Gay Visions of Ireland

review of Íde O'Carroll and Eoin Collins (eds.)
Lesbian and Gay Visions of Ireland. Towards the Twenty-First Century
Volume 4, p. 176

It is the nature of societies to constantly evolve and change, but by any standards the extent and nature of some of the recent developments in Irish society have been quite remarkable. The publication of this book in 1995 highlights certain of these changes, and illustrates the sort of progress that can be made over a relatively short period of time.

In 1986 a book entitled *Out for Ourselves – The Lives of Irish Lesbians and Gay Men* was published by Women's Community Press. Very few of the contributors to that volume are identifiable by name, and there is a pervasive feeling of defensiveness, alienation and even pessimism running through its pages. The book under review by contrast (but did it have to be published in England?) carries a more optimistic tenor. All the contributors identify themselves, and more hopefully claim their place as lesbians and gays in the Ireland of today and tomorrow. Lots of factors have contributed to this greater visibility and confidence, not least of which has been the personal bravery and tenacity of various lesbian and gay activists over the years. Recent and proposed legislative changes on homosexuality have merely reflected the greater tolerance of difference now evident in Irish society.

'Out and Proud and Strong' could be the motto of the book. Including the two editors, there are twenty-one always thoughtful, usually absorbing and often witty accounts of the experience of being lesbian and gay in contemporary Ireland. The editors made a good decision in asking their contributors for a personal perspective, and this provokes a sense of honest reflection and down-to-earth openness which is both refreshing and touching. I particularly liked the pieces by Marcy Dorcey and Louise Walsh about their personal experiences of lesbian/feminist activism and how their work as artists reflects that commitment. Also Brendí McClenaghan writes with integrity about his struggle as a gay republican activist, and Anne Maguire as an activist lesbian of the Irish diaspora.

There are numerous references in the book to the general sense of optimism generated throughout the country by the ceasefire in Northern

Ireland (still holding when this book was in gestation). Also, many writers mention the volcanic effect on them of Joni Crone's appearance as the 'first Irish lesbian' on The Late, Late Show in 1980 – she was responsible for a lot of 'coming out' it seems (regretfully I missed that occasion). The murder of Declan Flynn in Fairview Park and its aftermath in 1982–3, and of course the emergence of AIDS during the decade are both identified as key events in the development of the modern Irish lesbian and gay movements.

Though inevitably uneven, this is an absorbing collection of essays from inside one of the main forces for change within contemporary Irish society. Anyone with an interest in lesbian/gay issues, in honest and perceptive commentary, or in monitoring social change in society will find this book of great interest. Equally inevitably a few quibbles – the book cover is depressing and not at all reflective of the contents. Furthermore there could be more contributions from outside of the capital, where important work of national importance is going on too quietly. And there is much still to be done ...

Ann O'Kelly

WOMEN AND DISABILITY

Abstract: This article is an attempt to open the debate about the position of women with disabilities in Ireland today. Using data from interviews with a small group of disabled women, it records the lived reality of their lives in the following areas: the effects of disability on their everyday lives: friendships, relationships and motherhood; work; the women's movement and the provision of services. By exploring the historical treatment of people with disabilities in Ireland and internationally, a picture of their marginalisation within society emerges. The growth of the 'disability rights' movement throughout the western world and in Ireland is also examined, and the current position of Irish women with disabilities is set in this context. [....]

from 'Still Outside the Circle:
The Experience of Irish Women with Disabilities',
Volume 5, pp. 91-110

The Relevance or Otherwise of the Women's Movement

The women interviewed had mixed views on the women's movement, ranging from absolutely no knowledge, to indifference, to seeing a role for the women's movement in issues of concern to them:

> Delia: Prehaps if I was younger and wanted to work, some of the things they are talking about would matter, like having a child minded. The other thing is, I'm very lucky, I have my own home. Mind you, I can't stand arrogant, loud-mouthed women, trying to be a female version of a man.

The most suprising thing for me in the whole process of interviewing the women was the fact that the two deaf women did not understand what I was talking about when I mentioned the women's movement, even though they were involved in a women's group. I shall never forget the confusion on their faces as the sign language interpreter tried to explain what I was talking about:

> Patricia-Mary and Josephine: We meet each other and learn about things in the deaf women's group like about health and entitlements, also we did pottery classes, that was great. The women's movement, we never heard of it.

A gap between issues of importance to women with disabilities and the women's movement was highlighted by one of the women:

> Sabina: the important things for women with disabilities are not on the agenda of the women's movement. Things like personal care assistants for women who need them, women having to rely on their children for personal care, the provision of home helps and the issue of the income support for married women. Like when I think of… and the problems she has just getting to the toilet, and those little girls having to help her. Sure, they [women involved in the women's movement] have no idea.

Despite this, however, she sees a role for disabled women joining together, in order to highlight the concerns of all women with disabilities:

> Sabina: The women's group is great but, you say yourself, it was nearly all disabled women who came to the awareness day. Mind you, that was an eye-opener for me. You don't think of other people. It would be great to have a disabled women's group, with all the disabilities involved, not just MS, or even just physical.

Edel is actively involved in the disability rights movement, and highlighted some of the difficulties she encounters:

> Edel: You feel like you're constantly selling yourself – you're on the bandwagon all day and then in the pub you're doing the same, selling

the idea of integration. I got a phone call a few weeks ago from a woman asking me to set up a disabled women's group. I don't think that's right. All women's groups should just include women with disabilities, but not in a patronising way, like, aren't we great we're including women with disabilities. I'm not hung up about the women's movement, I'm more hung up in trying to get opportunities, disability comes into play. The women's movement should highlight the fact that there are more divorces if a woman has an acquired disability.

One woman was completely indifferent:

> Dorothy: it just doesn't seem to say anything to me. I've never even thought of it.

It is obvious that the women's movement does not impact to any great extent on the lives of the women interviewed. This finding conforms with Moran's findings. The women she spoke to saw the women's movement as "shutting the door on us because they are afraid of their own fears of disability" and that "the women's movement does not see disability as a civil rights issue. We have been excluded."[1]

The blame for disabled women's lack of involvement in the women's movement was laid squarely at the door of the women's movement by Wilson who delivered the keynote address at the 'Making Connections' conference organised jointly by the National Rehabilitation Board and the CSW in May 1992:

> ...the women's liberation movement failed to recognise disabled women's poverty, exclusion and silence ...through not challenging the inaccessibility of the environment ...relying on print and speech to exchange information effectively marginalised disabled women.[2]

This seemed to me to be an important issue to discuss with the women. The provision and delivery of services can impact greatly on the lives of all disabled people, but is particularly important for women who are normally seen as care-givers.

This is the one subject about which the women became angry during the interviews. Most of the women described the services provided by the state to people in their situation as being inadequate. [....] One of the women who had experience of working for a service organisation spoke of the difficulties encountered by women when they seek services:

> Sabina: I know how difficult it is for women to get services, when I think of ... and all the problems she has with home help, and even getting to the toilet, I just hope I'm never in that position. Carers can speak very loudly, especially if they're men, and husbands get a lot of sympathy if their wife is disabled.

Professional workers were criticised by some of the women, while acknowledging the difficulties they may experience:

> Edel: Professional are absolutely painful. It can take six months to get a wheelchair. Nurses in hospitals haven't a clue about physical disability – they're lovely women, but ... Disability awareness should be part of their study as well as teachers. [....]

Notes
1 B. Moran 1992, *Women with Disabilities in Ireland: A Double Disadvantage*, M Equality Studies thesis, UCD.
2 Wilson, 1992, 'Making Connections' Conference Report, Dublin, unpublished.

Claire McDonagh

DOMESTIC VIOLENCE IN GALWAY

Abstract: Violence against women is a violation of women's human rights which occurs across all political, economic, cultural and social divides. It is a grave social problem which threatens the safety, equality and bodily integrity of every victim. In Galway, 'Waterside House Refuge for Abused Women and Children' provides crisis refuge accommodation, counselling, advice and support to women and children who find themselves in violent home environment. Intimidation and fear are the main reasons women remain in a violent relationship. The aim of the refuge is to encourage each woman to determine her own future.

from 'Domestic Violence: The Galway Perspective',
Volume 4, pp. 109-116

[....] New developments regarding the issue of domestic violence occurred in the early 1970s. A shift in attitudes became noticeable in rural Ireland when refuges for abused women and children began to open in rural areas. The National Federation of Refuges was founded in 1979 with a view to strengthening individual refuges and providing a support and information network. There were 4 refuges in operation in the Republic at the time, in Dublin, Bray, Cork and Limerick. Other groups throughout the country were in the early stages of trying to establish refuges. [....]

Waterside House Refuge in Galway was opened by Galway Social Services on June 8th 1981. It was partly funded by the Western Health Board, while the shortfall was made up by fundraising and donations. [....] Waterside House was the first refuge to open in the West of Ireland. It has 7 self-contained units with 26 bed spaces; other facilities include a sitting room, laundry and a child care unit. Waterside House Refuge provides crisis accommodation for women and children, victims of domestic violence and abuse. Since June 1981 over 75,000 bednights have been recorded in the refuge. In Galway, women and children who were living in local authority housing and were forced out of their homes as a result of domestic violence were accepted on the local authority housing list for a second time, as a result of meetings between local authority representatives and the Waterside House team throughout the early 1980s. This was a major breakthrough for the families concerned.

In 1995 there was a substantial increase in the number of women looking for counselling, advice and information. Calls for assistance soared from an average of 20 calls per month to 60 calls per month, while the 4000 bednights recorded in 1994 rose to 5000 in 1995. The number of telephone enquiries have dramatically increased in recent times. The Women's Aid national helpline set up in March 1992 has received over 18,000 calls for help from abused women. The Special Domestic Violence and Sexual Assault, set up in 1994 by the Gardai in the Dublin Metropolitan area received 5,000 calls in one year. This figure becomes even more horrifying given that international research shows that only between 10–15% of women will report assault to the police. In 1993 a pilot study carried out in the Accident and Emergency Unit of St. James's Hospital revealed that 119 female admissions were made as a direct result of assault and attempted suicides. The injuries documented included 26 fractures, 40 cases of head injury, multiple bruising, lacerations and attempted strangulation. This was one pilot study in one Dublin Hospital[1] [....]

What Needs to be Done?

Providing adequate safe refuge for women and children is essential, but in addition to security, the provision of support and services is of central importance from the abused woman's perspective. A refuge should be a service in itself.

1   There is need for an education and awareness campaign to include all schools, to educate children at a young age on the problem of domestic violence, thus preventing domestic violence from continuing in subsequent generations.

2   Ongoing research into the nature of domestic violence is required. In recognition of this Waterside House Refuge in conjunction with The Family Guidance Institute has commissioned Ann-Marie Naughton B.A. M.A. to research domestic violence and abuse against women and children nationally.

3   Changes in legal matters and legislation are required in order to offer greater protection to women and their children.

4. An after care service is essential in order to provide on-going support for women and children after leaving refuges.

5   Preventive strategies are crucial: Emphasis should be on prevention, education and awareness. Training programmes for personnel working in the caring professions should be available outlining the horror of domestic violence.

6   Crisis services should be available on site in all refuges throughout the country. Statutory services, such as Community Care social workers finish at 5pm. There are no weekend services available. Refuges are open 24 hours each day and crisis services for victims of abuse should be available on request.

7   The provision of housing for women and children who are forced out of their homes because of violence is crucial. Safe housing is an essential part of the recovery of the abused woman. A safe and supportive environment is of vital importance. Self-help groups and training in Back to Work Training Courses are essential if the woman is to be empowered and enabled to start a new life for herself and her children.

According to Adam Jukes[2] who works with batterers at the Men's Centre in London, battering is a gender issue, entirely the responsibility of men. It is a political act and its underlying ideology is sexism. Violence will only cease when men stop being violent, and when the community as a whole stops condoning it. In consequence, everyone, everywhere must become intolerant of violence against women and uphold the belief that no woman deserves violence and that the use of violence is a crime. [....]

Notes
1   See Monica O'Connor 1995. *Zero Tolerance*, Women's Aid.
2   Adam Jukes 1990. 'Making Women Safe', *Social Work Today*.

Catherine Cronin

Women Engineers

Abstract: Why are there so few female engineers? Recent feminist analyses of technology have highlighted the potential conflict between feminine gender ideology and the masculine discourse and culture of technology. This study considers the experiences of first-year, female engineering students. These young women described a variety of alienating incidents ranging from male peers doubting their intelligence, abilities and motivation to lecturers marginalising them through exclusive use of male language and tolerance of male students' sexist and offensive behaviour. Overall the women were the subjects of crude remarks, jokes and teasing, much of which criticised their femininity, as expressed through their behaviour, attitudes and dress. The research findings illustrate the contradictions between feminine gender ideology and the overwhelmingly masculine culture of engineering/technology which are posed and faced by women in engineering.

from 'Is the 'Feminine Engineer' an Oxymoron? Women's Views and Experiences of Gender and Engineering', *Volume 3*, pp. 43-52

Introduction

I am a woman and an engineer. The project described in this paper emerged from reflection upon my own experiences as a woman in engineering and my growing awareness of feminist analyses of work, education, science and technology. Apart from my own personal stake in the matter, however, why does 'women and engineering' merit study, or even interest? One reason is the sheer disparity in numbers of female as compared with male engineers. While women represent roughly one-third of the total paid labour force in Ireland, only 3 per cent of engineers are women.[1] The proportion of women studying engineering is only slightly more encouraging. While women represent half of all university students, only 16 per cent of undergraduate engineering students are women.[2] This is the smallest proportion of female students in any course by far, making engineering the most male-dominated of all fields of study in Ireland, as in nearly all Western countries.[3]

The assumption that girls don't study engineering because most of them don't take Higher Mathematics is becoming less convincing, and still only partially explains the disparity. According to Department of Education statistics published in 1991, the proportion of girls taking Higher Maths at (then) Intermediate Certificate level exceeded the proportion of boys for the first time: 45 to 41 per cent.[4] In the same year, however, the proportion of girls taking Higher Maths at Leaving Certificate level was only 15 percent as compared with 26 per cent of boys.[5] While these statistics do not refer to the same cohort of pupils, the overall trend is clear. Roughly 1 in 3 girls demonstrating interest and ability in Higher Maths in junior cycle proceeds to Higher Maths in senior cycle, as compared with 2 in 3 boys. This would certainly help to explain the lower numbers of girls eligible to study engineering.

Yet even this disparity pales in comparison to the widely diverging proportions of girls and boys *choosing* to study engineering. Of all second-level pupils who took Higher Maths in the 1990 Leaving Certificate examination, 1 in 5 boys entered an engineering degree course, compared with only 1 in 17 girls.[6] There is clearly more at work deterring girls from engineering than there is keeping them away from Higher Maths alone.

I set out to answer some of the questions raised by these figures. Why, when other traditionally male-dominated fields of study such as commerce, law, medicine and science have become more balanced in make-up, has engineering remained a predominantly male bastion? Or, to put women back in the centre of the question, why don't young women choose to study engineering? [....]

Conclusion

So, is the 'feminine engineer' an oxymoron? The behaviour of some of the male engineering students and lecturers as cited in this study strongly confirms the theory that technology is still considered a masculine domain. Women who consider themselves feminine, like the women in this study, are entering the field, albeit in small numbers. However, a woman crossing into the masculine world of engineering is transgressing gender rules. The women in this study experienced the sanctions of this transgression: alienation, harassment, muting. Recognition of this contradiction between feminine identity and the masculine discourse and culture of technology is not a concession that women cannot or should not become engineers. As concluded by Ruth Carter and Gill Kirkup in their study of women in engineering:

> We must not avoid engineering issues because they seem too complex. Change is too important to leave to male' experts'; it should be effected through full participation of all social groupings.[7]

Without addressing specific strategies for change, these findings highlight the fact that simply encouraging more women into engineering is not going to resolve the problem of gender conflict. The problem of the underrepresentation of women in engineering is more than just an equality issue. Efforts which address only one part of the complex dynamic of gender and technology such as encouraging more women into the field, are doomed to failure, or at best limited success, if they are not also accompanied by efforts to address the harmful effects of gender roles for both sexes, efforts to deconstruct the gender symbolism throughout technology, and commitment to change the unequal gender division of labour, both private and public. [....]

Notes

1. Ireland 1991. *Statistical Abstract*. Dublin: Stationery Office.
2. In 1990/91 the proportion of full-time undergraduate enginerring students who were female was 15.9% (694/4373). Figures obtained by A. McQuillan at the HEA, Dublin in April 1992.
3. HEA 1989. *Report Accounts and Student Statistics*, Table 50.
4. Department of Education 1991. *Statistical Report 1988/89*. Tables 15.1, 15.2
5. *Ibid.* Tables 15.5, 15.6.
6. John Kelly 1991. 'Women, Engineering and Honours Maths', *The Irish Times*, (17 May).
7. Ruth Carter and Gill Kirkup 1990. *Women in Engineering*. London: MacMillan, p. 171.

Mary O'Malley-Madec

Travelling Women

Abstract: This paper highlights the importance of the role of Traveller women in maintaining Traveller culture through the observance of particular customs and in the telling of folklore. The author draws our attention to the necessity to preserve culture to ensure survival for ethnic minority populations, particularly if this minority is migrant. In this account, she provides information on protective customs in relation to maternity and childhood.

from 'The Irish Travelling Woman: Mother and Mermaid'
Volume 1, pp. 21–28

[....] In this paper I would like to look at some aspects of the folklore of the Irish Travellers which I believe indicate the ethnic identity of this group in terms of their social organisation and perception of reality. What I am going to focus on pertains in a particular way to women [....]

The women in the Travelling community are more aware than their male counterparts of the tugs which the settled life all around them presents and totter perilously between the values of their own culture and ours. We, in the settled community, are quick to make moral judgements on the social organisation of their group involving for example, matchmaking [....] Many of us would consider that Travelling women are oppressed; however, I think we have to look at this oppression (evidenced most forcibly in begging) as part of the cultural crisis involving male as well as female roles. [....]

Those of us who have had significant contact with the Travellers recognise the woman as the very backbone of Traveller society. She dominates in the camp and anywhere the family is not under public scrutiny; she is an important source of income (children's allowance and begging), and, in recent years, has become responsible for the education of young boys as well as young girls. [....]

Customs relating to mother and child point to a distinct, rich culture. They show how the world-view of these women developed. My informants were chiefly from the Galway area in the West of Ireland, where the traditions of the Travellers have remained intact compared to other places. I did not set out to elicit information on maternity or childhood; rather, it was my own pregnancy and my friendship with a young Travelling woman who was also expecting her first baby that opened the doors of their tradition to me. [....]

Pregnancy and birth [....] are both sacred and taboo. The mother's pregnant state and her act of giving birth are somehow seen to unleash supernatural forces in human life which pose a danger to everyone in the mother's entourage and particularly the male members of the camp. In the past it would appear that women gave birth away from the camp in some areas, although I am unable to establish whether this was common practice throughout the country. [....]

Some thirty years ago, a Travelling mother would have taken care not to put the clothes of a young baby out on the bushes to dry because she believed it would attract the attention of the fairies who would then come and abduct her baby and put a changeling in its place. The mother would not know immediately that her baby had been swapped for a changeling, because although the baby would have changed in nature, it would look the same. On November's Night a mother would take care to take in the clothes of all the family members so as to protect them from the fairies. [….]

Babies and children were in danger, not only from fairies, but also from the Evil Eye. The possessor of the Evil Eye was always a woman, often childless, and the victim was, at least in the accounts I got, a female child. The roles which the colour red plays in the customs of protection against the Evil Eye are rather unique. It is used primarily as a talisman, for example,. in certain families it is still customary to tie a piece of red cloth on the baby's cradle or clothes to protect the baby from the Evil Eye. This is also the reason why mothers, in the past, plaited the hair of their little girls with red ribbons and, although the protective function is rarely alluded to and even poorly remembered today, the fondness for red is still evident. [….]

The folk history of the Travellers remains for now a maze of unanswered questions. However, there are many clues to the past in the living folk memory. [….]

Liz Stanley

IRISH JOURNAL OF FEMINIST STUDIES

review of *Irish Journal of Feminist Studies*, Vol 1, No 1, *Volume 4*, pp. 170-171

How good it is to see a feminist journal that has been designed rather than just put together. The *Irish Journal of Feminist Studies* is stylish, with a strong and attractive design image running from its cover (commendably, each one will feature original artwork by an Irish woman artist) through its last page. Its distinctive design and clear uncluttered pages make the *IJFS* a pleasure to look at and to read. Cork University Press are to be greatly congratulated on such an excellent job.

Can you judge a book by its cover? Different and more complex questions arise over the journal's intellectual content. Specifically, is this to be a feminist journal produced in Ireland, or – more difficult to bring off, very much more to be desired and prized – is it to be a journal of Irish feminist studies? The editorial in the inaugural issue hedges its bets here. The statement of 'Editorial Policy' as well as the beginnings of the editorial introduction emphasise a programme of investigating and theorising Irish women's lives and Irish gender issues, but then also insists that the journal will not be 'exclusive to Ireland' but feature feminist ideas 'sans frontiere'.

This dual set of interests is evident in the interesting mix of articles and reviews in the first issue. To an outsider such as myself, what comes across is that duality remains, rather than a synthesis reached. This is not a matter of theoretical naivity or any simple failure of epistemological nerve. It is of course that these matters of theory and epistemology, apparently 'culture free', are in fact completely situated, located and indeed local, and mainly hail from those very small places indeed called Anglo-America and social theory. In effect, a synthesis is not possible when one local knowledge – the small place of feminist social theory – is premised upon epistemic privilege over Others, here the larger but still local place of Ireland.

What is needed, what would be fascinating to watch unfold, would be the making of Irish feminist theory, methodology, epistemology, as definitely specific and iconoclastically its own: not Other or marginal to the presumed centre (white, Anglo-American, elitist) of feminist social theory in all its implicit intellectual imperialism.

Is the *IJFS* the space to watch for this happening? These are early days, but I for one hope that each successive group of editors will grasp the nettle and be pro-active rather than reactive in their work here. Better honourable and distinctive 'in your face' failures than the grey 'know your place' respectability of the vast majority of instantly forgettable academic journals. Go for it!

Alan Hayes

WOMEN PUBLISHING FEMINISM

Abstract: This paper presents a short chronological account of second wave commercial feminist publishing in Ireland, focusing on the output of five self-defined feminist publishing houses, namely Arlen House (1975-1987), Irish Feminist Information Publications (1978-1997), Women's Community Press (1983-1988), Women's Education Bureau (1984-) and Attic Press (1984-).

from 'Big Women, Little Women: Towards a History of Second Wave Commercial Feminist Publishing in Ireland', *Volume* 6, pp. 139-150

[....] Women's Community Press (WCP) was a unique development in Irish publishing – following a co-operative model, using a non-hierarchical structure and sharing work equally. The original aim of the co-operative was to open up the print medium to people and groups usually denied access to it. As they stated in 1983, "we believe that the culture and creativity of groups such as working people, unemployed people, women, travelling people, children, prisoners, those without literacy skills and so on, have been denied expression through the established channels of communication. We use the term 'community publishing' to describe our efforts to rectify this." They also acted as an information resource for community groups, 'Third World' organisations, trade unions, women's groups and literacy groups wishing to undertake their own publishing, offering them workshops and practical advice. [....]

The aim of WCP was to "transfer skills with a view to fostering community self-reliance and cooperation", and they stated that "we believe that community publishing challenges and changes traditional notions of what constitutes 'literature', 'history' and 'culture' by adding the infinitely rich ideas and knowledge of those excluded from that narrow and elitist framework." In 1983 the press received substantial funding from the European Commission's Women's Bureau in Brussels and set about producing a series of feminist postcards as their first endeavour following the training course. These postcards were a significant development in 1980s Ireland. Intensely political and critical of society, they were funny as well as thought-provoking. The cards sold in tens of thousands.

The first book published by WCP was the best-selling *Pure Murder ...A Book about Drug Use,* edited by Noreen O'Donoghue and Sue Richardson, which presented personal accounts of drug users and their families. In 1984 *I Hate Mustard* was the first collection of non-sexist stories written by children for children to be published in Ireland (this was later joined in 1987 by *Talk about Weird).* The *Irish Feminist Review* which also appeared in 1984, was an account of feminist activity in Ireland during that year.

WCP had a strong relationship with community writing groups and was at the forefront of the immense development of that sector during the 1980s. In 1985 they published *Write Up Your Street: An Anthology of Community Writing,* which presented work by both women and men from different communities. However, probably their most important publication appeared in 1986. This was *Out for Ourselves: The Lives of Irish Lesbians and* Gay *Men,* compiled by the Dublin Lesbian and Gay Men's

Collectives, a publication which presented for the first time the thoughts of one of the largest minority groups in Ireland. This book was subjected to unofficial censorship with many bookshops refusing to stock it (even the so-called 'radical' ones), and some sectors of the media declining to give it publicity or review it. WCP was always a small publisher and it was a constant struggle to stay in business. When the surviving members of the collective decided to close its doors in 1988, a small group set up a similar venture called Spellbound which was in some ways a direct continuation of WCP, and reproduced WCP's postcards along with introducing new themes. [....]

A selection of covers from books produced by Irish feminist publishers between 1975-1987

Mary O'Malley

The Maighdean Mhara

It is always the same,
The men say little and the women talk,
Guessing what the men are saying
In the long gaps between words.
Always fishing for clues
They drop barbs, make humourous casts
In an endless monologue of lures.
They'll say anything for a bite.
The men look hunted and stay silent.

But I can make them sing out
A shower of curses and commands.
I challenge them to win
Against the sea and other men.
They listen for the slightest whisper
Between me and the wind. They understand
My slightest sigh, and respond.

Here in my belly where men feel safe
I draw out their soft talk,
Rising, falling, low as breath.
At ease and sure of their control
They are, in Irish, eloquent.
I never let on anything
But fall and rise and humour them.

Notes on Contributors

Luz Mar González Arias is a lecturer and researcher at the English Department, University of Oviedo (North of Spain), her field of research being contemporary Irish women writers. She has worked on the inscription of female corporeality in the Irish text, as well as on the contemporary revisions of Greek mythology by Irish women poets and playwrights. She has a special interest in Postcolonial theories and literary practises and has published two books on these topics: *Otra Irlanda. La estética postnacionalista de poetas y artistas irlandesas contemporáneas*, Universidad de Oviedo, 2000 (*Another Ireland. The postnationalist aesthetics of contemporary Irish women poets and visual artists*) and *Cuerpo, mito y teorías feminista. Revisiones de Eva en autoras irlandesas contemporáneas*, KRK ediciones, 1998 (*Body, Myth and Feminist Theory. Contemporary Revisions of the Myth of Eve by Irish women writers*).

Brian Arkins is Professor of classics at NUI, Galway. He was educated at Clongowes Wood College and at University College, Dublin, where he obtained a M.A. in classics and a Ph.D. in Latin. His books include *Sexuality in Catallas, Builders of my Soul: Greek and Roman Themes in Yeats, James Liddy: A Critical Study,* and *Hell Rising Ireland: Greek and Roman Themes in Modern Irish Literature.*

Wanda Balzano directs the Women's and Gender Studies Program at Wake Forest University, where she teaches Irish literature and film. She has published on Irish and British literature in Italy, Ireland and the USA and is currently editing, with Moynagh Sullivan, a special issue of *The Irish Review* on 'Feminism and Irish Studies'.

Gráinne Blair has an MA in Women's Studies from UCD. She has been a fulltime carer for her elderly mother for the last 8 years. She has published and lectured on the Salvation Army in Ireland since 1995. She is currently involved in activism for Carers rights.

Eoin Bourke is a former Professor of German the National University of Ireland, Galway. Born in Dublin, he lived in Germany for 14 years, working as a translator, broadcasting for Bavarian Radio, and studying at Munich University for his PhD. He has published widely in Ireland, Britain, Germany and Austria on a variety of literary themes. His latest book, *The Austrian Anschluss in History and Literature*, was published by Arlen House and is to form the first of a series on 'Literature and

Testimony'. Eoin is now prepared a collection of the accounts of male and female German travel writers in Ireland in the first half of the 19th century.

Eva Bourke is originally from Germany and has lived in Galway for many years. She is married to Eoin Bourke and they have three children. Eva is the author of *Gonella* (Salmon, 1985), *Litany for the Pig* (Salmon, 1989), *Spring in Henry Street* (Dedalus, 1996), *Travels with Gandolpho* (Dedalus, 2000) and has translated the poet Elisabeth Borchers in *Winter on White Paper* (Dedalus, 2002). She has also compiled two anthologies of contemporary Irish poetry translated into German. Her latest critically-acclaimed collection, *The Latitude of Naples* (Dedalus), was launched in April 2005.

Catherine Boyle is Reader in Latin American Literary and Theatre Studies at King's College London. She is the author of *Chilean Theater, 1973–1985. Marginality, Power and Selfhood* (1992), and has published widely on Latin American theatre. Her translation, *House of Desires (Los empeños de una casa* by Sor Juana Inés de la Cruz), was performed in 2004 by the Royal Shakespeare Company. She is a co-founder and editor of the *Journal of Latin American Cultural Studies. Travesía.*

Margaret Brehony graduated with a BA in Psychology in 1980, later training as a practitioner of Chinese medicine. Her studies took her to Nanjing, Chinia where she graduated with a Diploma in Clinical Practice. She specialised in paediatric acupuncture at the London School of Traditional Chinese Medicine, and taught acupuncture as part of a primary health care programme in Nicaragua. Margaret has recently completed an MA in Culture and Colonialism at NUI, Galway. Currently in practice in Galway, she also works with the Irish Refugee Council Focusing on anti-poverty, health and advocacy programmes with asylum seekers and refugees.

Catríona Brennan (BA Hons. Sociology, BA Hons. Psychology, MBA) is an experienced Gender and Conflict Resolution specialist, who has published research on women entrepreneurs and their children and is the author of *Gender Awareness and Life Skills: A training Manual for Educators*. Catríona is currently working as an independent research consultant with the aim of providing professional and specialist support to organisations. She is a member of the National Domestic Violence Intervention Agency (NDVIA) Advisory Committee and is also a

Director of the Charity Aid Africa, providing support for children affected by HIV/Aids in Africa.

Rose Tuelo Brock, a South African, has been living in Galway since 1979. She has written essays and taken part in discussions on topics to do with Justice and Fairness in Trade, World Debt crisis, Arm's Trade, Racism and Human Rights. She also writes poetry and short stories. Currently, she has a column on the local weekly paper, the *Connacht City Tribune*. She is a founder member of the Galway 'One World' centre.

Anne Byrne is a sociologist working in the Department of Political Science and Sociology, NUI, Galway, with research interests that span self and social identity, singleness studies, social exclusion, participative research methodologies, group work and community relations. She has published in the area of identity, single women, feminist research methodologies and on aspects of the history of social anthropology in Ireland. Anne is a board member of both the Women's Health Council and MACNAS – a Community Arts organisation, and is actively involved in both national and local research advisory groups. Recent publications include 'Developing a Sociological Model for Researching Women's Self and Social Identities' in the *European Journal of Women's Studies* (Special Issue on Identities), 2003, Vol. 10 (4); and co-written with Deborah Carr 'Caught in the Cultural Lag: The Stigma of Singlehood' in *Psychological Inquiry*, 2005.

Moya Cannon (Máire Ní Chanainn) was born in Dunfanaghy, Co. Donegal in 1956 and now lives in Galway. She studied history and politics at UCD, and International Relations at Corpus Christi College, Cambridge. She has published two collections of poems, *Oar*, (Salmon, 1990, 1994; Gallery, 2000) and *The Parchment Boat* (Gallery, 1997). A third collection, provisionally entitled *Carrying the Songs* is nearing completion. She has been an editor of *Poetry Ireland Review* and has held a number of residencies, most recently at the *Centre Culturel Irlandais,* Paris. She has been a recipient of the Brendan Behan Award and of the Lawrence O'Shaughnessy Award. She is a member of Aosdána.

Mary Clancy researches, teaches, writes and broadcasts on women's history. In 2000, she edited (with Caitríona Clear et al), *Women's Studies Review*, Volume Seven, on Oral History and Biography. Her current research interest is women's political and public work in county Galway, c1880-1925.

Nóirín Clancy is a feminist and has worked with women's groups over the past 10 years, both as a community develpment worker and in a training capacity. Based in Galway, she works on a part-time basis with the Women's Human Rights Alliance which raises awareness of international agreements, particularly CEDAW, the Convention on the Elimination of All Forms of Discrimination Against Women. Recently Nóirín attended the 33rd session of the CEDAW Committee in New York as part of a delgation of Irish NGOs.She continues to do freelance work and recenlty deliverd a Gender and Community Develoment module as part of a Certificate in Women's Studies for NUI, Galway. Nóirín is involved in the management committee of the Galway Refugee Support Group in a voluntary capacity.

Timothy Collins is a Chartered Librarian in the James Hardiman Library, NUI, Galway. A UCG graduate in the marine sciences, he has kept up his interest in the subject by researching, lecturing and publishing a significant number of books and papers on the history and bibliography of Irish science. His first book *Floreat Hibernia* was published by the RDS in 1985. Recent books include *Transatlantic Triumph and Heroic Failure*, a study of the shortlived Galway Line (Collins Press 2002); and *Decoding the Landscape* (3rd ed. 2002), popular as a primer in Irish Studies as well as Landscape Studies.

Terri Conroy has an M.Phil. in Irish Studies from UCG (now NUI, Galway). She has taught in third level and in adult education, and is currently a teacher in Clifden community school.

Francesca Counihan took her BA in UCG (now NUI, Galway) in 1982, She then spent six years in France before returning to take up a temporary post in UCG in 1988, and moved to a permanent post in NUI Maynooth in 1991. She completed a 'Doctorat ès Lettres' at l'Université de Paris VII and has published extensively on the work of Marguerite Yourcenar (*L'Autorité dans l'œuvre romanesque de Marguerite Yourcenar*, Lille, Presses Universitaires du Septentrion, 1998), and, more recently, on French women writers since 1990 ('Women writers in Contemporary France' in *Contemporary French Cultures and Societies*, ed. F. Royall, Oxford, Lang, 2003, pp 373–393).

Catherine Cronin lectures part-time in the Information Technology (IT) department at NUI, Galway, and is the Academic Co-ordinator of a recently established distance learning M.Sc. programme in the department. She has worked in the engineering and IT industries, higher education and community education in Ireland, Scotland and the U.S. Catherine has degrees in both Mechanical and Systems Engineering, and completed her M.A. in Women's Studies at the University of Limerick in 1992.

Catríona Crowe is a Senior Archivist in the National Archives of Ireland. She was a management committee member of the Women's History Project 1997–2002, and is currently President of the Women's History Association of Ireland. She is Chairperson of the SAOL Project, an education, rehabilitation and advocacy project based in Dublin's north inner-city for women who are in treatment for drug addiction.

Esther-Mary D'Arcy is a Chartered Physiotherapist and worked in Acute Hospitals in Dublin and Galway. She specialised in Women's Health and became a member of the Chartered Physiotherapists in Women's Health in 1989. Esther-Mary completed a Diploma in the Psychology of Counselling and a MA in Health Promotion at NUI, Galway and trained as a Facilitator. She is currently seconded from her post as Physiotherapy Manager in University College Hospital Galway to work as a joint union management partnership Facilitator with the Health Services National Partnership Forum. Esther-Mary has always maintained close links with her professional body and currently is President of the Irish society of Chartered Phsiotherapists.

Celia Davies is currently Professor of Health Care at The Open University. She is known in Women's Studies for her work 'Gender and the Professional Predicament in Nursing' (Open University Press 1995), and for a series of reports completed when she was Professor of Women's Studies and Director of the Centre for Research on Women at the University of Ulster between the mid 1980s and mid 1990s.

Aoife de Paor graduated from NUI, Galway with a BA in English and History in 1995 and in 1996 completed a Masters in Literature and Publishing. She taught for a number of years in Coláiste na Coiribe in Galway before returning to NUI, Galway in the 1998/99 academic year to study for the Higher Diploma in Communications. After graduation, she spent a year and a half working for the *Tuam Herald* as a staff reporter and, since 2001, has worked as a GAA journalist with *Ireland on Sunday* in Dublin.

Louis de Paor is Director of Irish Studies at NUI, Galway. He has published a number of poetry collections with Coisceim, and recently co-edited *Remembered Nations, Imagined Republics*.

Mary Dempsey is from Galway. She is a writer, filmmaker and photographer. Her poetry has been published in Cúirt Journal, *ROPES* (NUI, Galway), *Women's Studies Review*, (NUI, Galway), *Crannóg* and *Cork Literary Review*. She wrote and performed a dramatic Monologue, *Lily*, for the Irish Women Writers' Conference (UCD) 1999. She has given poetry readings and workshops in Italy and France under The Socrates Programme for Adult Education, organised by The Galway City Library. Mary has made three short films which have been shown at festivals in Ireland and abroad and have been broadcast on RTE and TG4. She has received funding awards from The Irish Arts Council, The Galway Film Centre and Screen Training Ireland.

Sheila Dickinson is a PhD candidate in the History of Art Department at UCD writing on gender and art practice in contemporary Irish art. She also lectures at the National College of Art a nd Design.

Bernadette Divilly has an MA in Dance Movement Therapy from the Somatic Psychology Department at Naropa University Boulder Colorado. She works in private practice as well as doing some teaching/training in Dance Movement Therapy. The Irish Assoication of Creative Arts Therapies is a great support as she works towards bringing Dance Movement Therapy to the West of Ireland. She is pioneering an approach called Dance Diversity that works with interculturalism and power differences. Her engagement with the healing power of movement runs deep and she loves the intelligence of our human tissue in action and stillness.

Freda Donoghue is Senior Research Fellow at the Centre for Nonprofit Management (CNM) in the School of Business Studies, Trinity College Dublin. She holds a PhD in Sociology and has worked in and published on non-profit research for the past decade. She was the chief researcher on the Irish team in the Johns Hopkins Comparative Non-Profit Sector Project producing the first systematic data on the size and scope of the non-profit sector in Ireland, and is now engaged on a large-scale mapping project with the CNM. She was a member of the National Committee on Volunteering set up under the White Paper *Supporting Voluntary Activity* and the *Programme for Prosperity and Fairness*, which reported to Government in 2002. She was elected to the Board of the International Society for Third Sector Research as Treasurer in 2003.

Orla Egan has been actively involved in a variety of lesbian groups amd activities since the early 1980s. She is currently researching the history of the Cork Lesbian community 1975-1999 as a doctoral student in Women's Studies at Trinity College, Dublin and for future publication. She has previously worked as the Director of the Higher Education Equality Unit and has edited a series of publications on educational equality issues. She has also been involved in the development and delivery of Women's Studies courses in University College Cork.

Bernadette Fallon holds a BA in English, Sociology & Politics from UCG (now NUI, Galway), and an MA in Modernism, Postmodernism and Representation from University College Dublin. She has written extensively, in the area of the arts and contemporary culture, for Irish and international newspapers, magazines, books, websites, radio and TV; and has worked as a broadcaster and editor in Ireland and abroad. She currently lives and works in London.

Irene Finn is a secondary teacher in Waterford. She graduated from UCD and has also completed an MA in Women's Studies from UL. Her main research interest is in women's role in public health in late nineteenth and early twentieth century Ireland. She is the author of 'Women in the Medical Profession in Ireland, 1876-1919', in Bernadette Whelan (ed) *Women and Work in Ireland, 1500-1933* (Four Courts, Dublin, 2000).

Jo. George is a Senior Lecturer in the English Department at the University of Dundee. She teaches Old and Middle English and also runs the Joot Theatre Company, a drama group she established with her students in 1992. A graduate of Vassar College, Jo obtained her PhD from King's College, University of London. She has published widely in the fields of Old English poetry, mediaeval drama, the Pre-Raphaelites and translation theory. Before teaching in Dundee, she held posts at the National University of Ireland, Galway as well as UCD. She is currently on the editorial board of *The Grove*, working papers on English studies.

Maria Gibbons lives in Co. Leitrim and works in media and research, amongst other things.

Kerry Hardie is the author of several works, among them *In Sickness* (The Honest Ulsterman, 1995), *A Furious Place* (Gallery Press, 1996), *Cry for the*

Hot Belly (Gallery Press, 2000) and *The Sky Didn't Fall* (Gallery Press, 2004). Her first novel *Hannie Bennet's Winter Marriage* appeared in 2000 from HarperCollins and her next, *The Bird Woman*, is forthcoming. She is joint winner of the Michael Hartnett Poetry Award 2005.

Alan Hayes is a member of staff at NUI, Galway, where he is an activist for equality. He is the co-editor of *The Irish Women's History Reader* (Routledge, London/New York, 2001) and *Irish Women's History* (Irish Academic Press, Dublin 2004). He is publisher of Arlen House, Ireland's oldest feminist publisher, and is currently writing a biography of the six Gifford sisters and a history of feminist publishing.

Chris Head lives in the seaside town of Portstewart on the Antrim Coast. She is a practising visual artist, doodle diarist, writer and singer/songwriter. Her most recent project has been the production of a CD entitled *'Namaste'*. She is an accredited group facilitator whose work focuses on creative processes. In her experience too many of us have bought into the disabling myth that 'creativity is a gift bestowed on the few' and do not recognise or value the creativity within ourselves. For her it is vital that the gap that separates cultural life and experience from ordinary life, be closed.

Rita Ann Higgins was born in 1955 in Galway. She published her first five collections with Salmon, *Goddess & Witch* (1990), which combines *Goddess on the Mervue Bus* (1986) and *Witch in the Bushes* (1988), *Philomena's Revenge* (1992) and *Higher Purchase* (1996). From Blackstaff in 1996 appeared *Sunny Side Plucked: New & Selected Poems*, a Poetry Book Society Recommendation, *An Awful Racket* (2001) and *Throw in the Vowels: New and Selected Poems* (2005). Her plays include *Face Licker Come Home* (1991) and *Down All the Roundabouts* (1999). She was Galway County's Writer-in-Residence in 1987, Writer in Residence at NUI, Galway, in 1994-95, and Writer in Residence for Offaly County Council in 1998-99. In October 2000 she was Green Honors Professor at Texas Christian University. Her many awards include a Peadar O'Donnell Award in 1989 and several Arts Council bursaries. She is a member of Aosdána.

Myrtle Hill is currently Director of the Centre for Women's Studies at Queen's University, Belfast. A senior lecturer in social, religious and women's history, she has published widely in these areas. Her books include *Women in Ireland: A Century of Change*, Belfast, 2003, *The Time of the End: Millenarian Beliefs in Ulster,* Belfast, 2001, *Women of Ireland, Image & Experience c1880–1920* (2nd edtn.) Belfast, 1999 (with V. Pollock) and

Evangelical Protestantism in Ulster, 1740–1900, London, 1992 (with David Hempton). Recent articles on feminism and women's history include: 'Challenging the State we're in: The Feminist Seventies in 'Troubled' Northern Ireland', Helen Graham, Ann Kaloski, Ali Neilson and Emma Robertson, (eds.), *The Feminist Seventies*, York, 2003, pp. 75–90; 'Revisioning Women's Studies', *Feminist Theory*, Volume 4 (3) December, 2003, pp. 355–8;

Margaret Hodgins holds a BA (Mod.), MA and PhD from TCD. She was self-employed in a Dublin-based training company, a lecturer in Waterford IT, a distance education tutor for DCU, and, since 1995, has been employed by NUI, Galway in the Department of Health Promotion. Her research interests include workplace Health Promotion, bullying and work life balance, traveller health, and quality of life of older people.

Eileen Kane is president of GroundWork, an NGO that helps communities in Third World countries to identify and implement their own priorities. She developed the first department of anthropology in Ireland, and is a former chair of the Irish government's advisory body on development aid. In recent years, she has focused on girls' education in Africa. She was Visiting Irish Professor at the World Bank and is the author of *Seeing for Yourself* and *Girls' Education in Africa* (World Bank 1995, 2004) and *Doing Your Own Research* (Boyars, 2000).

Constantina Katsari is lecturing at the History Department of the National University of Ireland, Galway. She is the co-editor of the book *Patterns in the Economy of Roman Asia Minor* (Classical Press of Wales 2005) and the co-author of the book *The Mint of Amorium and the Coin Finds, Amorium Reports V* (BAR International Series 2006, forthcoming). She has also published articles and reviews in both refereed journals and edited collections on all aspects of the society, economy and ideology of the Roman Empire.

Nuala Keher is the Chief Executive Officer of Líonra. This relatively new Network consists of the seven third-level Colleges in Ireland's Border Midlands and Western (BMW) Region. She is a member of the Board of Skillnets, a body established by the Department of Enterprise Trade and Employment to support enterprise-led training and networking and is a Director of IDEAS Institute, a SIPTU subsidiary. A former Manager of the National University of Ireland, Galway's Open Learning Centre and of the National Executive Council of SIPTU, Nuala has a particular interest in the area of collaboration between higher education and enterprise and building networks between the Social Partners, Educationalists, Trainers and the Adult Worker/Learner population. She holds a Masters degree in Sociology and has published in the area of Organisational Change and Labour Rights.

Cecily Kelleher was appointed to the foundation chair of Health Promotion at NUI Galway in 1990 and over the next decade developed an inter-disciplinary research programme that included the direction of Ireland's first ever national lifestyle survey, SLAN (Survey of Lifestyles, Attitudes and Nutrition) and numerous intervention programmes to improve health among vulnerable groups and in settings like the workplace and primary care. She took up the chair of public health medicine and epidemiology in UCD in January 2003. Her interests are in the contribution of social factors to the development of chronic ill-health, particularly cardiovascular disease. She is presently chair of the statutory Women's Health Council and a member of the National Council for Bioethics at the Royal Irish Academy. She has published 20 reports, 3 books and 100 peer published papers.

Catherine Kelly graduated from Exeter University in 2002 with a PhD in Drama. Her interest is in contemporary Irish Theatre and her thesis considered the theme of the 'internal exile' in this context. Currently, she is pursuing her interest in drama through creative writing. She was among the prize winners in RTE's P.J. O'Connor Radio Drama Awards (2004). Her first play Iona was broadcast in autumn 2004. She teaches in a secondary school in Northern Ireland.

Anne Kennedy (née Hoag) was born in Los Angeles in 1935. She was educated at Stanford and worked as a high school teacher and freelance journalist. With her close friend, Rex Stewart, a former trumpet player in the Duke Ellington Band, she recorded a series of interviews with jazz musicians which is now housed in Ellington's archive in the Smithsonian Museum of American History. She moved to the San Juan Islands in the Pacific Northwest in 1972 and from there to Galway in 1977. A talented photographer, her work includes a series inspired by Nora Barnacle and another by Irish proverbs. Her first poetry collection, *Buck Mountain Poems* (Salmon, 1989) was inspired by the thousand year old *Cold Mountain Poems* by the Chinese poet Han Shan and is set in the San Juan Islands. Her second volume, *The Dog Kubla Dreams My Life* (Salmon, 1994), is a haunting exploration of memory and belonging, notable for its fragile and evocative imagery. Anne Kennedy died in 1998 and is survived by four daughters and a son.

Mary Kierse is presently working with the National Educational Welfare Board in Ennis as an Educational Welfare Officer. She holds a BA, MA, and H.Dip from UCG (now NUI, Galway).

Siobhán Kilfeather was born and raised in Belfast. She studied at Cambridge and at Princeton where she completed a PhD on eighteenth-century Irish women writers. She has taught at Columbia University, the University of Chicago (as a Visiting professor), and at the University of Sussex. She now teaches Irish writing in the English Department, Queen's University Belfast. She was an editor of *The Field Day Anthology of Irish Writing: Irish Women's Writing and Traditions* and has published essays on Irish feminism and on eighteenth and nineteenth-century Irish literature. She is currently writing a book on the Irish gothic.

Jessie Lendennie is a poet, and publisher with Salmon Publishing. She was born in Arkansas and moved to Galway in 1981. Widely anthologized, her collection *Daughter* was published by both Salmon Publishing and Signpost Press in the USA. Jessie was a co-founder of *The Salmon* magazine and the Cúirt International Festival of Literature in Galway. She currently lives near the Cliffs of Moher in Clare.

Ronit Lentin is director of the MPhil in Ethnic and Racial Studies, Department of Sociology, Trinity College Dublin. Her books include *Conversations with Palestinian Women* (1982), and *Israel and the Daughters of the Shoah: Reoccupying the Territories of Silence* (2000). Her edited collections include *Gender and Catastrophe* (1997), *(Re)searching Women: Feminist Research Methodologies in the Social Sciences in Ireland* (with Anne Byrne, 2000), *Racism and Anti-racism in Ireland* (with Robbie McVeigh, 2002), *Women and the Politics of Military Confrontation: Palestinian and Israeli Gendered Narratives of Dislocation* (with Nahla Abdo 2002), *Re-presenting the Shoah for the 21st Century* (2004), and *Representing Migrant Women in Ireland and the EU* (with Eithne Luibhéid, special issue of Women's Studies International Forum, vol 27/4, 2004). Ronit has published extensively on racism and gender, gender and genocide, Israel and the Holocaust, Israeli and Palestinian women.

Maria Luddy is Reader in History at Warwick University. She has published extensively on the history of women in Ireland in the nineteenth and twentieth centuries. She was Director of the Women's History Project from 1997 to 2001, and co-editor of the *Field Day Anthology of Irish Writing: Irish Women's Writings and Traditions*, vols4 and

5 (Cork/New York, 2002). She is currently working with Dr Gerardine Meaney on an AHRB-funded project which will create a database of all Irish women writers, writing in the Irish and English languages, between 1800 and 2000.

Victor Luftig is Associate Professor and Director of the Centre for the Liberal Arts at the University of Virginia. He wrote *Seeing Together: Friendship Between the Sexes in English Writing, from Mill to Woolf* (Stanford UP, 1993) and co-edited a collection of essays on Joyce and history. He is interested in intersections between literature and government: the piece included here will become part of a book on the Kennedys and literature, a sequel to his current project on the search for Poet Laureate in the years after the death of Tennyson.

Joan McBreen is from Sligo and lives in Tuam. Her poetry collections are *The Wind Beyond the Wall* (Story Line Press) and *A Walled Garden in Moylough* (Story Line Press and Salmon Publishing). Awarded an MA Degree from UCD in 1997, she compiled and edited *The White Page/An Bhileog Bhán: Twentieth Century Irish Women Poets* (Salmon Publishing 1999, 2000, 2001). Her latest collection, *Winter in The Eye: New and Selected Poems*, was published by Salmon in 2003. Her first CD, *The Long Light on the Land: Selected Poems by Joan McBreen with Traditional Airs and Classical Music*, was launched in 2004.

Emer McCarthy is a graduate in geography and sociology from Maynooth University and has a Masters in Health Promotion. She has worked as a researcher in Health Promotion in NUI, Galway and as co-ordinator of the Galway Health Project, and is currently a teacher in Galway.

Claire McDonagh was born and educated in Galway. She has two adult children, is widowed and lives in County Galway. She was involved with the foundation of 'Waterside House Refuge for Distressed Women and Children' and was employed there from 1981-2002. She also managed 'Westside House Hostel for Homeless Women' for ten years. She was chairperson of the National Federation of Women's Refuges for six years and in 1996 was selected as 'Galway Person of the Year'. Claire is currently running her own counselling practice part-time.

Anne MacFarlane graduated with a B.A. (Psychology and Sociology) from University College Cork in 1992. She then completed her MA (1995) and Ph.D (1998) in the Department of Health Promotion, NUI, Galway. After working as a Research Fellow in University College London for two years (2000–2002), Anne returned to Galway and held a Health Research Board Health Services Research Fellowship in the Department of General Practice, NUI, Galway (2002–2004). Anne was appointed Lecturer in Primary Care at the Department of General Practice in August 2004. Anne's research programme is underpinned by a strong interest in the sociology of health and illness, particularly people's perspectives and experiences of accessing and using primary healthcare services. Her current research programme includes studies of refugee and asylum seeker health issues, telehealthcare, anti-microbial prescribing behaviour and medical education research.

Hannagh McGinley has recently graduated with a masters from NUI Galway. In her view, she has to date only written poetry from the heart, but some day she hopes to write from the intellect.

Mary Mangan is originally from Dublin and seeing her family reared returned to education as a mature student in 1999, embarking on the Certificate/Diploma in Women's Studies in NUI Galway. She completed her BA in 2004 with a degree in English and History and then gained valuable research skills as a trainee genealogical researcher with Galway Family History (West). She is returning to an area of specific interest to her with the challenge of an MA in Women's Studies in 2005/2006.

Stephen Mannix graduated from UCD in 1996 with a Masters degree in Psychological Research. He currently works at Computer Associates International, as a Technical Specialist in the field of Data Warehousing.

Catherine Marshall is Senior Curator, Head of Collections at the Irish Museum of Modern Art. She is an art-historian, and a graduate of Trinity College Dublin and University College Dublin. She lectured in the History of Art Department at Trinity College, Dublin from 1987 to 1996 and taught programmes at the National College of Art and Design and at University College Dublin. She has been twice elected to the Chair of the Irish Association of Art Historians, served on the Board of the Douglas Hyde Gallery, 1990–1995, and was a member of the executive committee of the Centre for Gender and Women's Studies at TCD (1992 –2002). She has served on various national committees, participated in a number of Public Art Selection processes and been guest speaker at conferences and events from the Burren Law School to the 'Re-Imagining Ireland' Conference in Virginia, U.S.A, 2003. In 2004 she curated 'Views from an Island', Contemporary Irish Art from the Collection of the IMMA' which was shown at the Millenium Monument Museum in Beijing and the Shanghai Art Museum.

Helen Mortimer has a background in teaching and adult education. She has worked as a counsellor/psychotherapist in Galway and in Mayo and is a regular contributor to newspapers on issues relating to women.

Peter Moser is the head of the Archives for rural history in Zollikofen/Bern (www.agrararchiv.ch) and is currently working (together with Tony Varley) on a biography of Elizabeth Bobbett (1898–1971), the forgotten farmer, feminist and strike leader from Wicklow, who was a founder and longtime General Secretary of the Irish Farmers' Federation.

Philomena Mullen was born in Ireland to an Irish mother and a Nigerian father. She is a graduate of Trinity College Dublin, where she read English and Philosophy. She undertook the M.Phil. in Women's Studies with a dissertation theorising Rwandan women's use of violence during the 1994 genocide. In recent years she has become involved in the issue of race within an Irish context and is formerly a member of the National Consultative Committee on Racism and Interculturalism. She works in Dublin with the Legal Unit of the Irish Traveller Movement.

Singer/songwriter *Sharon Murphy* grew up in Connemara and now lives in Galway city. Many of her songs deal with personal and social issues, and her début CD, *Invisible Walls*, containing thirteen original songs, is on release in Ireland.

Nóirín Ní Riain is an internationally acclaimed spiritual singer. She has recently completed a Doctorate at the University of Limerick, the first in theology awarded by that University. The subject of her thesis was towards a theology of listening and sound for which she coined the word 'Theosony', which embraces all aspects of 'The Sound of God'. Nóirín travels worldwide giving experiential workshops on this subject. Furthermore, she is currently writing a book on the subject for publication in 2006 by Veritas Publications, Dublin.

Ana Nunes studied English and Portuguese University of Coimbra. A period of graduate study followed at University College Dublin before she completed her MA in American Studies at the University of Coimbra in 2000. She is currently finalising her doctorate at University College Dublin. Her research focuses on African American History fiction. Recent publications include 'Memory Recreated: Let Me Give Witness the Only

Way I Can' published in *Landscapes of Memory* (2004). Forthcoming publications include articles on historical fiction, Sherley Anne Williams, and Dessa Rose for a *Feminist Encylopaedia of African American Litterature* edited by Elizabeth Ann Beaulieu (Greenwood Press). Ana is a senior tutor in the School of English at University College Dublin, where she also teaches a seminar on African American fiction.

Helen O'Donoghue graduated in Fine Art from the National College of Art and Design, Dublin in 1979. She initiated the first formal arts intervention at primary school level with the artist Dervil Jordan: (*Paint on the Wall*, a murals in primary schools scheme) with the Arts Council of Ireland (1985). Helen also formed a co-operative film and video company 'City Vision' and was one of its directors until 1989. With this company she directed a series of video projects with and about children. In 1991, Helen was appointed Senior Curator/Head of Education and Community Programmes at the Irish Museum of Modern Art (IMMA). Her projects with IMMA included work with the formal education sector and with communities living in the Museum's locality. Since 1999, Helen has travelled throughout the country with the Museum's National Programme. She curated the exhibition *Once Is Too Much* in 1997 at the Irish Museum of Modern Art.

Mary O'Donoghue grew up in Co. Clare and now lives in Boston. Her first collection *Tulle* is published by Salmon Poetry, and her poems have appeared in a wide range of European and North American periodicals and anthologies. She is also a writer of fiction, and her stor ies have appeared in *The Dublin Review*, *The Stinging Fly*, *The Cuirt Annual* and *AGNI*. She is assistant professor of English at Babson College, Massachusetts.

Orla O'Donovan is a lecturer in the Department of Applied Social Studies in University College Cork. Her current research focuses on the cultures of action of social movement organisations mobilised around health issues, and debates about corporate colonisation of health activism.

Christine O'Dowd-Smyth is lecturer in French and Francophone Studies at Waterford Institute of Technology. She has just completed a PhD in North African Francophone Literatures and a chapter of her thesis is devoted to the coming to writing of Algerian and Moroccan women. Her research interests include the comparative study of the problematic of postcolonial identity in both North African writing in French, and Irish writing in English; Diasporic writing; Women's autobiography; Contemporary French society; Womens Studies.

Riana O'Dwyer is senior lecturer in the English Department at the National University of Ireland, Galway. She edited the section on 'Women's Narratives 1800–1840' in the *Field Day Anthology of Irish Writing*, Vol. 5. Riana was elected Chair of the International Association for the Study of Irish Literatures (IASIL) for the period 2003–6. She has lectured and published on Joyce, modern Irish drama, Irish studies, and Irish women novelists of the nineteenth century.

Pádraig Ó Héalaí is senior lecturer in the School of Irish at the National University of Ireland, Galway. He obtained his M.A. in Modern Irish at University College Dublin and his PhD from the National University of Ireland for a dissertation on legends concerning New Testament characters in Irish tradition. His research interests include Irish folklore with special emphasis on religious narratives and on beliefs and customs associated with the supernatural in Irish tradition. He has published widely on these topics and was Editor of *Béaloideas*, the journal of the Folklore of Ireland Society from 1981–95.

Aine O'Healy is Professor of Modern Languages and Literatures at Loyola Marymount University, Los Angeles. She specializes in Italian feminism, history and theory of film, and cultural studies. She was formerly Professor of Italian at NUI Galway.

Ann O'Kelly lectures in the Centre for Nursing Studies at NUI, Galway. She has previously worked in the Centre for Health Promotion on the Social Care programme, and as co-ordinator of a HORIZON project.

Jane O'Leary was born in America, and is a leading figure in the promotion, performance and composition of new music in Ireland. She is a graduate of Vassar College and Princeton University (PhD). An Irish resident since 1972, Jane created the distinguished contemporary music ensemble *Concorde* in 1976, and is their director and pianist. Her compositions have been widely performed internationally and her orchestral work 'From Sea-Grey Shores' was selected for performance by the National Symphony Orchestra of Ireland on their debut American tour in 2003. She is a founder member of *Aosdána*, a founder member of *Music for Galway*, and was Composer-in-Residence at the Royal Irish Academy of Music in Dublin from 2000–2003.

Mary O'Malley is the author of four collections of poetry published by Salmon Press and *The Boning Hall: New and Selected Poems* published by Carcanet. She grew up in Connemara, has received a Hennessy award for her poetry, as well as three Arts Council bursaries. She has two children, lives in Galway and is a member of Aosdana. She was 2003 writer in residence in the Irish Cultural Centre in Paris and has been Director of the Douglas Hyde Conference for the past two years.

Mary O'Malley-Madec is director of the Villanova University Centre at NUI, Galway. She is a poet and researcher and completed her Ph.D. on socio-linguistics at the University of Pennsylvania.

Rosaleen O'Neill lectures in the Department of German at NUI, Galway. Her research interests include 18th century German language and literature and translation studies. She was co-editor of volume six of the *Women's Studies Review*.

Karen Offen is a historian and independent scholar, affiliated as a Senior Scholar with the Institute for Research on Women and Gender, Stanford University. She is a founder and past secretary/treasurer of the International Federation for Research in Women's History, and currently serves on the Board of Directors for the International Museum of Women (San Francisco). Her article, 'Defining Feminism: A Comparative Historical Approach,' *Signs: Journal of Women in Culture and Society,* 14:1 (Fall 1988), has been translated in French, Spanish, German, Japanese, and Italian. Her most recent book is *European Feminisms, 1700–1950: A Political History* (Stanford University Press, 2000). She is completing a book on the 'woman question' debate in modern France

Mary Owens worked in the Centre for Development Studies and the Department of Adult and Continuing Education at NUI, Galway from 1989–2000. During that period she was involved in the Rural Women's Research Project at the Women's Studies Centre. She is now an independent radio producer.

Mike Power graduated from Waterford RTC, (WIT) in 1980, and worked in UCD, for six months. He also worked in the Department of fisheries in Abbotstown for three months on mussel (fish) diseases. Mike graduated from UCG (now NUI, Galway) with a first class honours degree in Biochemistry in 1982. He then worked in the diagnostics industry in Galway for five years, and completed his PhD in 1989 in Immunodiagnostics on bone diseases. Mike works, almost exclusively, in bone-related studies in the field of biochemistry.

Mary Pruitt worked for the Welfare Department in the late 1960s, and learned that the face of poverty in America is a face of color, and its people are women and children. She became a feminist and a fighter for civil rights. In 1973, at Minneapolis Community College, Mary was a Founding Mother of the Women's Studies Program. She completed her MA in College Counselling, at Hunter College, City University of New York, and her PhD in American Studies, at the University of Minnesota.

Christina Quinlan is currently completing her PhD in the School of Communications at Dublin City University. Her thesis is a feminist ethnographic study of women in prison in Ireland. In this work Christina is focusing on an examination of different constructions and representations of the identities of the imprisoned women. Christina's background is in social research. From a master's degree in Rural Development, both Irish and third world development, as Research Officer in the Community Office at DCU, Christina undertook a great deal of research, working generally with marginalised populations. Christina teaches Research Methods at DCU, both quantitative and qualitative. She has a particular interest in visual research methods.

Mary Quinn is a lecturer in the Department of Management in NUI, Galway, primarily in the area of industrial relations. She has been interested in gender equality in employment for many years. In 2002, she completed a PhD on the process and outcomes of Equality Officer investigation under the Employment Equality Act, 1977. She currently lectures on a number of courses on the B.Comm. and the M.B.S in Industrial Relations and Human Resource Management. She is currently working on research on workplace health and safety in the Irish hotel industry.

Maggie Ronayne is Co-ordinator of the Global Women's Strike in Ireland. The Strike is a network of grassroots women in over 60 countries, independent of political parties.She is a lecturer in Archaeology at NUI, Galway. Her expertise is on the archaeological case against cultural destruction by war and large development projects; her work has helped support Kurdish villagers fight against dam construction. Her academic work, highlighting women's essential role in creating and defending culture, is informed by her commitment to and involvement in the Strike.

Her most recent book is *The Cultural and Environmental Impact of Large Dams In Southeast Turkey.*

Eilish Rooney is a feminist community activist and academic in the School of Sociology and Applied Social Studies, University of Ulster. Her work on women in the northern Irish conflict has appeared in a range of publications. Recent contributions have included *Feminist Theory* and the *Community Development Journal*. She contributed a section on contemporary Northern Irish women's writing to the *Field Day Anthology of Irish Writing, Vol. V: Irish Women's Writing & Traditions*. She is currently working with the Transitional Justice Institute in the university on women and gender equality in the transition process that has followed the Good Friday Agreement. She is Co-ordinator of Academic Affairs: Community Studies and Programme Director of the BSc (Hons) Community Development.

Caitríona Ruane is a deeply committed human rights and community activist. Caitríona worked for a US-based aid foundation from 1983–87 in Central America. On her return to Ireland she worked full-time for Trocaire before co-founding the Center for Research and Documentation, which studied conflict resolution in South Africa and Central America and hosted Nobel Peace Prize winners (Rigoberta Menchu from Guatemala and Jose Ramos Horta from East Timor) on a visit to Ireland. Caitríona has been an international observer for elections in South Africa, and was a member of the Committee on the Administration of Justice and organised the Belfast Forum on Policing conference in 1994. From 1997–2001 Caitríona was the Director of Feile an Phobail (the West Belfat Festival and Europe's biggest Community Festival) and a founder of the St. Patrick's Day Parade, during which time she took unionists in the city hall to court on grounds of funding discrimination. In 2000 President Mary McAleese presented Caitríona with the Aisling Person of the Year Award. Caitríona was elected MLA for South Down in November 2003 and since then has been an integral participant in the Peace Talks.

Angela Ryan is a lecturer in French at UCC. Her research interests include French and comparative literature and thought, psychoanalysis and philosophy applied to literature; myth and subjectivity; theory; art history; women and the media; the rhetoric of the body and representation and mimetics of the tragic heroine.

Christiane Schönfeld completed her PhD in Germanic Languages and Literatures at the Pennsylvania State University in 1994. She currently teaches German and Film at the National University of Ireland, Galway. She has published a book on the prostitute in German expressionism entitled *Dialektik und Utopie* (Würzburg: Königshausen & Neumann, 1996), edited *Commodities of Desire: The Prostitute in German Literature* (Rochester: Camden House, 2000), and co-edited *Denkbilder. Festschrift für Eoin Bourke* (Königshausen & Neumann, 2004). She has published articles on expressionism, autobiography, confessional narratives, 19th and 20th century women writers, and German film.

Lorna Shaughnessy lectures in the Department of Hispanic Studies, NUI, Galway, teaching on BA and BComm programmes, the Diploma in Spanish and the taught MA on Latin American Literature. Research interests include modern Spanish poetry, particularly the Generation of '27, also political poetry by women poets from Central America and contemporary Mexican Poetry. She is currently preparing the publication of translations of contemporary Mexican poetry for Edwin Mellen Press (2005) and Arlen House (2006). Other areas of interest include political participation by women in Central America from 1970–1990s, postcolonial theory, and the uses of Mesoamerican mythologies in the political literature of the Region.

Ethna Shryane RGN., SCM., M.A., is a graduate of NUI, Galway. She is currently working as Nurse/Medical Researcher with the Department of General Practice, NUI, Galway on the CoHeart Study, and she also works with Nursing Support Services at the University College Hospital Galway.

Jane Sixsmith is a lecturer in Health Promotion at the Department of Health Promotion NUI, Galway, and a contributing member of The Centre for Health Promotion Studies, NUI, Galway. Jane previously completed twelve years professional registered nursing experience, including community-based practice, which focused on aspects of women's health, community and public health. Subsequent to undertaking an MA in Health Promotion in 1994/5, Jane worked as a researcher within the Department of Health Promotion NUI, Galway prior to gaining a teaching post in 1999 and a lectureship in 2001.

Ailbhe Smyth has been Director of WERRC at UCD since 1990, and has worked in Women's Studies since the early 1980s. She lectures and writes mainly about women and gender in contemporary Ireland, feminist, lesbian and radical politics, and cultural issues. She has served on numerous State boards including the Higher Education Authority and as a Trustee of the National Library, and as a consultant on a wide range of equality issues in Ireland and Europe. Active in feminist, lesbian and gay and other radical politics for many years, she is currently Co-Chair of the National Lesbian and Gay Federation. Her articles and essays have been published widely, and she has written and edited books on feminist issues.

Liz Stanley is Professor of Sociology at the University of Edinburgh, and is very committed to collaborative projects, including as former editor of four journals – *Women's Studies International Forum, Sociology, Sociological Research Online* and *Auto/Biography*. Her current research interests are concerned with memory and state commemoration, particularly in South Africa. Relevant publications are *Imperialism, Labour and the New Woman: Olive Schreiner's Social Theory* (Durham, Sociology Press, 2002) and *Mourning Becomes...: Post/Memory and Commemoration of the Concentration Camps of the South African War 1899–1902* (Manchester: Manchester University Press; & New Brunswock: Rutgers University Press).

Sheila Street is a graduate of NUI Galway and NUI Maynooth. She worked with AIDS West in a voluntary capacity and as a staff member for a number of years. In 1998 she moved to Dublin where she spent six years working in local drug services for heroin users, their families and communities. The work involved community development, family support, drug education and outreach work to women working in prostitution. The birth of her daughter prompted a delightful career change and a return to the West, and she is currently exploring the possibility of returning to work that involves less use of crayons!

Marian Tannam is a consultant, trainer and researcher. She has a B.A. in Communication and a Masters in Equality Studies. She has been involved in anti-racism in Ireland for over twenty-years and was a founding member of Harmony (1986-98), an anti-racist/intercultural family organisation. In her work with the Dominican Justice Office she recently co-ordinated an NGO Alliance project which produced and presented a Shadow Report to the Irish Government's First Report to the UN Committee on the Elimination of All Forms of Racial Discrimination. She is a partner in Harnett Tannam Consultancy which provides consultancy and training in anti-racism, intercultural communication and diversity management. See www.htconsultancy.com for details. Her experience of being in an intercultural family has given her insight into issues of culture and racism in Irish society.

Jane Tynan currently teaches Cultural Studies at Central Saint Martins College of Art and Design in London. She studied in Belfast and Dublin and has written extensively on gender and identity. Her current research explores British masculinities through First World War representations of men in uniform.

Diane Urquhart has a PhD and MA from the Queen's University of Belfast. She is a former fellow of the Institute of Irish Studies of Queen's and has worked as a researcher for the Women's History Project. She is currently the Deputy Director and Senior Lecturer in Modern Irish History at the Institute of Irish Studies of the University of Liverpool. Her publications include *Women In Ulster Politics, 1890–1940: A History Not Yet Told* (Dublin, 2000) and *The papers of the Ulster Women's Unionist Council and Executive Committee, 1911–40*. She is also the co-editor of *Coming Into the Light: The Work, Politics and Religion of Women in Ulster, 1840–1940* (Belfast, 1994); *The Irish Women's History Reader* (London, 2001) and *Irish Women's History* (Dublin, 2003). She is currently researching aristocratic Anglo-Irish women's use of political patronage in the 19th and 20th centuries.

John Waddell is Professor of Archaeology at NUI Galway. Among his publications are *The Bronze Age Burials of Ireland* and *The Prehistoric Archaeology of Ireland*.

Sylvia Walby is Professor of Sociology at Lancaster University. She is interested in both theoretical development and policy impact, and enjoy engaging in collaborative research. My research is situated within the tension between general social theory and specific forms of inequality, especially gender. Over the years this led me from theories of patriarchy to a current concern to mainstream difference into social theory. Substantively, I have an interest in economic matters, a fascination with new political forms, and concern with marginalised groups (domestic violence matters). Today, all of these issues are framed by globalisation, the understanding of which requires new forms of social theory, especially complexity theories.

Eilís Ward is lecturer in the Department of Political Science and Sociology in NUI, Galway where she teaches in the areas of of gender, development, human rights and politics. She has published on women's political participation, the women's movement in Ireland, Irish refugee policies and citizenship. Her current research topics include women and the sex industry in Ireland.

UCG Women's Studies Centre Review
Volume One, 1992

EDITORS: Anne Byrne, Jane Conroy, Sean Ryder,

Introduction

Women and Irish Society
Anne Byrne / Statistics – What Do They Tell us About Women?

Mary Owens / Women in Rural Development: A Hit or Miss Affair?

Mary O'Malley / The Irish Travelling Woman: Mother and Mermaid

Women's History
John Waddell / Women in Ancient Europe

Timothy Collins / Irish Women Scientists

Alan Hayes / The *Real* Maud Gonne

Women and the Arts
Angela Mehegan / The Representation of Women in Fine Art

Jane O'Leary / Swimming Against the Stream: Women Composers Then and Now

Margaret E. Fogarty / Images of God in Women's Writing

Jodi-Anne George / The Women's Art: May and Jane Morris and their Embroidery

Catherine M. Boyle / The Creative Force in Marginality: Women in Latin American Writing

Bernadette Fallon / Sylvia Path: The Double in the Woman

Christian D. Stevens / Editorial Restraint in *The Revelations of Divine Love*

UCG Women's Studies Centre Review
Volume Two, 1993

EDITORS: Anne Byrne, Jane Conroy, Sean Ryder

Introduction

Women and Difference
Eileen Kane / Women: Mismeasured and Misunderstood?

Nuala Keher / Women and Trade Union Restructuring: Women Must Wait?

Rosaleen O'Neill / An End to Privilege? East German Women and German Unification

Peter Moser / Rural Economy and Female Emigration in the West of Ireland 1936–1956

Celia Davies / The Equality Mystique: The Difference Dilemma and The Case of Women Academics

Women and Creativity
Eva Bourke, Moya Cannon, Anne Kennedy, Jessie Lendennie, Joan Mc Breen, Mary O'Malley / Salmon Poets

Nóirín Ní Riain / Sound Women: An Irish Perspective on Female Musical Creativity in Song

Francesa Counihan / At Last, A Woman in the Academy? Marguerite Yourcenar as Woman Writer

Ailbhe Smyth / Borderline Crosstalk

Women and The Body
Tom O'Malley / Perceptions of Sexual Violence

RuthRiddick / Irish Abortion Rights: 1992, A Year of Achievement

Cecily Kelleher / Hormone Replacement Therapy: Is it Good for Women's Health?

Esther-Mary D'Arcy / Able-Bodied Women?

Imelda Leahy / The Sport of Kings-and Queens? A Brief Review of Women's Status in Irish Racing

UCG Women's Studies Centre Review
Volume Three, 1995

EDITORS: Pat Byrne, Jane Conroy, Alan Hayes

Introduction

Women, Feminism and the Academy
Ronit Lentin / Explicitly Feminist? Feminist Research Methodologies Re-Visited

Liz Stanley / Speaking 'as a…', Speaking 'for the…': On the Mis/Uses of the Category 'Experience' in recent Feminist Thought

Mary Brigid Kelly / Exploring Feminist Teaching – Teaching Feminism

Catherine I. Cronin / Is the 'Feminine Engineer' an Oxymoron? Women's Views and Experiences of Gender and Engineering

Karen Offen / Reflections on National Specificities in Continental European Feminisms

Women's History
Brian Arkins / The Reign of the Phallus: Women in Fifth Century Athens

Aoife de Paor / The Status of Women in Medieval Ireland

James Lewton-Brain / Witches and Gender

Mary Clancy / '… it was our joy to keep the flag flying': A Study of the Women's Suffrage Campaign in County Galway

Women and Literature
Karen Robertson / Considering the Black Woman in *The White Devil*

Riana O'Dwyer / Woman and her Master: Lady Morgan and Feminism

Anne Colman / Nineteenth-Century Irish Women Writers: An Overview

Victor Luftig / Power all the Way: Poetry, Presidents, and the Centre

Women, Rights and Powers
Lorna Shaughnessy / Military Participation and Moral Authority: Women's Political Participation in Nicaragua, 1975–95

Mary C. Pruitt / 'At the Center of Resistance': Contemporary North American Indigenous Women

Catherine Itzin / Pornography, Harm and Human Rights: The European Context

Monica O'Connor and *Niamh Wilson* / Violence against Women: A Human Rights Issue

Anne Byrne / Making Development Work for Women

Book Reviews

Sean Ryder on Eva Cherniavsky, 1995, *That Pale Mother Rising: Sentimental Discourses and the Imitation of Motherhood in 19th Century America.*

Orla Ní Chomhraí on Natalie Zemon Davis and Arlette Farge (eds), 1995, *A History of Women in the West. III: Renaissance and Enlightment Paradoxes.*

Stephen Mannix on Karen Green, 1995, *The Woman of Reason: Feminism Humanism and Political Thought.* Susan J. Hekman, 1995, *Moral Voices, Moral Selves: Carol Gilligan and Feminist Moral Theory.*

Timothy Collins on John Mahon, 1995, *Kate Tyrell 'Lady Mariner': The Story of the Extraordinary Woman Who Sailed the Denbighshire Lass.*

Clare Leon on Ngaire Naffine (ed.), 1995, *Gender, Crime and Feminism.*

Elizabeth Tilley on Nancy Owen Nelson, (ed.), 1995, *Private Voices, Public Lives: Women Speak on the Literary Life.*

Conor Pentony on Andrea Nye, 1994, *Philosophia: The Thought of Rosa Luxemburg, Simone Weil and Hannah Arendt.*

Eilís Ward on Annelise Orleck, 1995, *Common Sense and a Little Fire: Women and Working-Class Politics in the United States, 1900–1965.*

Caitriona Clear on Kathyrn Kish Sklar, 1995, *Florence Kelley and the Nation's Work: The Rise of Women's Political Culture 1830–1900.*

Marie Boran on Molly Ladd-Tylor, 1994, *Mother-Work: Women, Child Welfare, and the State, 1890–1930.*

Patricia Hanna on Anne Thurston, 1995, *Because of her Testimony: The Word in Female Experience.*

Fionnuala Byrne on Betty S. Travitsky and Adele F. Seeff (eds), 1994, *Attending to Women in Early Modern England.*

Jane Conroy on Lynne Vallone, 1995, *Disciplines of Virtue: Girl's Culture in the Eighteenth and Nineteenth Centuries.*

Aine Ni Leime on Imelda Whelehan, 1995, *Modern Feminist Thought: From the Second Wave to 'Post-Feminism'.*

Notes on New Books

UCG Women's Studies Centre Review
Volume Four, 1996

EDITORS: Alan Hayes, Ann Lyons, Aine Ni leime, Lorna Shaughnessy

Introduction

Defining the Political
Eilis Ward and Orla O'Donovan / Networks of Women's Groups and Politics in Ireland: What (Some) Women Think

Jane Tynan / Redefining Boundaries: Feminism, Women and Nationalism in Ireland

Diane Urquhart / In Defence of Ulster and the Empire: The Ulster Women's Unionist Council, 1911–1940

Perspectives on Citizenship
Sylvia Walby / Women and Citizenship: Towards a Comparative Analysis

Mary Quinn / Women and Employment: Norway and the Republic of Ireland

Mary Owens and Anne Byrne / Family, Work and Community – Rural Women's Lives Rural Women's Research Project: Summary Account

Kathleen Barry / The Prostitution of Sexuality: A Cause for New International Human Rights

Claire Mc Donagh / Domestic Violence: The Galway Perspective

Beijing and After
Caitriona Ruane / Obstacles to Peace and Human Security in Ireland

Nóirín Clancy / Experiences of Beijing

Rachel Doyle / Making their Voices Heard – Traveller Women and Beijing

Different Voices
Stephen Mannix / Women, Stories and Feminist Moral Psychology: Listening to the Voices of Experience

Berni Divilly / Down to Earth Meeting the Dancer Within: Women's Studies in Movement

Kate Wolf / See Here, She Said

Book Reviews

Eithne McDermott on Sue Bridger, Rebecca Kay and Kathryn Pinnick. 1996. *No More Heroines? Russia, Women and the Market.*

Timothy P. Foley on Anne Ulry Colman. 1996. *Dictionary of Nineteenth-Century Irish Women Poets.*

Liz Stanley on Dolores Dooley and Liz Steiner-Scott (eds). 1996. *Irish Journal of Feminist Studies.*

Ger Moane on Timothy P. Foley, Lionel Pilkington, Sean Ryder and Elizabeth Tilley (eds.) 1995. *Gender and Colonialism.*

Denise Waldron on Noel Harvey and Adrian F. Twomey. 1995. *Sexual Harassment in the Workplace. A Practical Guide for Employers and Employees.*

Kate Soudant on Sylvia D.Hoffert. 1995. *When Hens Crow: The Women's Rights Movement in Antebellum America.*

Francesca Counihan on Alex Hughes and Kate Ince (eds). 1996. *French Erotic Fiction: Women's Desiring Writing 1880–1990.*

Eileen Foley on Beryl Madoc-Jones and Jennifer Coates (eds). 1996. *An Introduction to Women's Studies.*

Marie McGonagle on Anne Morris and Susan Nott. 1995. *All My Wordly Goods: A Feminist Perspective on the Legal Regulation of Wealth.*

Maria Gibbons on Íde O'Carroll and Eoin Collins (eds). 1995. *Lesbian and Gay Visions of Ireland. Towards the Twenty-First Century.*

Mary Clancy on Kit and Cyril Ó Céirín. 1996. *Women of Ireland: A Biographic Dictionary.*

Sean Ryder on Laura Pietropaolo and Ada Testaferri (eds). 1995. *Feminisms in the Cinema.*

Jane Conroy on Anne T. Quartararo. 1995. *Women Teachers and Popular Education in Nineteenth-Century France. Social Values and Corporate Identity at the Normal School Institution.*

Marie Morrissey on Jenny Shaw. 1995. *Education, Gender and Anxiety.*

Mary Cawley on Simon Szreter. 1996. *Fertility, Class and Gender in Britain 1860–1940.*

Ruth Curtis on Karen Fraser Wyche and Faye J. Crosby (eds). 1996. *Women's Ethnicities: Journeys Through Psychology.*

Notes on New Books

Women's Studies Review
Volume Five, 1997

Women and Health

EDITORS: Margaret Barry, Jane Conroy, Alan Hayes, Ann O'Kelly, Lorna Shaughnessy

Cecily Kelleher / Preface

Introduction

Health and Tradition
Pádraig Ó Héalaí / Pregnancy and Childbirth in Blasket Island Tradition

Anne MacFarlane / The Changing Role of Women as Health Workers in Ireland

Health and Health Care
Margaret Hodgins and Cecily Kelleher / Health and Well-Being in Social Care Workers

Jane Sixsmith, Emer McCarthy and Ethna Shryane / Women's Attitudes to the Menopause, HRT, Breast Cancer and Mammography Screening

Mike Power / Osteoporosis: An inevitable Consequence of Ageing?

Sheila Street / Women and HIV

Health, Culture and Society
Ann O'Kelly / Still Outside the Circle: The Experience of Irish Women and Disabilities

Helen Mortimer / For Women Only – Why Fat is a Gender Issue

Lorna Shaughnessy / Female Genital Mutilation: Beyond Mutilating Mothers and Foreign Feminists

Margaret Brehony / The Health Crisis and Women in Nicaragua

From Private Philanthropy to Public Policy
Note: Lady Dudley's Scheme for the Establishment of District Nurses in the Poorest Parts of Ireland

Anne Broekhoven / Review Essay I: A Plan for Women's Health, 1997–1999

Orla O'Donovan / Review Essay II : The Plan for Women's Health and the Politics of Knowledge – A Brief Commentary

Epilogue
Maureen Joyce / Counting

Book Reviews
Myrtle Hill on Anne Byrne and Madeline Leonard (eds). 1997. *Women in Irish Society: A Sociological Reader*

Jane Conroy on Diane Cousineau. 1997. *Letters and Labyrinths: Women Writing/Cultural Codes*

Catherine Cronin on Julia Evetts. 1996. *Gender and Career in Science and Engineering*

Margaret Tumelty on Ronit Lentin, Lia Mills, Mary Montaut, Clare Toolan, Ailbhe Smyth (eds). 1997. *f/m*

Ann Lyons on Sharon Hays. 1996. *The Cultural Contradictions of Motherhood/* Donna Bassin, Margaret Honey and Meryle Kaplan (eds). 1996 [1994]. *Representations of Motherhood*

Lorraine Shannon on *Thamyris: Gender in the Making: Indian Contexts*

Diane Urquhart on Margaret Kelleher and James H. Murphy (eds). 1997. *Gender Perspectives in Nineteenth-Century Ireland: Public and Private Spheres*

Catherine Davies on Lois M. Smith and Alfred Padula. 1996. *Sex and Revolution: Women in Socialist Cuba*

Rosaleen O'Neill on Chris Weedon (ed.). 1997. *Postwar Women's Writing in German*

Dr. Una Fallon on Miriam M. Wiley and Barry Merriman. 1996. *Women and Health Care in Ireland: Knowledge, Attitudes and Behaviour*

Women's Studies Review
Volume Six, 1999

EDITORS: Jane Conroy and Rosaleen O'Neill

Introduction

Minorities in Ireland: Theory and Experience
Ronit Lentin / Racialising (our) Dark Rosaleen: Feminism, Citizenship, Racism, Antisemitism

Marian Tannam / At Home from Abroad: The Experience of Some Migrant Women in Ireland

Shalini Sinha / Studying Racism Within Women's Studies in Ireland

Philomena Mullen / On Being Black, Irish and a Woman

Literature of Otherness and Identity
Mary Gallagher / Revisiting the 'Others' Others', Or the Bankruptcy of Otherness as a Value in Literature in French

Christine O'Dowd-Smyth / Silence and Exile in the Works of Three Algerian Women Writers: Nina Bouraoui, Soraya Nini and Malika Mokeddem

Ana P.L.N. Nunes / Marked at Birth: History and Identity in Gayl Jones's *Corregidora*

Poetry

Mary O'Malley	Louis de Paor
Eva Bourke	Hannagh McGinley
Sharon Murphy	Aileen Kelly
Mary Dempsey	Rita Ann Higgins

Varia
Rose Brock / Labelling to Exploit: One Woman's View of Global Market Practices

Brian Arkins / Women in Rome

Aine O'Healy / Nemesis and her Sisters: Feminist Filmmakers in Naples and Rome

Alan Hayes / Big Women, Little Women: Towards a History of Second Wave Commercial Feminist Publishing in Ireland

Book Reviews
Eithne MacDermott on Toby W. Clyman and Judith Vowles (eds). 1996. *Russia Through Women's Eyes: Autobiographies from Tsarist Russia*
Patricia O'Byrne on Catherine Davies. 1998. *Spanish Women Writing 1849–1996*
Ann Lyons on Julia Grant. 1998. *Raising Baby by the Book: The Education of American Mothers*
Maureen Langan-Egan on Máirín Nic Eoin. 1998. *B'ait Leo Bean: Gneithe den Ideeolaiocht Inscne I dTraidisiun Liteartha na Gaeilge*
Caoilfhionn Vaughan on Geraldine Mitchell. 1997. *Muriel Gahan, Champion of Rural Women and Craftworkers*
Liz Steiner-Scott on Pat O'Connor. 1998. *Emerging Voices: Women in Contemporary Irish Society*
Ronit Lentin on Dalia Ofer and Lenore J. Weitzman. 1998. *Women in the Holocaust*

Notes on New Books

Women's Studies Review
Volume Seven, 2000

EDITORS: Mary Clancy, Caitriona Clear, Triona Nic Giolla Choille
REVIEWS EDITOR: Alan Hayes

Guest Introduction
Catríona Crowe

Introduction

Oral History

Maura Cronin / Experience Of Supervising Undergraduate Oral History Research

Anne Byrne / Singular Identities: ManagingStigma, Resisting Voices

Terri Conroy-Baker / Oral Research in Ballyconneely

Mary Kierse / 'We Taught and Went Home': Women Teachers in Clare 1922–1958

Caitríona Clear / Oral History and Women's Household Work in Ireland 1922–1961: Some Reflections

Sources for Women's Lives
Maria Luddy / The Women's History Project

Biography
Irene Finn / From 'Case Study' to 'Life': Mary Strangman (1872–1943) Doctor, Suffragist, Public Health Activist, Town Councillor

Martina Ann O'Doherty / Dreams, Drear, and Degradation: The Representation of Early Twentieth-Century Irishwomen in Selected Plays of Teresa Deevy (1894–1963)

Gráinne Blair / Looking for Lola: I, Lola Montez and Others – A Multiography

Work in Progress
Mary Clancy, Caitríona Clear / Introduction

Veronica Fitzgerald / I: A Change of Habit

Mary Mangan / II: Woman of the House

Kitty Dillon Monaghan / III: The Farm - The Heart of the Country

Liz Nolan / IV: Delia Kerrigan, 1895–1963

Oral History Interview
Kathleen Gormley / A Personal Account of Life in Inner-City Dublin in the 1940s, 50s, and 60s

Review Essays
Alan Hayes / Introduction

Mary Clancy: Tony Varley / Political Women – Women … Politically

Síle de Cléir / Bright Sparks from Attic

Gifford Lewis: Alan Hayes / Grace Gifford in Irish History

Kimberely A. LoPrete / Pre-Modern Women

Reviews
Niall Crowley on *(Re)searching Women: Feminist Research Methodologies in the Social Sciences in Ireland*
Vivienne Batt on *Arguing with the Phallus*
Monica Cullinan on *Women's Studies Serials*
Eva Bourke on the poetry of Rita Kelly

Notes on New Books

Women's Studies Review
Volume Eight, 2002

Making a Difference: Women and the Creative Arts

EDITORS: Vivienne Batt, Jane Conroy, Sheila Dickinson, Ann Lyons, Lorna Shaughnessy
REVIEWS EDITOR: Alan Hayes

Introduction

Transforming Icons
Constantina Katsari / Public Images of Roman Imperial Women During the Julio-Claudian Period: A Review Article

Angela Ryan / Camille Claudel: The Artist as Heroinic Rhetorician

Christiane Schönfeld / Women On Screen: A Short Jistory of the *Femme fatale*

Siobhán Kilfeather / Editing *The Field Day Anthology*

Transgressing Conventions
Shelia Dickinson / Multiplicity in Art Practice: Alice Maher in Conversation With Shelia Dickinson

Wanda Balzano / The Veiled Subject: Figuring the Feminine Through Una Troy's/Elizabeth Connor's 'The Apple' and Siobán Piercy's Screenprints

Catherine Marshall / 'I'll Spin You a Yarn, I'll Weave You a Tale...': Subverting Patriarchy Through Art and 'Women's Work'

Luz Mar González Arias / Beyond Categorisations: A Conversation with Carmel Benson

Translating Experience
Helen O'Donghue and Catherine Marshall / Alternative Representations Create Alternative Possibilities

Catherine Kelly / Breaking the Mould: Three Plays by Marina Carr

Mary Dempsey / Visa to Rejoin the Human Race: A Twelve-minute Film Script

Chris Head / Creativity Workshop

Poetry
Eva Bourke, Moya Cannon, Mary Dempsey, Kerry Hardie, Mary O'Donoghue

Book Reviews
Tracy Holsgrove on Alan Hayes and Diane Urquhart (eds), *The Irish Women's History Reader*, 2001; and Linda Connolly, *The Irish Women's Movement: From Revolution to Devolution*, 2002

Adrienne Anifant on Andrea Dworkin, *Scapegoat: The Jews, Israel and Women's Liberation*, 2000; Ronit Lentin, *Israel and the Daughters of the Shaoh: Reoccupying the Territories of Silence*, 2000; Margaret McCarthy, *My Eyes Only Look Out: Experiences of Irish People of Mixed Race Parentage*, 2001.

Fiona Bateman on Fidelma Farley, *Anne Devlin*, 2001

Sheila Dickinson on Pauline Bewick and Rita Kelly, *Kelly Reads Bewick*, 2001

Caitríona Clear on Phil Kilroy, *Madeleine Sophie Barat: A Life*, 2000

Marie Mulholland on Nahla Abdo and Ronit Lentin (eds), *Women and the Politics of Military Confrontation: Palestinian and Israeli Gender Narratives of Dislocation*, 2002

Mary Cullen on Caitríona Clear, *Women of the House: Women's Household Work in Ireland, 1922-1961*, 2000

Mary Clancy on Geraldine Curtin, *The Women of Galway Jail: Female Criminality in Nineteenth-Century Ireland*, 2001

Women's Studies Review
Volume Nine, 2004

Women's Activism and Voluntary Activity

VOLUME EDITOR: Vivienne Batt
GENERAL EDITOR: Rebecca Pelan
REVIEWS EDITOR: Alan Hayes

Introduction

Freda Donoghue / Women and Volunteering – A Feminised Space?

Caitríona Brennan / Factors Impacting on the Motivations of Staff Working in Domestic Violence Shelters

Elena Kim / Women's Involvement in Religious Fundamentalism: A Case Study of Hizb Ut-Tahrir, Kyrgyzstan

Christina Quinlan / A Journey Into the Women's Prison

Orla Egan / Searching for Space: Cork Lesbian Community 1975–2000

Mary Dempsey / It Really Happened

Eoin Bourke / From a Proletarian Aesthetic to Social Agitation. Käthe Kollwitz's Protrayal of Women as Revolutionaries, Victims and Protectors in Her Art and Poster Work

Myrtle Hill / Lessons and Legacies: Feminist Activism in the North c1970–2000

Eilish Rooney / Counting Women's Equality in West Belfast and Finding Failings in the Northern Ireland Equality Commission

Mary Paul Keane / Exploring Difference – Women's Cross-border/Cross-community Cultural Exchange and Activism

Maggie Ronayne / Invest in Caring Not Killing: An Interview with Phoebe Jones, Global Women's Strike, Philadelphia

Hazel Healy / Women's Global Action – Gender Politics and Grass-roots Resistance

Book Reviews

Nuala Ní Chonchúir on Éilís Ni Dhuibhne, *Midwife to the Fairies,* 2003

Constantina Katsari on Konstantinos Kapparis, *Abortion in the Ancient World,* 2002

Pat Jourdan on Deirdre Brennan, Maighread Medbh and Nuala Ní Chonchúir, *DIVAS! New Irish Women's Writing,* 2003

The *Women's Studies Review* also cultivated business relationships with

Women: A Cultural Review (Routledge)
Australian Feminist Studies (Carfax)
Frontiers: A Journal of Women's Studies (University of Nebraska Press)
The European Journal of Women's Studies (Sage)
Gender and History (Blackwell Publishers)
Feminism and Psychology (Sage)
Feminist Studies (University of Maryland)
Gender and Society (Sage)
Journal of Gender Studies (Carfax)
Feminist Review (Routledge)
Signs (University of Chicago Press)
Gender and Education (Carfax)
U.S.-Japan Women's Journal (Palo Alto, CA)
Studies on Women Abstracts (Carfax)
Sexualities (Sage)
Gender, Place and Culture (Carfax)
Women's News (Belfast)
Trouble and Strife (Norfolk)
Ms.chief (Dublin)
Queen's University of Belfast
University of Limerick
University of Dublin, Trinity College
Tir Eolas, Kinvara, County Galway
Kenny's Book
shop, Galway
Attic Press, Dublin
The Feminist Press, City University of New York